STANDARD CATALOG OF®

CIVIL WAR FIREARMS

by John F. Graf

©2008 Krause Publications, Inc.,
a subsidiary of F+W Media, Inc.

Published by

Gun Digest®Books
An imprint of F+W Media, Inc.
700 East State Street • Iola, WI 54990-0001
715-445-2214 • 888-457-2873
www.gundigestbooks.com

Our toll-free number to place an order or obtain
a free catalog is (800) 258-0929.

Cover Photo Courtesy Benelli USA Corporation

Library of Congress Control Number: 2008937702
ISBN-13: 978-0-89689-613-0
ISBN-10: 0-89689-613-7

Designed by Elizabeth Krogwold
Edited by Dan Shideler

Printed in CHINA

CONTENTS

DEDICATION

To my grandmother, Celine (Coninx) Robertson. Though she is gone, I carry that which she taught me: the love of the Civil War, pursuit of scholarship, and always trying to do the right thing.

ABOUT THE AUTHOR

John F. Graf has a master of arts degree in historical administration and has been a military collector for more than 30 years. He is the long-time editor of *Military Trader* and *Military Vehicles Magazine* and is the author of *Warman's Civil War Collectibles, Badgers for the Union, Warman's Civil War Field Guide,* and *Warman's WWII Collectibles* as well as numerous articles on nineteenth century material culture. He currently resides in Missouri.

ACKNOWLEDGMENTS

Undertaking this book would have been inconceivable without relying on the scholarship and dedication to antique firearms of Norm Flayderman. His Guide to Antique Firearms, now in its ninth edition, is unsurpassed for accuracy in both identification and pricing. It was inconceivable to me that my publisher would ask me to assemble a book that would ever come close to the scope of Norm's work. With trepidation, I approached him for assistance. Always the consummate gentleman, Norm respectfully declined, explaining that he was going through his own authorship struggles as he completed the proofs of his current edition of the Guide. He did, however, express his good wishes and expedience with the research. Having obtained his "blessing," I felt as though I could proceed. My thanks—or that of the hobby—to Norm cannot be measured.

I wish to thank Thomas Kailbourn for his hours and hours of research. I have known Tom for more than 20 years and through all that time, I have had nothing but the very highest regard for his scholarship, thoroughness and professionalism. I count him among my closest friends, in addition to being a fine colleague.

The accumulation of information included in this book has occurred over nearly 40 years, so an accurate listing of those who aided is nearly impossible. Indeed, many who have contributed to this work are no longer around to see the results. This saddens me. However, I do want to thank the following: Alya Alberico, Jeff Anderson, Bill Brewster, Weldon Brudlos, William K. Combs, Joseph S. Covais, David Doyle, Jason Devine, David Fagan, Paul Goodwin, Larry Hicklin, Patrick F. Hogan, Randy Jackson, James D. Julia, Turner Kirkland, H. Michael Madaus, Anna McCoy, Denise Moss, John M. Murphy, Steve Osman, Patrick Quinn, Robert M. Reilly, Celine Robertson, Frank Reile, Harold St. Mary, Thomas Shaw, Jefferson Shrader, Perk Steffen, Donald L. Ware, Bill Weber, and Jaime M. Wood.

I want to take this opportunity to acknowledge the strength I receive from my family. First, and foremost, I must thank my parents, John Milton and Helen Graf. Without their accepting my fascination with the Civil War as a young boy, and then helping me to discover the possibilities that scholarship, study, and perseverance provide, I could never have followed my passion for history and the Civil War. When I was 12, they gave me my first gun: A reproduction Model 1863 Remington rifle.

I am blessed with the finest brothers and sister: Tom, Joe, Jim, and Celine. Even though I am now old and gray-haired, I will always be their baby brother. The number of times they let me tag along to go shooting, borrow books, or explain history to me are countless. All I can say is, "Thank you."

And finally, there are two women who stand out: My partner, Diane Adams-Graf, and my daughter, Trisha Lynn Graf. You were both so patient and supportive as I worked on this book. I am, indeed, a fortunate man.

INTRODUCTION

Between the bombardment of Fort Sumter on April 12, 1861, and the final surrender of Confederate troops on May 26, 1865, the way wars were fought and the tools soldiers used changed irrevocably. When troops first formed lines of battle to face each other near Bull Run Creek in Virginia on June 21, 1861, they were dressed in a widely disparate assemblage of uniforms. They carried state-issued, federally-supplied, or brought-from-home weapons, some of which dated back to before the War of 1812. They marched to the orders and rhythms of tactics that had served land forces for at least the previous 100 years. Four short years later, the generals and soldiers had perfected the art of warfare on the North American continent, having developed such leaps as the use of the repeating rifle and widely dispersed infantry formations.

This change levied a toll on the nation, however, in the form of more than one million casualties (over 620,000 war-related deaths). At that rate, nearly one in four soldiers experienced the pains of war firsthand. It was impossible for the war to not impact every one of the 34.3 million residents of the United States and former Confederate States. Over the ensuing years, the pain—for most—subsided, but the memory remained strong. Families still pay homage to their veteran ancestors, grade school students memorize the Gettysburg address, we bow our heads on Memorial Day, and many hold dear the original sentiments represented by the Confederate battle flag.

THE CIVIL WAR EXPERIENCE

Many Americans satisfy their desire to feel connected with the Civil War by exploring battlefields or cemeteries or researching their own family ancestors who served. Some people even read countless biographies, regimental histories, or battle accounts, even joining Civil War study groups or "Round Tables." For many, these very private explorations are enough to satiate their need to learn about the conflict and the lives of its participants.

For some though, simply memorializing the war isn't sufficient to satisfy that need to remain connected to the events of 1861-1865. Some will painstakingly recreate uniforms and equipment to don on weekend campaigns and refight battles, this time firing at their fellow countrymen with muskets

and cannons charged with powder and paper instead of canisters of grape shot or loads of buckshot. For these "reenactors," such events help them come close to experiencing the daily work, inconveniences, and feelings of Civil War soldiers. Of course, at the end of the weekend, these modern "Sessesh" and "Billy Yanks," return to their twenty-first-century lives, leaving the recreated image of maimed fellow soldiers, dysentery, and lice-infested clothing behind.

And finally, for another group of Civil War enthusiasts, the best medium for understanding the heritage and role of thousands who served is by collecting war firearms. For these collectors, holding an 1861 Taunton-produced Springfield rifled musket, studying the detail of a Tarpley carbine, or feeling the heft of a Spiller & Burr revolver are connectors to the Civil War. The pistols, revolvers, rifles, muskets, and carbines represent direct links to a comprehensive understanding of the depth of commitment, sacrifice, and engagement that the soldiers felt.

COLLECTORS AND ACCUMULATORS

Collecting firearms from the Civil War is not a new hobby. Even before the war ended, people were already picking up weapons dropped on the battlefield. The first collectors, as with any period of warfare, were the participants themselves. Soldiers sent home "captured" or "liberated" guns. When the war ended, many were given the opportunity to buy their weapon upon mustering out of the service.

After the war, the passion for owning a piece of it did not subside; early collectors gathered representative weapons. Simultaneously, and not unlike the time following any major conflict, a grand scale of surplus sales emerged. This was the heyday of Civil War collecting. Dealers such as Francis Bannerman made hundreds of Civil War weapons available to the general public. For as little as $3.50, a person could buy a Springfield musket. Ten dollars would secure a Confederate Richmond-made version. Though a lot of sales were made

to early collectors, much of the surplus was sold in bulk to other governments, outdoors enthusiasts, and a lot was sold simply for its scrap value.

Following World War II, a new wave of collecting emerged. Reveling in the victories in Japan and in Europe, Americans were charged with a renewed sense of patriotism and heritage. At the same time, the newspapers started to track the passing of the last few veterans of Civil War. As the nation paid tribute to the few survivors of the Rebellion, it acknowledged that the 100-year anniversary of the war was fast upon them. In an effort to capture a sense of the heritage, Civil War buffs began to collect in earnest. With the high profile of the Civil War Centennial in the 1960s, thousands of outstanding relics seemingly emerged from closets, attics, and long-forgotten chests. Collectors eagerly bought and sold firearms, swords, and uniforms.

By the end of the twentieth century, Civil War collecting had peaked. Some thought, "all the good stuff is gone!" Little did these skeptics realize, collectors are not the end user. Rather, a collector is merely the caretaker who provides a good home for an object until that time when they choose, or no longer are able, to care for the item. Then, these relics, thought to be gone, suddenly reemerge on the market. And it is this era of Civil War relic reemergence in which we currently live.

The fabulous collections of firearms that were assembled in the late 1940s and early 1950s are reappearing. Granted, the prices have increased considerably. Nevertheless, Civil War firearms (and relics in general!) like no one has seen available for fifty years are suddenly appearing at auctions, shows, and on private dealer's lists.

Today, we benefit from the many years of research that has resulted from the earlier collecting frenzies. Books that the first generation of collectors could only have dreamed of are now available on specialized topics such as Gwyn & Campbell carbines, Sharps carbine and rifles, or the weapons of the Palmetto Armory. At no moment in time since the Civil War has so much information and material been available at a single instant.

As we enter this "glory period" of Civil War collecting, though, many lessons need to be relearned. Whereas an old-time collector could look at a saber and recognize offhandedly that it was the product of the Griswold factory or quantify the variations of percussion conversion done to flintlock muskets at Federal arsenals, many of these outstanding artifacts have not been available for study for years. Collectors are learning many of the nuances that affect desirability and value for the first time (often at the expense of the old-timer's patience!).

USING THIS BOOK

This book is organized into nine chapters representing different types of Civil War firearms. Today, so many weapons are sold as "Civil War" that never saw the American continent until at least a hundred years after the war concluded. The weapons represented in this book are those can be documented as having been purchased and carried between 1860 and 1865 by Union or Confederate troops. Though many indiduals carried exotic weapons during the war, some collectors may be disappointed to not see them listed in this book. Generally, production and issue of a weapon had to exceed 75 to be included in this work.

To make the best use of this book, it is important to understand just a few basic terms:

MUSKET: A muzzle-loading, smooth bore long arm that is equipped to support a bayonet.

RIFLED MUSKET: A musket originally built as a smoothbore but later rifled and fitted with long range sights.

RIFLE-MUSKET: A muzzle-loading long arm that was originally built with a rifled barrel in approximately .58 caliber and was equipped to support an triangular bayonet.

RIFLE: A two-banded, rifled weapon (or of similar length to a two-banded weapon) equipped to support a saber bayonet.

CARBINE: A breech or muzzle-loading shoulder arm having a smooth or rifled bore, using externally primed ammunition. Originally designed for horse-mounted troops.

MUSKETOON: A muzzle-loading shoulder arm having a smooth or rifled bore and a maximum barrel length of 26.5 inches.

PRICING

Pricing in this book follows the standard set forth by Norm Flaydermann in his ground-breaking and essential *Guide to Antique American Firearms.* Only two ratings are listed for each weapon that most represents what is available. These ratings are part of the 7-step system adopted by the National Rifle Association.

The values printed within this work are simply representative of the prices paid at auction during the past eight years. As all collectors know, price values are just a guide and are never intended to be the final word on the price of a particular piece. Many factors, foremost of which is condition followed by provenance, will drastically change the value of a weapon. The values here are for a weapon assumed to be as issued with no known provenance, alterations. or additional markings

Comparing prices of similar items, the reader will discover that known provenance will almost always dramatically affect the price of a Civil War firearm. Both dealers and collectors like to refer to such items as "identified," meaning that the name of the original Civil War soldier who owned the firearm t is still known. Although it has always been important to collectors to know who carried or used what items during the war, now, more than ever, premium prices are being paid today for an item with a "proven history." Not only are guns being touted as to who originally used them during the war, dealers are attempting to add value by making claims as to what prominent collectors have previously owned the artifacts as well! Pieces that once sat in a prominent collection have gained a degree of legitimacy (and value) greater than an identical object with no known history.

Provenance has probably affected price more than any other factor in recent years, so it stands to reason that many items have "acquired" a provenance. When you are paying for an item and its history, be careful. It is easy for a seller to tell a story when handing over an object, but it is a lot more difficult to verify or prove it. The best provenance will be in the form of period inscriptions or written notes attributing an object to a particular soldier.

THE WEAPON'S PLACE IN HISTORY

Finally, it is the goal of this book to help the collector understand the context of the firearm. Depending on how it is viewed, the context can be varied. For example, a Model 1861 Springfield rifle in average condition is, in the most base of contexts, an item worth about $900. Stepping up the ladder, it represents the strides in rifled firearms development made in a few short years of the Civil War. Even higher up the ladder of consciousness, it might represent the need of a modern society to feel connected with its past.

Context is, obviously, a very personal consideration. Feelings and emotions aside, however, it is factually correct that these firearms represent a time in the United States's history when a pervasive feeling of states rights and isolation from its government caused a people to sever themselves from the nation. What ensued was the overwhelming willingness of the masses to die to protect that right or to protect the integrity of the Union. This is the context that we, as collectors of firearms of this great struggle, can never forget.

CHAPTER 1

MUSKETS

I n terms of Civil War weaponry, a "musket" is any smooth-bore, muzzle-loading shoulder arm of a minimum length of 50" that was made to support a bayonet. That is to say, "the standard weapon carried by the world's infantry in the 17th, 18th and early 19th centuries."

By 1861, the musket was an antiquated weapon. In the decade prior, many of the major world armies, including that of the United States, had adopted rifled weapons. Rifled muskets, rifle-muskets, rifles, and rifled carbines were changing the way war was fought.

As rifled weapons reached the troops, hundreds of thousands of smoothbore muskets were relegated to arsenal gun racks. When buyers for the Union and Confederacy searched, the world's governments were eager to sell the obsolete muskets. With few alternatives, the buyers reluctantly snatched up the stocks hoping that armories back in the States (whether United or Confederate) would be able to rifle the weapons before issuing them to the troops. Whereas this did happen, it was the exception more than the rule.

The same process occurred in the United States. Government and state armories were full of obsolete muskets, some dating back to the War of 1812. On November 12, 1859, Colonel of Ordnance H.K. Craig stated that 23,894 flintlock muskets were still unaltered and in the possession of the United States armories and arsenals. Two months later, he reported 499,554 .69-caliber percussion muskets and muskets altered to percussion were on hand and suitable for service. However, of that number, 60,878 muskets and rifles were in arsenals in South Carolina, Alabama, and Louisiana, and would be lost if the southern states decided to seize them. At that time, the U.S. arsenals reported little more than 35,000 rifled weapons on hand.

Work had been in progress to convert the smoothbores to rifled weapons and flintlock ignitions to percussion, but that work had proceeded rather slowly. Desperate for arms, many states sent their troops off to war armed with whatever weapons they had.

However, by 1863, manufacturing in the north was closing in on meeting demand. Troops who had entered the war with old, state-provided smoothbores or received sub-standard European arms began to receive new issues of rifle-muskets. In the South, where demand out-paced supply, this transition took a bit longer. Nevertheless, the smoothbore musket is best quantified as an "early war weapon."

AUSTRIAN MODEL 1842, .70 CALIBER, PAPER CARTRIDGE, PERCUSSION

Made by Austrian National Armory and private gun manufactories, ca. 1842-1849 Total imported: Unknown, but more than 135,000.

Overall length: 58".

Muzzleloader, single shot.

Markings are uncommon. Each lock plate was stamped with a small Austrian eagle and the year of manufacture (with the first digit omitted, e.g., "843"). A few examples have the year of manufacture stamped on the barrel near the breech in addition to "IB" in an oval. Some arms bear the mark of a private manufacturer, "RS Heretta".

Originally fitted with a tube-lock ignition system developed in Austria, the three-band, Model 1842 muskets were produced as smoothbores. All iron furniture was left bright. Later, many were rifled to fire a conical bullet. The U.S. Ordnance Department purchased approximately 68,500 Model 1842 muskets in various configurations. Conversions from the original tube-lock include a U.S. cone seated in the barrel, bolster or cone seat brazed on the breech, patent breech with forged bolster, or a U.S. Maynard conversion style. The firm of Kruse, Drexel and Schmidt supplied 25,000 in the original tube-lock configuration to General John Frémont. Herman Boker imported two shorter versions: A cadet model that was 52-1/2" overall and an engineer model measuring 48-1/2". It is unknown how many Model 1842 muskets the Confederate government purchased, though it was, most likely, a weapon utilized by southern troops.

GOOD—$375   FINE—$1,250

Amoskeag Auction Company, Inc.

BRITISH PATTERN 1839 MUSKET, .75 CALIBER, PAPER CARTRIDGE, PERCUSSION

Made by various English manufactures, London, England, 1839-1851 Total imported: Unknown, but likely more than 10,000.

Overall length: 55".

Muzzleloader, single shot.

Lock plates vary dependant on year of manufacture. Generally, the lock plate will be stamped with a crown over "VR," the British "broad arrow" and the year of manufacture in addition to "Enfield" or "Tower," depending on place of manufacture. Barrels are stamped with either the Enfield proof mark, a crown over "VR" or "MR" above a set of crowned scepters or the London and Birmingham mark consisting of a crown over "TP" over a broad arrow in addition to a crown over "B" surmounting a "7" over a crowned broad arrow.

Rock Island Auction Company

Originally designed as a flintlock musket, the P39 musket can be recognized by the three round pins and upper swivel screw that retain the barrel to the stock. The P39 was produced without a rear sight, though several examples clearly have had sights added. Though records do not specifically indicate pattern models, it is very likely that both Confederate and U.S. Ordnance purchasing agents obtained P39 muskets.

GOOD—$920   **FINE—$1,350**

BRITISH PATTERN 1842 MUSKET, .76 CALIBER, PAPER CARTRIDGE, PERCUSSION

Made by various English manufactures, London, England, 1842-1855. Total imported: Unknown, but likely several thousand.

Overall length: 55".

Muzzleloader, single shot.

Lock plates vary depending on year of manufacture. Generally, the lock plate will be stamped with a crown over "VR", the British "broad arrow" and the year of manufacture in addition to "Enfield" or "Tower", depending on place of manufacture. Barrels are stamped with either the Enfield proof mark, a crown over "VR" or "MR" above a set of crowned scepters or the London and Birmingham mark consisting of a crown over "TP" over a broad arrow in addition to a crown over "B" surmounting a "7" over a crowned broad arrow.

The P42 musket can be recognized by the three flat keys and upper swivel screw that retain the barrel to the stock. The P42 was produced with a notched rear sight. The ramrod head is slightly concave. Rather than a side plate like that found on the P39, the lock plate screws pass through two brass washers with rectangular extensions on opposite sides. Though records do not specifically indicate pattern models, it is very likely that both Confederate and U.S. Ordnance purchasing agents obtained P39 muskets.

GOOD—$950   **FINE—$1,350**

CONFEDERATE CONTRACT PERCUSSION CONVERSIONS

Converted by various gunsmiths, Richmond, Virginia, 1861. Total production: 50,000.

Muzzleloader, single shot.

In 1861, the Commonwealth of Virginia contracted six Richmond gunsmiths to convert approximately 50,000 flintlock muskets: S.B. Cocke, Thomas Addams Jr., Francis Perpignon, Samuel C. Robinson, Samuel Sutherland, and the Union Manufacturing Company. The contractors all employed the brazed bolster configuration.

James D. Julia Auctioneers, Fairfield, Maine

James D. Julia Auctioneers,
Fairfield, Maine

Confederate Brazed Bolster, Type I. Percussion bolster brazed over the flintlock vent. An iron plug blocks the hole drilled through the bolster to connect the cone hole to the old vent hole.

James D. Julia Auctioneers,
Fairfield, Maine

Confederate Brazed Bolster, Type II. Percussion bolster brazed over the flintlock vent. A screw blocks the hole drilled through the bolster connect the cone hole to the old vent hole.

The "Confederate brazed bolsters" do not add significantly to the value of the particular converted musket. For values, refer to the particular type of weapon.

U.S. MUSKET, .69 CALIBER, CONTRACT CONVERSIONS TO PERCUSSION IGNITION

W hen the U.S. Ordnance Department determined to convert its firearms from flintlock to percussion ignition systems in the 1840s, it had 600,000 muskets deemed suitable for altering to percussion. Many of those muskets were converted from the late 1840s until the beginning of the Civil War, using three basic systems:

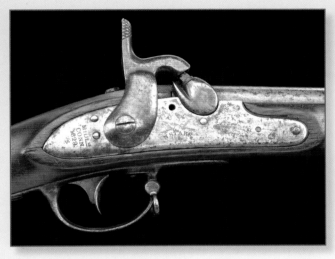

James D. Julia Auctioneers, Fairfield, Maine

The French-style (or side-lug, or drum-and-nipple).

This was the earliest type of conversion and was performed by private contractors until the early 1850s. All exposed lock parts were removed, the flash pan cut and ground off almost flush with the lock plate, the touch hole enlarged, and screw holes plugged. A cylindrical bolster and nipple was screwed into the touch hole and a new hammer installed.

GOOD—$700   FINE—$1,300

James D. Julia Auctioneers, Fairfield, Maine

Virginia cone-in-barrel contract conversion. James D. Julia Auctioneers, Fairfield, Maine

New York State Hitchcock contract cone-in-barrel conversion.

The Belgian-style (or cone-type). This conversion, performed insofar as is known by only the national armories in the early 1850s, involved removing all exposed lock components, filling screw holes, and removing the pan and filling the resulting hole with brass, flush with the lock plate surface. A nipple was screwed into a threaded hole near the top of the barrel, slightly right of center, and a new hammer installed.

GOOD—$700   **FINE—$1,300**

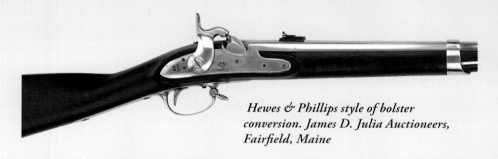

Hewes & Phillips style of bolster conversion. James D. Julia Auctioneers, Fairfield, Maine

New Jersey Patent Breech (Type I) bolster alteration. James D. Julia Auctioneers, Fairfield, Maine

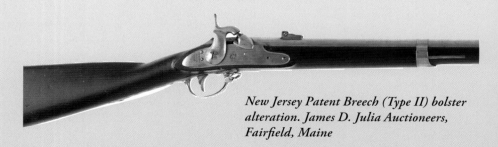

New Jersey Patent Breech (Type II) bolster alteration. James D. Julia Auctioneers, Fairfield, Maine

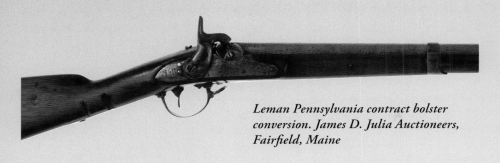

Leman Pennsylvania contract bolster conversion. James D. Julia Auctioneers, Fairfield, Maine

Butterfield Pennsylvania contract bolster conversion. James D. Julia Auctioneers, Fairfield, Main

Virginia Manufactory bolster conversion. James D. Julia Auctioneers, Fairfield, Maine

U.S. Contract patent breech. Rock Island Auction Company

The bolster-style. Private contractors carried out this conversion, which was deemed necessary to structurally strengthen muskets converted to rifled muskets, from around the mid-1850s to the early months of the Civil War. All external parts were removed from the lock, and holes filled. Two variations then occurred: the barrel was cut off near the breech, the bore was threaded, and a new breech with integral nipple bolster was screwed in; or, a bolster was brazed over the touch hole. A new hammer completed the alteration.

GOOD—$700   FINE—$1,300

FRENCH MODEL 1822 MUSKET, .69/.71 CALIBER, PAPER CARTRIDGE, PERCUSSION

Made by royal arsenals at Tylle, Charleville, Mutzig and St. Etienne and copied by Liege manufacturers, ca. 1822-ca. 1842. Total imported: Unknown, but Union records show over 147,000 French and Belgium muskets were purchased.

Overall length: Type I, 58".

Type II, 55-4/5".

Muzzleloader, single shot.

Lock plate markings reflect arsenals where manufactured. The barrel tang is engraved with the model designation, "M 1822" and year of manufacture. Liege-made examples have only the year of manufacture proof marks. A "T" will follow the model number on weapons altered in French arsenals. French barrels may also be stamped with the date of alteration and caliber in millimeters in addition to the usual proof marks.

French regular line infantry carried the longer, Type I Model 1822 muskets. Voltiguers (light infantry) carried the shorter, Type II muskets. Both were originally configured as smoothbore, flintlock muskets, but were later converted to percussion by replacing the hammer and inserting a cone directly in the top of the barrel and plugging the vent or by brazing a bolster over the vent. Many were rifled and received long-range rear sights at the same time. Union gun buyers purchased at least 147,000 French and Belgian muskets during the Civil War. However, their records do not indicate model designations, making it impossible to know exactly how many Model 1822 muskets made it to the United States. The U.S. Ordnance Department rated French and Belgian smoothbore muskets as 3rd class. No record of Confederate purchases is known.

BOTH TYPES: GOOD—$350   FINE—$900

FRENCH MODEL 1842 MUSKET, .70/.71 CALIBER, PAPER CARTRIDGE, PERCUSSION

Made by French royal and Imperial arsenals and copied by Liege manufacturers, ca. 1842-ca. 1855. Total imported: Unknown, but Union records show over 147,000 French and Belgium muskets were purchased.

Overall length: Type I, 58-1/4".

Type II, 56".

Muzzleloader, single shot.

Lock plate markings reflect arsenals where manufactured. Between 1848 and 1852, French lock plates are inscribed with "Mre. Nle. de" followed by a city name. After 1852, this was changed to "Mre. Impale. de" followed by the city name. The barrel tang is engraved with the model designation, "M 1842" and year of manufacture. Liege-made examples have only the year of manufacture proof marks. A "T" will follow the model number on weapons altered in French arsenals. French barrels may also be stamped with the date of alteration and caliber in millimeters in addition to the usual proof marks.

Originally configured as smoothbore muskets, the Model 1842 was the first percussion long arm that the French Army adopted. French regular line infantry carried the longer, Type I Model 1842 muskets. Voltiguers (light infantry) carried the shorter, Type II muskets. The Model 1842 can be recognized by its back-action lock. All iron fittings are bright Many Model 1842 were subsequently rifled and received long-range sights. Union gun buyers purchased at least 147,000 French and Belgian muskets during the Civil War. However, their records do not indicate model designations making it impossible to know exactly how many Model 1842 muskets made it to the United States. The U.S. Ordnance Department rated French and Belgian smoothbore muskets as 3rd class. No record of Confederate purchases is known.

BOTH TYPES: GOOD—$350   FINE—$900

MORSE "INSIDE LOCK" MUSKET, .69 CALIBER, PAPER CARTRIDGE, PERCUSSION

Made by George W. Morse, Greenville, South Carolina, ca. 1863-1864. Total production: Fewer than 200.

Overall length: 53-3/4".

Muzzleloader, single shot.

Lower brass trigger tang stamped, "MORSE'S LOCK / STATE WORKS / GREENVILLE, S.C." together with a serial number. The date (for example, "1863") is stamped on the brass finial in front of the trigger bow.

The three-band, smoothbore musket incorporate a centrally located lock mechanism inside the stock. A shaft runs horizontally through the lock, terminating at an oval brass plate on the left side of the stock and attached to the hammer on the right.

GOOD—$25,000   FINE—$65,000

MECHANICAL AND AUTO PRIMING PERCUSSION CONVERSIONS

During the 1840s and 1850s there was a rush to produce efficient and affordable percussion conversion systems for the thousands of flintlock muskets in federal arsenals. Designers proposed mechanical priming systems as time-savers by eliminating the need to manually place a percussion cap on the cone. In practice, these systems were troubled and none, other than the Maynard Tape Primer, received wide acceptance.

BUTTERFIELD DISC PRIMER

The Butterfield primer consisted of a tube mounted to the center of the lock plate. The tube held tiny fulminate detonation discs. Internal mechanisms permitted a disc to be placed on the nipple when the user cocked the hammer.

Jesse Butterfield received a contract to convert 5,000 arms with this system in 1859. Deliveries, however, were very limited. Converted weapons were usually marked on the lock plate, forward of the hammer, "BUTTERFIELD'S / PATENT DEC. 11, 1855 / PHILADA".

GOOD—$2,500   FINE—$8,000

James D. Julia Auctioneers, Fairfield, Maine

MAYNARD TAPE PRIMER

The Maynard device is quickly recognized from the door placed on the lock plate forward of the hammer. To accommodate the mechanism, a special humped-shape hammer had to be used. The Maynard system fed a narrow strip of varnished paper with spots of fulminate at regular intervals.

Remington Arms Co. fulfilled a contract for the conversion of 20,000 U.S. Model 1816 muskets to the Maynard system between 1856-1859. The contract also called for the muskets to be rifled and receive long-range sights. The lock plates on these conversions are stamped, "REMINGTON'S / ILION, N.Y. / [date] / N.Y." Some are known to be marked "HERKIMER" instead of "ILION".

GOOD—$900   FINE—$1,850

The Frankford Arsenal's "Type I" Maynard conversion included a rear sight and rifling.

D.S. NIPPES CONVERSION

D.S. Nippes received two contracts each for the conversion of 1,000 U.S. Model 1835/1840 muskets. Nippes alteration built on the principal of the Maynard tape primer but could also be manually primed with a single conversion. Markings encountered on Nippes conversions include, "EDWARD MAYNARD / PATENTEE / 1845" and "MAYNARD'S PATENT / WASHINGTON / 1845".

GOOD—$2,100   FINE—$4,000

The "Type II" Maynard conversion was not sighted. Rock Island Auction Company

WARD TAPE PRIMER

The Ward system incorporated a swivel door on the upper section of the hammer. This covered the receptacle for a roll of tape primers. An internal mechanism fed the tape over the nipple when the user cocked the hammer. Ward conversions are found on U.S. Model 1816 (and even earlier Model 1812) muskets. The right side of the hammer is marked "J.N. WARD. U.S.A. / PATENTED JULY 1, 1856." Although the total quantity produced is unknown, the State of New York contracted for 1,200 conversions in 1857.

GOOD—$2,500   FINE—$4,750

James D. Julia Auctioneers, Fairfield, Maine

*Rock Island
Auction
Company*

PRUSSIAN MODEL 1809 MUSKET, .71 OR .72 CALIBER, PAPER CARTRIDGE, PERCUSSION

Made by several different private gun manufactories, ca. 1809-1839 Total imported: Unknown, but at least 100,000.

Overall length: 56-1/2".

Muzzleloader, single shot.

Lock plates stamped either "Potsdam", "Saarn", "Neiße", or "Suhl" beneath a Prussian crown. The large number of imports bearing the Potsdam stamp give the weapon its common designation. The year of conversion to percussion will often be found stamped on the left side of the barrel as will "[crown] / FW." Butt plates exhibit an array of markings including the year of conversion from flint, rack number, and regimental designation.

Originally produced as a flintlock, smooth-bore musket, the Model 1809

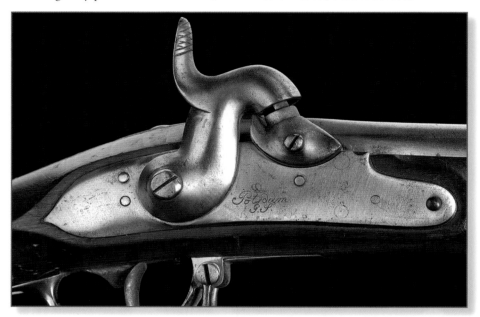

Rock Island Auction Company

was converted to percussion before being replaced by the Model 1839 rifled musket. All steel parts were left bright. The U.S. Ordnance Department purchased 100,300 Prussian arms identified as "smooth bore." There are no known records of Confederate purchases.

GOOD—$350   **FINE—$900**

U.S. MODEL 1841 CADET MUSKET .57 CALIBER, PAPER CARTRIDGE, PERCUSSION

James D. Julia Auctioneers, Fairfield, Maine

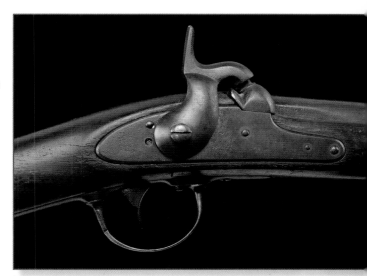

Manufactured by Springfield Armory, Springfield, Massachusetts, 1844–45. Total production: 450.

Muzzleloader, single shot.

Eagle over "US" on lock plate to front of hammer; "SPRING / FIELD / [year] vertically on lock plate to rear of hammer; "V / P / [eagle head]" on barrel.

This musket was intended for use by the Corps of Cadets at the U.S. Military Academy and was in service through 1856. Although it had a 40" round barrel secured to the stock with three iron bands, there is evidence that there were also three-band examples with 31" and 34" barrels. All metal parts were browned, except the casehardened lock. The bayonet stud was on the underside of the muzzle; there was no rear sight. Sling swivels were on the center band and front of the trigger guard bow.

GOOD—$6,500   FINE—$18,000

James D. Julia Auctioneers, Fairfield, Maine

U.S. MODEL 1842 MUSKET, HARPERS FERRY ARMORY, .69 CALIBER, PAPER CARTRIDGE, PERCUSSION

James D. Julia Auctioneers, Fairfield, Maine

Manufactured by Harpers Ferry Armory, Harper's Ferry, Virginia (now West Virginia), 1843–55. Total production: approximately 103,000.

Overall length: 57-13/16". Weight: 9 lbs. 3 oz.

Muzzleloader, single shot.

Eagle over "US" on lock plate in front of hammer; "HARPERS / FERRY / [year]" vertically on lock plate to rear of hammer; "V / P / [eagle head]" proof mark on left side of barrel near breech; inspector's initials forward of proof marks on some examples; "US" on tang of butt stock.

With the exception of the armory markings on the lock plate, the U.S. Model 1842 Muskets originating from Harpers Ferry Armory were virtually identical to those manufactured at the Springfield Armory. In addition, the musket parts from both armories were interchangeable. A variant of the U.S. Model 1842 Musket was the 3,200 reported to have been altered with shortened, rifled barrels and long-range rear sights for an expedition by John Charles Frémont in 1847. These rifled muskets had 33" barrels and an overall length of 48-1/2".

GOOD—$950   FINE—$2,750

U.S. MODEL 1842 MUSKET, SPRINGFIELD ARMORY, .69 CALIBER, PAPER CARTRIDGE, PERCUSSION

Manufactured by Springfield Armory, Springfield, Massachusetts, 1844–55. Total production: approximately 172,000.

Overall length: 57-13/16". Weight: 9 lbs. 3 oz.

Muzzleloader, single shot.

Eagle over "US" on lock plate in front of hammer; "SPRING / FIELD / [year]" vertically on lock plate to rear of hammer; "V / P / [eagle head]" proof mark on left side of barrel near breech; inspector's initials forward of proof marks on some examples; "US" on tang of butt plate.

Rock Island Auction Company

The U.S. Model 1842 musket was the first regulation percussion firearm and the last .69-caliber musket to be manufactured in U.S. armories. They were used in large numbers in the Mexican War and in the early months of the Civil War. They featured all-iron furniture, finished bright; a flat lock plate with beveled edges; 42" bright barrel fastened to the 55" black walnut stock with three barrel bands, the center of which held the upper sling swivel; and lower sling swivel riveted to the forward part of the trigger guard bow. A bayonet lug was located on the underside of the barrel near the muzzle. There was no rear sight; the forward sight was a brass blade on the upper barrel band. The butt plate was flat and 4-1/2" long. Many U.S. Model 1842 Muskets were rifled and equipped with long-range rear sights after 1855, and redesignated the U.S. Model 1842 Rifled Musket.

GOOD–$950   FINE–$2,750

U.S. MODEL 1842 MUSKET, B. FLAGG & COMPANY CONTRACT, .69 CALIBER, PAPER CARTRIDGE, PERCUSSION

Manufactured by B. Flagg & Co., Millbury, Massachusetts, 1849. Total production: at least 640.

Overall length: 57-3/4". Weight: approximately 9 lbs. 3 oz.

Muzzleloader, single shot.

Eagle over "U.S." on lock plate in front of hammer; "B. FLAGG & CO. / MILLBURY / MASS. / 1849" vertically on lock plate to rear of hammer ("1849" is marked horizontally on some specimens); "US" in italics on butt plate tang; serial number on butt plate tang, top of each band, and top of barrel near breech.

Benjamin Flagg's version of the U.S. Model 1842 Musket was a virtual copy of the government-manufactured original. The musket had a short production run, evidently during only 1849, and South Carolina purchased 640 stands the following year. The lock plates of some specimens have a nonstandard shape, in which the surface forward of the percussion cap bolster cutout continues at about the same, nearly horizontal angle as the bolster cutout, but slightly below its level. This extension was beveled like most of the rest of the plate.

GOOD–$1,200   FINE–$3,800

U.S. MODEL 1842 MUSKET, PALMETTO ARMORY CONTRACT, .69 CALIBER, PAPER CARTRIDGE, PERCUSSION

James D. Julia Auctioneers, Fairfield, Maine

Manufactured by Palmetto Armory, Columbia, South Carolina, 1852-53. Total production: at least 6,020.
Overall length: 57-3/4". Weight: approximately 9 lbs. 3 oz.
Muzzleloader, single shot.
"PALMETTO ARMORY S*C" in a circle around a palmetto tree, on lock plate to front of hammer; "COLUMBIA / S.C. 1852" vertically on lock plate to rear of hammer; "V / P / [palmetto tree]" proof mark on barrel near breech; "SC" on tang of butt plate.
In April 1851 the Palmetto Armory secured a contract with South Carolina to produce 6,000 copies of the U.S. Model 1842 Musket. The armory completed the contract by the end of 1853, on machinery purchased from Benjamin Flagg's factory in Millbury, Massachusetts, that had previously been used to manufacture the A. H. Waters and B. Flagg versions of the U.S. Model 1842 Musket. The Palmetto Armory version was very similar to the standard U.S. model, with variations in some examples including brass barrel bands instead of iron and a bayonet stud on top of the barrel rather than the bottom. In addition, some examples had long-range rear sights or browned barrels.

GOOD—$3,500   FINE—$7,000

U.S. MODEL 1842 A. H. WATERS CONTRACT MUSKET, .69 CALIBER, TYPE I (STANDARD BUTT PLATE), PAPER CARTRIDGE, PERCUSSION.

Made by A. H. Waters & Co., Milbury, Massachusetts, ca. 1844. Total production: probably over 100.
Overall length: 57-3/4". Weight: approximately 10 lbs. 4 oz.
Muzzleloader, single shot.
"A. H. WATERS & CO. / MILBURY, MASS" vertically on lock plate behind hammer; eagle and italic "US" on lock plate to front of hammer; "V", "P", and eagle head on barrel near breech.
This musket was produced by the private armory of Asa H. Waters in a very small quantity, probably in or after 1844. The locks were unhardened iron, flat with a beveled edge. The browned barrel was 42" long. Some examples had all-iron furniture, like the U.S. Model 1842 Musket, while others had all-brass furniture. The Type I musket had a standard butt plate, and the Type II a heavily textured brass "Sea Fencible" butt plate.

GOOD—$950   FINE—$3,400

U.S. "NAVY CONTRACT" MUSKET, .69 CALIBER, PAPER CARTRIDGE, PERCUSSION

Manufactured by A. H. Waters, Millbury, Massachusetts, and Eli Whitney, Jr., New Haven, Connecticut, ca. 1817–36; alterations ca. 1842–51. Total production: unknown.
Overall length: 57-11/16". Weight: 9 lbs. 15 oz.
Muzzleloader, single shot.
Waters version: "US / A WATERS" on lock plate to front of hammer; "MILLBURY / [year]" on lock plate to rear of hammer. Whitney version: "U.S. / [crossed arrow and olive branch] / E. WHITNEY" on lock plate in front of hammer; "NEW / HAVEN / [year]" on lock plate to rear of hammer.
At some point, probably between around 1842 and 1851, one or more arsenals or contractors altered an unknown number of U.S. Model 1816 flintlock muskets, .69 caliber. These muskets incorporate the "cone," or "Belgian" percussion system, with a nipple set directly on the breech instead of on a bolster, as well as a heavy, curved, brass butt plate (some iron plates have been reported) with a prominent protrusion at the heel. Since the butt plate was noticeably narrower than the stock version, the butt stock was correspondingly narrowed. Various sources have designated this alteration as a "Navy Contract," "Sea Fencible," or "Massachusetts Militia" musket.

GOOD—$950   FINE—$3,400

CHAPTER 2
RIFLED MUSKETS

I t is easy to confuse the terms "rifled musket," "rifle-musket," "rifle," and "musket." So easy, in fact, that the terms were often used interchangeably during the Civil War—and still are today among collectors!

In an effort to equip armies with modern arms, the practice of rifling smoothbore muskets emerged in the 1840s. A smoothbore musket that was subsequently rifled is referred to as a "rifled musket."

U.S. armories undertook rifling smooth-bore muskets during the 1855s, but these efforts were never really maximized until the prospect of civil war loomed. In February 1861, Colonel of Ordnance H.K. Craig reported that there were 24,300 .69 Model 1822 muskets altered to percussion at the Kennebec Arsenal and more than 100,000 .69 Model 1842 muskets ("much superior to the altered arms") at other arsenals. Furthermore, he explained to his superior, Secretary of War J. Holt, that preparations to rifle the latter had been begun but were suspended by the Secretary's predecessor in the late 1850s. He promised Lincoln's government that the work would immediately recommence.

Meanwhile, northern and southern buyers scoured European arsenals and armories hoping to find quality weapons to purchase and import. The European governments had undertaken the similar strategy of rifling old smoothbore muskets. However, as the European gun manufacturer's delivered stocks of newly made rifle-muskets and rifles, the old rifled muskets were retired to the gun racks. In most cases, these are the weapons the American buyers were able to purchase.

Rifled muskets remained in the hands of troops right up until the end of the Civil War. Today, they represent an interesting collision of old world linear tactics when the smooth-bored musket was supreme, with the new style of combat of identifying individual targets that is still practiced today.

U.S. Model 1842 Rifled Musket, Types I and II, 69 Caliber, Paper Cartridge, Percussion

Original muskets manufactured by Harpers Ferry Armory, Harper's Ferry, Virginia (now West Virginia), 1843–55, and Springfield Armory, Springfield, Massachusetts, 1844–55; altered to rifled muskets at the same armories, 1855–59. Total altered: 55,290.

Overall length: 57-13/16". Weight: 9 lbs. 4 oz.

Muzzleloader, single shot.

Eagle over "US" on lock plate in front of hammer; "HARPERS / FERRY / [year]" or "SPRING / FIELD / [year]" vertically on lock plate to rear of hammer; "V / P / [eagle head]" proof mark on left side of barrel near breech; inspector's initials forward of proof marks on some examples; year on barrel tang; "US" on tang of butt stock.

Government armories and arsenals carried out a program from 1855 to 1859 to rifle the barrels of U.S. Model 1842 Muskets (.69 caliber). The barrels were rifled with three broad grooves, with lands of the same width. In addition, long-range rear sights were installed on most units. These rifled muskets are designated "Type I."

Model 1842 Type II rifled muskets do not have rear sights.

A subset of the U.S. Model 1852 Rifled Muskets, Type I, were the 500 units that were browned at Harper's Ferry Armory in 1856.

Type II rifled muskets were the up to 20,074 weapons that were not fitted with rear sights.

Good—$1,200   **Fine—$3,500**

Model 1842 Type I rifled musket. Rock Island Auction Company

*Rock Island
Auction
Company*

GREENWOOD ALTERATION OF U.S. MUSKET TO RIFLED MUSKET, .69 CALIBER, PAPER CARTRIDGE, PERCUSSION (BELGIAN OR "CONE" TYPE)

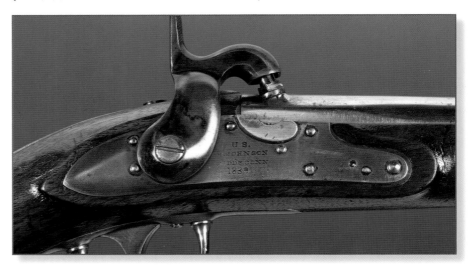

Muskets manufactured by various national and private armories; altered to rifled muskets by Miles Greenwood & Company, Cincinnati, Ohio, 1861. Total altered: 16,918.

Overall length and weight depend on model.

Muzzleloader, single shot.

Markings according to original maker.

In 1861 Miles Greenwood & Company of Cincinnati, Ohio, converted to rifled muskets 16,918 U.S. muskets which previously had been altered with cone-in-barrel (or Belgian style) percussion systems. The rifling was with four narrow grooves, and a rear sight similar to that on the British P1853 rifle-musket was soldered to the barrel.

GOOD—$900   **FINE—$2,000**

GREENWOOD ALTERATION OF U.S. MODEL 1842 MUSKET TO RIFLED MUSKET, .69 CALIBER, PAPER CARTRIDGE, PERCUSSION

Original muskets manufactured by Harpers Ferry Armory, Harper's Ferry, Virginia, 1843–55, and Springfield Armory, Springfield, Massachusetts, 1844–55; altered to rifled muskets by Miles Greenwood & Company, Cincinnati, Ohio, 1861. Total altered: approximately 8,400.

Overall length: 57-13/16". Weight: approximately 9 lbs. 4 oz.

Muzzleloader, single shot.

Eagle over "US" on lock plate in front of hammer; "HARPERS / FERRY / [year]" or "SPRING / FIELD / [year]" vertically on lock plate to rear of hammer; "V / P / [eagle head]" proof mark on left side of barrel near breech; inspector's initials forward of proof marks on some examples; year on barrel tang; "US" on tang of butt stock.

In 1861 the State of Ohio contracted with Miles Greenwood & Company to alter a quantity of U.S. Model 1842 smoothbore muskets to rifled muskets with long-range rear sights. Greenwood reportedly altered 8,406 of these weapons, rifled with four narrow grooves, and with rear sights similar to the British P1853 rifle-musket soldered to the barrel.

GOOD—$1,200   **FINE—$3,500**

GREENWOOD ALTERATION TO AUSTRIAN MODEL 1842 MUSKET TO RIFLED MUSKET, APPROXIMATELY .70 CALIBER, PAPER CARTRIDGE, PERCUSSION

Manufactured by Austrian national armory, alteration by Miles Greenwood & Co. and Hall, Carroll, & Co., Cincinnati, Ohio, 1861. Total production: approximately 10,000.

Overall length: 57-3/4".

Muzzleloader, single shot.

Three-digit date (omitting the first digit "1") to front of hammer on lock plate; Austrian imperial double-headed eagle to rear of hammer on lock plate; most metal parts stamped with identical numbers.

In 1861, Miles Greenwood & Company contracted to alter 10,000 Austrian Model 1842 smoothbore muskets destined for Gen. John Charles Frémont's Missouri troops. Greenwood subcontracted 5,000 of the units to Hall, Carroll, & Company, also of Cincinnati. Reportedly, the alteration consisted of replacing the Austrian tubelock ignition apparatus with a percussion system, possibly of the cone-in-barrel (or Belgian) type, as well as installing a long-range rear sight soldered to the barrel. This model of musket had a 43" barrel and easily identifiable lock markings.

GOOD—$400   **FINE—$1,500**

Rock Island Auction Company

U.S. MODEL 1851 RIFLED CADET MUSKET, .57 CALIBER, PAPER CARTRIDGE, PERCUSSION

Manufactured by Springfield Armory, Springfield, Massachusetts, ca. 1851–53, rifled by Springfield Armory, 1857. Total production: ca. 341.

Overall length: 55-1/4".

Muzzleloader, single shot.

"SPRING / FIELD / [year]" on lock plate to rear of hammer; eagle over "US" on lock plate to front of hammer; year on top of breech plug tang; "V," "P," and eagle head near breech.

Springfield Armory's records for 1857 reported that 341 Model 1851 Cadet Muskets, smoothbore, were rifled and equipped with long-range rear sights. These rifled muskets had 40" barrels and iron furniture, finished bright; and three barrel bands (upper band with double strap).

GOOD—$850   **FINE—$2,000**

P.S. JUSTICE RIFLED MUSKET, .69 CALIBER, TYPE I, PAPER CARTRIDGE, PERCUSSION

Made by Philip S. Justice, Philadelphia, 1861. Total production: Unknown.

Overall length: 54-3/4".

Muzzleloader, single shot.

"P.S. JUSTICE / PHILADA" on lock plate to front of hammer and on top of barrel near breech; on some specimens, a number to rear of bayonet stud and eagle on lock plate to front of hammer.

Philip S. Justice supplied 2,174 .69-caliber rifled muskets in three distinctive types to the U.S. Ordnance Department in the fall of 1861. Similar in appearance to the U.S. Model 1816 musket converted to percussion, the Type I rifled musket was assembled from old-stock parts, with a new (and often unseasoned) black walnut stock. The 39" barrel was rifled with three wide lands and shallow grooves. It included a long-range rear sight, Model 1816 lock and trigger, and three Model 1840 or 1842 barrel bands with springs and sling swivel on the bottom of the middle band.

GOOD—$800   **FINE—$1,700**

P.S. JUSTICE RIFLED MUSKET, .69 CALIBER, TYPE II, PAPER CARTRIDGE, PERCUSSION.

Made by Philip S. Justice, Philadelphia, 1861. Total production: Unknown.
Overall length: 55". Weight: 7 lbs. 6 oz.
Muzzleloader, single shot.

"P.S. JUSTICE / PHILADA" on lock plate to front of hammer and on top of barrel near breech; on some specimens, a number to rear of bayonet stud and eagle on lock plate to front of hammer.

At least one weapons expert has called the Justice Type II rifled musket perhaps the poorest firearm submitted to the U.S. Ordnance Department in the Civil War, and possibly the only martial shoulder arm of the war with the barrel pinned to the stock, in lieu of barrel bands. The 39" browned barrel was fitted with a long-range rear sight or a fixed, V-notch sight. All furniture was brass, and included a patch box in the butt stock, two ramrod thimbles, and a trigger guard bow with a distinctive reverse curve on the bottom. There were no provisions for sling swivels. The black walnut stock was crudely manufactured, often of unseasoned wood.

GOOD—$800   FINE—$1,700

P.S. JUSTICE RIFLED MUSKET, .69 CALIBER, TYPE III, PAPER CARTRIDGE, PERCUSSION.

Made by Philip S. Justice, Philadelphia, 1861. Total production: Unknown.
Muzzleloader, single shot.

"P.S. JUSTICE / PHILADA" on lock plate to front of hammer and on top of barrel near breech; on some specimens, an eagle on lock plate to front of hammer.

Of the three types of Justice Rifled Musket, .69 caliber, the Type III appears to have survived in the greatest numbers. Unlike the other two types, it was built entirely of new parts, and included a 39" browned barrel, prominent brass front blade sight, and two-leaf rear sight soldered to the barrel. The barrel was secured to the 52" black walnut stock with three 1/2"-wide, split-clamping oval bands; upper sling swivel on the middle band. The bayonet stud was on the bottom of the barrel, 1" from the muzzle. The furniture was brass, including a patch box and distinctive, reverse-curve trigger-guard bow.

GOOD—$900   FINE—$1,800

*Rock Island
Auction
Company*

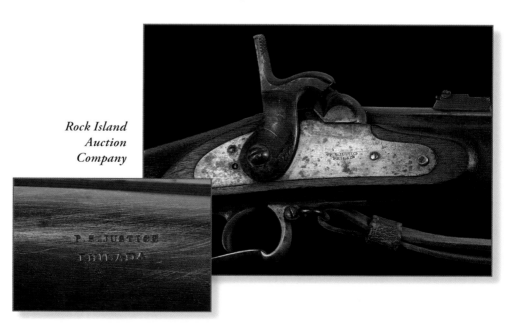

U.S. MODEL 1842 MUSKET, PALMETTO ARMORY CONTRACT, .69 CALIBER, PAPER CARTRIDGE, PERCUSSION

Manufactured by Palmetto Armory, Columbia, South Carolina, 1860-1861. Total production: at least 3,700.

Overall length: 57-3/4". Weight: approximately 9 lbs. 3 oz.

Muzzleloader, single shot.

"PALMETTO ARMORY S*C" in a circle around a palmetto tree, on lock plate to front of hammer; "COLUMBIA / S.C. 1852" vertically on lock plate to rear of hammer; "V / P / [palmetto tree]" proof mark on barrel near breech; "SC" on tang of butt plate.

In April 1851 the Palmetto Armory secured a contract with South Carolina to produce 6,000 copies of the U.S. Model 1842 Musket. The armory completed the contract by the end of 1853, on machinery purchased from Benjamin Flagg's factory in Millbury, Massachusetts, that had previously been used to manufacture the A. H. Waters and B. Flagg versions of the U.S. Model 1842 Musket. The Palmetto Armory version was very similar to the standard U.S. model, with variations in some examples including brass barrel bands instead of iron and a bayonet stud on top of the barrel rather than the bottom. In February 1860, the State of South Carolina contracted the Palmetto Armory to add a fixed rear sight and rifle 3,700 of the Model 1842 muskets then at the Armory. The Armory completed the contract by August 1861. All of the rifled muskets are dated 1852.

GOOD—$2,500   **FINE—$5,000**

PRUSSIAN MODEL 1839/55 RIFLED MUSKET, .69 TO .72 CALIBER, PAPER CARTRIDGE, PERCUSSION

Made by government armories and several different private gun manufactories, ca. 1839-ca.1860. Total imported: Unknown, but at least 65,000.

Overall length: 57".

Muzzleloader, single shot.

Lock plates stamped with the Prussian crown over place of manufacture such as "SUHL / S & C", "Potsdam / GT", "Zella", or "Mehlis," which is over the year of manufacture.

Though originally designed as a smoothbore, manufacturers began to turn out rifled versions of the Model 1839 in 1855, hence the designation "Model 1839/55." The barrel is fitted with a patent breech that accepts a screwed in cone. The U.S. Ordnance Department purchased 65,000 Prussian arms identified as "smooth bore." There are no known records of Confederate purchases.

At least two variants of the standard Model 1839/55 are known:

Type I: Nearly identical to the standard Model 1839/55 except that it is fitted with a back-action lock. Type I rifled muskets vary in bore from .69" to .715". The union gun dealer, Herman Boker, imported 4,286 of this variant during the Civil War.

Type II: This variant is early identical to the standard Model 1839/55 but measures only 55-1/2" overall and is chambered for a .615"-caliber ball. The Type II has a bayonet stud beneath the barrel in place of the retaining spring. Type II variants are fitted with a long range sight very similar to the type used on the British Pattern 1853 rifle-musket. U.S. importer John Hoey purchased 1,810 Prussian rifles, "caliber .615" on March 6, 1862.

ALL TYPES: GOOD—$375   FINE—$1,100

James D. Julia Auctioneers, Fairfield, Maine

HANSEATIC LEAGUE MODEL 1840 RIFLED MUSKET, .70 CALIBER, PAPER CARTRIDGE, PERCUSSION

Made by Carl Phillip Crause, Hertzberg, Germany, ca. 1839-? Total imported: Unknown.

Overall length: 55-1/2".

Muzzleloader, single shot.

Lock plate inscribed "Crause of Hertzberg". Monogrammed "T", "S", or "R" have also been observed.

Though originally designed as a smoothbore, most were rifled during the 1850s. The barrel was browned while other iron parts were left bright. It is unknown how many were imported during the war, but it has been reported that 2,680 were transferred to the State of Ohio by the Federal government.

GOOD—$375 FINE—$1,100

SAXON MODEL 1844 RIFLED MUSKET, .71 CALIBER, PAPER CARTRIDGE, PERCUSSION

Made by several manufacturers, Liege, Belgium, ca. 1844-? Total imported: Unknown.

Overall length: 57".

Muzzleloader, single shot.

Lock plate stamped to reflect individual manufacturing companies, including "[crown] / BF" for Beuret Freres, "[crown] / AF" for August Francotte and "P.J. MALHERBE- A LIEGE". A Liege proof mark is usually stamped on the right side of the breech. Assembly numbers mark the barrel, breech, bands and other major components.

Though originally designed as a smoothbore, most were rifled during the 1850s. Two types of sights have been observed on Model 1844 rifled muskets: the first is a notched, block-mounted sight on the breech plug tang. The second style has a folding leaf pierced with three sighting holes mounted on the barrel. Metal furniture can be either brass iron. The barrel and any iron furniture was left bright. Because gun buyers (or sellers) did not make a great effort to differentiate between the muskets of various German states, it is unknown how many Saxon Model 1844 rifled muskets were imported during the war. There are no known records of Confederate purchases.

GOOD—$375 FINE—$900

BAVARIAN MODEL 1842 RIFLED MUSKET, .70 CALIBER, PAPER CARTRIDGE, PERCUSSION

Made by national armory, Amberg, Germany, ca. 1842-ca. 1858. Total imported: Unknown.

Overall length: 56-1/4".

Muzzleloader, single shot.

Lock plate stamped "AMBERG" with the year of manufacture over a crown.

Originally produced as smooth bore muskets, the Model 1842s were rifled with five grooves in the early 1850s. They were the first percussion weapons adopted by the Bavarian army. The three-band weapon has a simple blade front sight just to the rear of the front barrel band. The rear sight is a simple notched block of iron mounted to the breech tang. Examples have been observed with a hinged rear sight. Though Marcellus Hartley commented on the availability of Bavarian muskets in his communications with the Secretary of War, no evidence of any purchase has been discovered. No records of Confederate purchases are known.

GOOD—$375 FINE—$900

FRENCH MODEL 1816 RIFLED MUSKET, .71 CALIBER, PAPER CARTRIDGE, PERCUSSION

Made by a variety of French and Belgium gun manufactories, ca. 1816-ca. 1822. Total imported: at least 2,000.

Overall length: 58-1/8".

Muzzleloader, single shot.

A wide variety of lock plate markings have been observed. The barrel tang is engraved with the model designation, "M 1816."

After the French government retired its flintlock, smooth-bore Model 1816 muskets, the German State of Wurttemberg acquired them. The Germans converted the muskets to percussion by replacing the flintlock hammer, pan, and frizzen, with a bolster brazed to the breech, a cone threaded into it, and a new hammer. Furthermore, they rifled the barrel and added a long-range rear sight. When Union purchasing agent Marcellus Harley purchased 2,000 of the rifled muskets in Liege, he called them "Wurttemberg government guns." No records of Confederate purchases are known

GOOD—$375 FINE—$900

FRENCH MODEL 1822 RIFLED MUSKET, .69/.71 CALIBER, PAPER CARTRIDGE, PERCUSSION

Made by royal arsenals at Tylle, Charleville, Mutzig and St. Etienne and copied by Liege manufacturers, ca. 1822-ca. 1842. Total imported: Unknown, but Union records show over 147,000 French and Belgium muskets were purchased.

Overall length:Type I, 58".
Type II, 55-4/5".
Muzzleloader, single shot.

Lock plate markings reflect arsenals where manufactured. The barrel tang is engraved with the model designation, "M 1822" and year of manufacture. Liege-made examples have only the year of manufacture proof marks. A "T" will follow the model number on weapons altered in French arsenals. French barrels may also be stamped with the date of alteration and caliber in millimeters in addition to the usual proof marks.

French regular line infantry carried the longer, Type I Model 1822 muskets. Voltiguers (light infantry) carried the shorter, Type II muskets. Both were originally configured as smoothbore, flintlock muskets, but were later converted to percussion by replacing the hammer and inserting a cone directly in the top of the barrel and plugging the vent or by brazing a bolster over the vent. Many were rifled and received long-range rear sights at the same time. Union gun buyers purchased at least 147,000 French and Belgian muskets during the Civil War. However, their records do not indicate model designations making it impossible to know exactly how many Model 1822 muskets made it to the United States. The U.S. Ordnance Department rated French and Belgian rifled muskets as 2nd class. No record of Confederate purchases is known.

BOTH TYPES: GOOD—$375   FINE—$900

FRENCH MODEL 1842 RIFLED MUSKET, .70/.71 CALIBER, PAPER CARTRIDGE, PERCUSSION

Made by French royal and Imperial arsenals and copied by Liege manufacturers, ca. 1842-ca. 1855. Total imported: Unknown, but Union records show over 147,000 French and Belgium muskets were purchased.

Overall length:Type I, 58-1/4".
Type II, 56".
Muzzleloader, single shot.

Lock plate markings reflect arsenals where manufactured. Between 1848 and 1852, French lock plates are inscribed with "Mre. Nle. de" followed by a city name. After 1852, this was changed to "Mre. Impale. de" followed by the city name. The barrel tang is engraved with the model designation, "M 1842" and year of manufacture. Liege-made examples have only the year of manufacture proof marks. A "T" will follow the model number on weapons altered in French arsenals. French barrels may also be stamped with the date of alteration and caliber in millimeters in addition to the usual proof marks.

Originally configured as smoothbore muskets, the Model 1842 was the first percussion long arm that the French Army adopted. French regular line infantry carried a 58-1/4" long version of the Model 1842 musket. Voltiguers (light infantry) carried a shorter, 56" long version. Either sized of the Model 1842 can be recognized by its back-action lock. All iron was left bright. In 1853, many Model 1842 muskets were rifled and received long-range sights. The longer infantry line weapons were shortened to 56" at this time. Union gun buyers purchased at least 147,000 French and Belgian rifled and smoothbore muskets during the Civil War. However, their records do not indicate model designations, making it impossible to know exactly how many Model 1842 rifled muskets made it to the United States. The U.S. Ordnance Department rated French and Belgian rifled muskets as 2nd class. No record of Confederate purchases is known.

BOTH TYPES: GOOD—$375   FINE—$900

PIEDMONTESE MODEL 1844/60 RIFLED MUSKET, .69 CALIBER, PAPER CARTRIDGE, PERCUSSION

Made by state arsenals at Torino, Italy, and Liege, Belgium, ca. 1855. Total imported: Unknown but Union records show at least 2,000 were purchased.

Overall length: 56".
Muzzleloader, single shot.

The weapons imported by the U.S. were manufactured at one of three Liege, Belgium arsenals. Lock plate markings reflect arsenals where manufactured: Those made by August Francotte & Co. are marked with his cypher and "[crown] / AF. Some of the stocks of these will be stamped with a circular "A. Francote-Liège" mark. Falisse and Trapmann stamped lock plates that the produced, "Liège / F&T / 1861. Finally, those produced by Ancion are stamped, "Ancion & Cie / a Liège".

The Piedmontese Model 1844/60 was the first percussion long arm adopted by the Kingdom of Piedmont. Originally designed as a copy of the French Model 1822 Musket, the Piedmontese weapons were rifled in 1860. Marcellus Harley reported to Secretary of War Stanton in 1862 that he was ready to ship 2,000 Piedmontese Rifled Muskets. No known record of Confederate purchase.

GOOD—$375   FINE—$900

CHAPTER 3
RIFLE-MUSKETS

I n the mid-1850s, the United States embarked on a new era in military hardware. By approving the manufacture and issuing of rifle-muskets to its infantry, they were keeping up in an international arms race to field the most modern armed forces.

Whereas rifled muskets were already in the hands of some troops, the smoothbore musket was still the most prevalent. Rather than focusing all efforts on reboring the old weapons, the federal arsenals at Harpers Ferry and Springfield would begin the manufacturing of the modern, purpose-built, Model 1855 rifle-musket.

A rifle-musket is a long arm that was originally built with a rifled barrel. Generally—but not exclusively—manufacturers produced rifle-muskets in approximately .58 caliber. Finally, the third characteristic of a rifle-musket is that it is equipped to support an angular bayonet.

By far, rifle-muskets were the most common weapons of the Civil War. Contractors and arsenals in both the north and south turned out tens of thousands of rifle-muskets, making this a ripe area for collectors today.

U.S. Model 1855 Rifle-Musket, .58 Caliber, Harpers Ferry, Paper Cartridge, Percussion

Rock Island
Auction Company

Harpers Ferry Model 1855 Rifle-Musket, Type I. Rock Island Auction Company

Proof marks found on Harpers Ferry-manufactured Model 1855 rifle-muskets. Rock Island Auction Company

Manufactured by Harpers Ferry Armory, Harpers Ferry, Virginia (now West Virginia), 1859–61. Total production: 12,158.

Overall length: 56". Weight: 9 lbs. 3 oz.

Muzzleloader, single shot.

"U.S. / HARPERS FERRY" in front of lock plate in front of hammer; year to rear of lock plate; spread eagle on primer door; "V / P" over eagle head on upper left flat of barrel; year on top of barrel near breech.

The Harpers Ferry version of the U.S. Model 1855 Rifle-Musket, .58 caliber, was similar to the Springfield version, with the exception of different maker's mark on the lock plate.

Three principal types existed:

Type I: Included a long-base rear sight marked "US," 5-1/2" from the breech; furniture was iron, except for a brass fore-tip.

Type II: In early 1855, a smaller long-range, two-leaf sight was adopted; it was mounted 2-3/4" from the breech.

Type III: Same as the Type II, except the fore-tip was changed to iron, and an iron patch box was installed in the right side of the butt stock.

All types: Good—$1,450   Fine—$5,000

Springfield Model 1855 Rifle-Musket, Type III, with iron patchbox. Amoskeag Auction Company, Inc.

James D. Julia Auctioneers, Fairfield, Maine

U.S. MODEL 1855 CONTRACT RIFLE-MUSKET, SPRINGFIELD, .58 CALIBER, PAPER CARTRIDGE, PERCUSSION

Manufactured by Springfield Armory, Springfield, Massachusetts, ca. 1856–61. Total production: 47,115.

Overall length: 56". Weight: 9 lbs. 3 oz.

Muzzleloader, single shot.

"U.S. / SPRINGFIELD" to front of lock plate in front of hammer; year to rear of lock plate; spread eagle on primer door; year on top flat of barrel near breech; "V / P" over eagle head on upper left flat of barrel; "U" on right side of each barrel band; "US" on tang of butt plate.

This model of rifle-musket, manufactured by the Springfield and Harpers Ferry Armories, saw extensive service in the Civil War and was significant for being the first officially adopted U.S. firearm to use the .58-caliber Minié bullet. It incorporated the Maynard tape primer system and had a 40" round barrel rifled with three grooves. All hardware was finished bright. The oil-finished black walnut stock had inspector's initials stamped on the left side opposite the lock.

Three principal types existed:

Type I: Included a long-base rear sight marked "US," 5-1/2" from the breech; furniture was iron, except for a brass fore-tip.

Type II: In early 1855, a smaller long-range, two-leaf sight was adopted; it was mounted 2-3/4" from the breech.

Type III: Same as the Type II, except the fore-tip was changed to iron, and an iron patch box was installed in the right side of the butt stock.

ALL TYPES: GOOD—$1,650   FINE—$5,500

U.S. MODEL 1855 WHITNEY CONTRACT RIFLE-MUSKET, .58 CALIBER, PAPER CARTRIDGE, PERCUSSION

Manufactured by Eli Whitney, Jr., New Haven, Connecticut, ca. 1857–58. Total production: approximately 350.

Overall length: 56". Weight: 9 lbs. 3 oz.

Muzzleloader, single shot.

"E. WHITNEY / N. HAVEN" to front of lock plate in front of hammer; year (usually "1858"; some examples lack dates) to rear of lock plate; spread eagle on primer door; letter over number on barrel near breech.

The Whitney Contract version of the U.S. Model 1855 Rifle-Musket, .58 caliber, was similar to the Springfield and Harpers Ferry versions, with these exceptions in the Whitney arms: the barrel was rifled with seven grooves instead of three; the fore-tip was pewter of the Enfield pattern; the band-retaining springs were slightly longer; and side-screw ferrules were brass of the Enfield type. Specimens exist with both the Type I long-base rear sight and the smaller Type II rear sight.

GOOD—$1,550   FINE—$3,500

U.S. MODEL 1858 CADET RIFLE-MUSKET, SPRINGFIELD, .58 CALIBER, PAPER CARTRIDGE, PERCUSSION

Manufactured by Springfield Armory, Springfield, Massachusetts, ca. 1858–60. Total production: 2,501.

Overall length: 53".

Muzzleloader, single shot.

"U.S. / SPRINGFIELD" to front of lock plate in front of hammer; year to rear of lock plate; spread eagle on primer door; year on top flat of barrel near breech; "V / P" over eagle head on upper left flat of barrel; "U" on right side of each barrel band; "US" on tang of butt plate.

The U.S. Model 1858 Cadet Rifle-Musket was similar to the U.S. Model 1855 Rifle-Musket, Type I, except for a shortened, 38" barrel and stock shortened 1" at the butt, yielding an overall length 3" shorter than the Model 1855 Rifle-Musket.

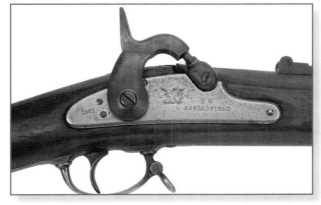

James D. Julia Auctioneers, Fairfield, Maine

GOOD–$1,500   FINE–$4,500

U.S. MODEL 1861 RIFLE-MUSKET, SPRINGFIELD, .58 CALIBER, PAPER CARTRIDGE, PERCUSSION

Manufactured by Springfield Armory, Springfield, Massachusetts, 1861–62. Total production: 265,129.

Overall length: 56". Weight: 9 lbs. 2 oz.

Muzzleloader, single shot.

"U.S. / SPRINGFIELD" to front of lock plate in front of hammer; spread eagle at center of lock plate; year to rear of lock plate; year on top flat of barrel near breech; "V / P" over eagle head on upper left flat of barrel; "U" on right side of each barrel band; "US" on tang of butt plate; inspector's initials on left side of stock opposite the lock.

Considered the principal longarm in the Federal service in the Civil War, the U.S. Model 1861 Rifle-Musket was similar to the U.S. Model 1855 Musket-Rifle, Type II, except with an iron fore-tip and a standard percussion cap nipple and bolster, instead of the Maynard tape-primer mechanism. The round, 40" barrel was rifled with three broad grooves. All metal parts were bright finished, but blued rear sights are sometimes found. The rear sight was a two-leaf type graduated to 500 yards, but reportedly some early examples of the arm were fitted with Model 1858 sights. The black walnut stock was 53" long and oil finished.

GOOD–$1,200   FINE–$3,500

U.S. MODEL 1861 EAGLEVILLE CONTRACT RIFLE-MUSKET, .58 CALIBER, PAPER CARTRIDGE, PERCUSSION

Manufactured by Eagle Manufacturing Company, Mansfield, Connecticut, ca. 1861–63. Total production: at least 5,500; possibly as many as 20,000.

Overall length: 56". Weight: 9 lbs. 2 oz.

Muzzleloader, single shot.

"U.S. / EAGLEVILLE" on lock plate below bolster cutout; spread eagle at center of lockplate; year toward rear of lockplate.

In late December 1861, the Federal government contracted with the Eagle Manufacturing Company for 25,000 U.S. Model 1862 Rifle-Muskets, reducing that number to 20,000 in May 1862. The company is known to have delivered 5,500 units between April 14 and September 30, 1862, but documents indicate that the contract was fulfilled.

GOOD–$950   FINE–$3,000

Rock Island Auction Company

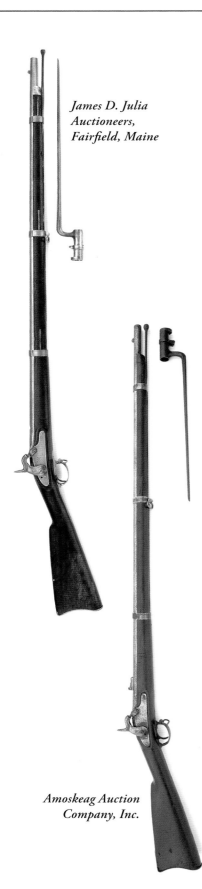

*James D. Julia
Auctioneers,
Fairfield, Maine*

*Amoskeag Auction
Company, Inc.*

U.S. MODEL 1861 CONTRACT RIFLE-MUSKET, ALFRED JENKS & SON, .58 CALIBER, PAPER CARTRIDGE, PERCUSSION

Manufactured by Alfred Jenks & Son, Philadelphia, Pennsylvania, 1861–62. Total production: 98,464.

Overall length: 56". Weight: 9 lbs. 2 oz.

Muzzleloader, single shot.

Three lock plate markings existed: 1) "U.S. / BRIDESBURG / 1861" below bolster cutout and spread eagle at center of lock plate (extremely rare); 2) "U.S. / PHILADELPHIA" below bolster cutout; spread eagle at center of lock plate; year of manufacture to rear of lock plate; 3) "U.S. / BRIDESBURG" below bolster cutout of lock plate, spread eagle at center of lock plate, year near rear of lock plate (most common).

Alfred Jenks & Son's Bridesburg Machine Works delivered U.S. Model 1861 Rifle-Muskets under five contracts between July 13, 1861, and February 1, 1865.

GOOD—$900   FINE—$1,300

U.S. MODEL 1861 RIFLE-MUSKET, "MANTON" CONTRACT, .58 CALIBER, PAPER CARTRIDGE, PERCUSSION

Manufactured by Whitneyville Armory, New Haven, Connecticut, ca. 1862–63. Total production: probably fewer than 2,000.

Overall length: 56" and 55". Weight: approximately 9 lbs.

Muzzleloader, single shot.

"MANTON" engraved in Old English letters below bolster cutout on lock plate; year stamped vertically near rear of lock plate; "V / P" over eagle head on barrel (design of eagle head varied, and it was absent on some examples); inspector's mark "G.W.Q." on barrel of most examples.

The "Manton" Contract U.S. Model 1861 Rifle-Musket was actually the product of Eli Whitney, Jr.'s Whitneyville Armory. It is unclear why Whitney delivered these arms with markings inferring that they were the product of the London armory of J. Manton & Son, but it has been speculated that Whitney was attempting to pawn-off substandard weapons by attaching the name of a respected foreign manufacturer to them. Barrel lengths of 39" and 40" have been observed, and the "Manton" had a single-leaf rear sight different from the Springfield version of the arm.

GOOD—$950   FINE—$3,000

U.S. MODEL 1861 RIFLE-MUSKET, WILLIAM MASON CONTRACT, .58 CALIBER, PAPER CARTRIDGE, PERCUSSION

Manufactured by William Mason, Taunton, Massachusetts, ca. 1862–63. Total production: 30,000.

Overall length: 56". Weight: 9 lbs. 2 oz.

Muzzleloader, single shot.

"U.S. / WM MASON / TAUNTON" below bolster cutout on lock plate; spread eagle at center of lock plate; year at rear of lock plate.

The version of the U.S. Model 1861 Rifle-Musket produced by the factory of William Mason was very similar to the Springfield version of the weapon, with the exception of the lock plate markings.

GOOD—$900   FINE—$2,750

U.S. MODEL 1861 RIFLE-MUSKET, "MILLBURY" CONTRACT, .58 CALIBER, PAPER CARTRIDGE, PERCUSSION

Presumed manufactured by A. H. Waters, Milbury [sic], Massachusetts, 1861–62. Total production: unknown.

Overall length: 56". Weight: 9 lbs. 2 oz.

Muzzleloader, single shot.

"U.S. / MILLBURY" below bolster cutout on lock plate; spread eagle (rearward facing) at center of lock plate; year at rear of lock plate.

It is uncertain who manufactured examples of the U.S. Model 1861 Rifle-Musket marked "MILLBURY," but it is assumed these were the products of A. H. Waters and Company of Milbury, Massachusetts. The unusual rear-facing eagle is similar to the eagle stamped on U.S. Model 1842 muskets produced under contract by Benjamin Flagg, who after the death of Asa Waters, Jr., became the superintendent of the Waters factory.

GOOD—$1,200   FINE—$3,250

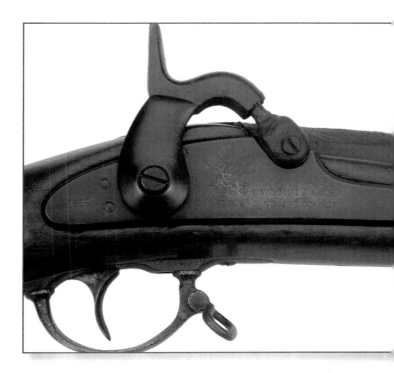

U.S. MODEL 1861 RIFLE-MUSKET, JAMES D. MOWRY CONTRACT, .58 CALIBER, PAPER CARTRIDGE, PERCUSSION

Manufactured by James D. Mowry, Norwich, Connecticut, 1861–64. Total production: 22,000.

Overall length: 56". Weight: 9 lbs. 2 oz.

Muzzleloader, single shot.

"U.S. / JAS D. MOWRY / NORWICH, CONN." below bolster cutout in lock plate; spread eagle at center of lock plate; year at rear of lock plate.

James D. Mowry Contract U.S. Model 1861 Rifle-Muskets were assembled from a mix of Mowry's own parts and those acquired from subcontractors.

GOOD—$900   FINE—$2,750

U.S. MODEL 1861 RIFLE-MUSKET, MUIR CONTRACT, .58 CALIBER, PAPER CARTRIDGE, PERCUSSION

Manufactured by William Muir and Company, Windsor Locks, Connecticut, ca. 1861–64. Total production: 30,000.

Overall length: 56". Weight: 9 lbs. 2 oz.

Muzzleloader, single shot.

"WM MUIR & CO. / WINDSOR LOCKS, CT." below bolster cutout on lock plate; spread eagle over "U.S." at center of lock plate; year at rear of lock plate.

The Muir Contract Model 1861 rifle-muskets were assembled from parts mostly obtained from subcontractors. A large number of the arms were substandard, and the government accepted those units at a discount of almost 25 percent. Muir made deliveries between January 22, 1863, and November 3, 1864.

GOOD—$900   FINE—$2,750

U.S. MODEL 1861 RIFLE-MUSKET, NORRIS & CLEMENT CONTACT, .58 CALIBER, PAPER CARTRIDGE, PERCUSSION

Manufactured by S. Norris & W. T. Clement, Springfield, Massachusetts, ca. 1863–64. Total production: approximately 11,000 (?).

Overall length: 56". Weight: 9 lbs. 2 oz.

Muzzleloader, single shot.

"S.N. & W.T.C. / FOR / MASSACHUSETTS" below bolster cutout on lock plate; spread eagle over "U.S." at center of lock plate; year toward rear of lock plate.

In 1863 and 1864, Samuel Norris and W. T. Clement fulfilled two or more contracts for Model 1861 rifle-muskets. An 1864 Massachusetts Adjutant General's report noted that the state had purchased 11,000 "Springfield Rifle Muskets & Appendages" from Norris & Clement, but this number may have included a mix of Model 1861 and Model 1863 rifle-muskets.

GOOD—$900   FINE—$2,750

U.S. MODEL 1861 RIFLE-MUSKET, "PARKER'S SNOW & CO." (JAMES MULHOLLAND CONTRACT AND PARKER, SNOW & CO. CONTRACT), .58 CALIBER, PAPER CARTRIDGE, PERCUSSION

Amoskeag Auction Company, Inc.

Manufactured by Parker, Snow & Company, Meriden, Connecticut, ca. 1863–64. Total production: 5,502, Mulholland Contract; 15,000, Parker, Snow & Co. Contract.

Overall length: 56". Weight: 9 lbs. 2 oz.

Muzzleloader, single shot.

"PARKERS' SNOW & CO. / MERIDEN, CONN." stamped on lock plate below bolster cutout; spread eagle over "U.S." at center of lock plate; year toward rear of lock plate ("1863" probably Mulholland Contract; "1864" Parker, Snow & Co. Contract).

Documentary evidence indicates that specimens of this contract rifle-musket dated 1863 were most likely manufactured for James Mulholland of Reading, Pennsylvania, under a subcontract by Parker, Snow, Brooks & Co. (later, Parker, Snow & Co.) of Meriden, Connecticut. Mulholland delivered 5,502 of these arms to the U.S. government between July 7 and October 31, 1863.

In November 1864, Parker, Snow & Co. completed delivery of 15,000 Model 1861 rifle-muskets to the U.S. government under the firm's own contract of September 28, 1863.

GOOD—$900   **FINE—$2,750**

U.S. MODEL 1861 RIFLE-MUSKET, "NORFOLK" MODEL (WELCH, BROWN & CO. CONTRACT), .58 CALIBER, PAPER CARTRIDGE, PERCUSSION

Manufactured by Welch, Brown and Company, Norfolk, Connecticut, ca. 1861–64. Total production: 16,000.

Rock Island Auction Company

Overall length: 56". Weight: 9 lbs. 2 oz.

Muzzleloader, single shot.

"U.S. / NORFOLK" below bolster cutout on lock plate; spread eagle at center of lock plate; year to rear of lock plate.

Welch, Brown and Company contracted to produce 18,000 Model 1861 rifle-muskets in November 1861, but delivered only 16,000 units, from September 1862 to December 1863. The government accepted only 2,940 of these as up to standard, purchasing the balance at discount.

GOOD—$900   **FINE—$2,750**

U.S. MODEL 1861 RIFLE-MUSKET, NORWICH ARMS

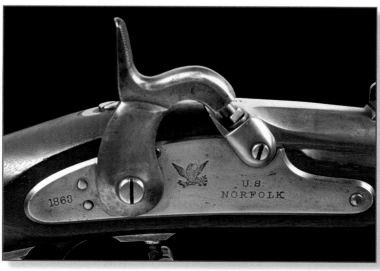

Co. Contract, .58 Caliber, Paper Cartridge, Percussion

Manufactured by Norwich Arms Company, Norwich, Connecticut, ca. 1863–64. Total production: 25,000.

James D. Julia Auctioneers, Fairfield, Maine

Overall length: 56". Weight: 9 lbs. 2 oz.

Muzzleloader, single shot.

"U.S. / NORWICH" on lock plate below bolster cutout; spread eagle at center of lock plate; year at rear of lock plate.

Norwich Arms Company fulfilled two contracts, dated April 1, 1863 and October 16, 1864, to supply 25,000 Model 1861 Rifle-Muskets to the U.S. government. In addition, a shortened variant existed with a 36" barrel and two Model 1863 barrel bands.

Good—$900   **Fine—$2,750**

U.S. Model 1861 Rifle-Musket, "Providence" Contract, .58 Caliber, Paper Cartridge, Percussion

Probably manufactured by Providence Tool Co., Providence, Rhode Island, 1862. Total production: unknown.

Overall length: 56". Weight: 9 lbs. 2 oz.

Muzzleloader, single shot.

"U.S. / PROVIDENCE" below bolster cutout on lock plate; spread eagle at center of lock plate; "1862" toward rear of lock plate.

It is not certain who manufactured Model 1861 rifle-muskets stamped "PROVIDENCE," but it is assumed that it was the Providence Tool Company, with a smaller possibility that the maker was C. D. Schubarth of Providence, Rhode Island.

Good—$900   **Fine—$2,750**

U.S. Model 1861 Rifle-Musket, Providence Tool Co. Contract, .58 Caliber, Paper Cartridge, Percussion

Amoskeag Auction Company, Inc.

Manufactured by Providence Tool Co., Providence, Rhode Island, ca. 1862–65. Total production: 70,000.

Overall length: 56". Weight: 9 lbs. 2 oz.

Muzzleloader, single shot.

"U. [spread eagle] S. / PROVIDENCE TOOL CO / PROVIDENCE R I" at center of lock plate; "1863" or "1864" (and possibly "1865") toward rear of lock plate.

The Providence Tool Company delivered to the U.S. government 70,000 stands of Model 1861 rifle-muskets from December 1862 to May 1865. They were considered high-quality arms. Note that it is possible, but not certain, that Model 1861 rifle-muskets marked "U.S. / Providence" and "1862" on the lock plates were early-production examples of the Providence Tool Co. Contract.

Good—$900   **Fine—$2,750**

U.S. MODEL 1861 RIFLE-MUSKET, REMINGTON CONTRACT, .58 CALIBER, PAPER CARTRIDGE, PERCUSSION

Manufactured by E. Remington & Sons, Ilion, New York, ca. 1864–65. Total production: 40,000.
Overall length: 56". Weight: 9 lbs. 2 oz.
Muzzleloader, single shot.
"REMINGTON'S / ILION, N.Y." below bolster cutout on lock plate; inspector's initial near front of lock plate; spread eagle over "U.S." at center of lock plate; "1864" or "1865" at rear of lock plate.
Under a contract of December 14, 1863, E. Remington & Sons supplied the U.S. government with 40,000 Model 1861 musket-rifles, with deliveries from May 31, 1864 to May 24, 1866. Specimens dated 1864 and 1865 have been reported.

GOOD—$900   FINE—$2,750

U.S. MODEL 1861 RIFLE-MUSKET, E. ROBINSON CONTRACT, .58 CALIBER, PAPER CARTRIDGE, PERCUSSION

Manufactured by Edward Robinson, New York City, ca. 1863–64. Total production: 30,000.
Overall length: 56". Weight: 9 lbs. 2 oz.
Muzzleloader, single shot.
Markings were in two styles: 1) first 12,000 examples: "E. ROBINSON" in straight line over "NEW YORK" under bolster cutout of lock plate; spread eagle over "U.S." at center of lock plate; "1863" at rear of lock plate; and 2) last 18,000 examples: "E. ROBINSON" in arc over "NEW YORK" below bolster cutout; spread eagle over "U.S." at center of lock plate; "1864" to rear of lock plate.
Edward Robinson delivered 30,000 Model 1861 rifle-muskets under four contracts dated June 10 and December 29, 1863, and February 23 and October 4, 1864. The U.S. government paid substantially below the contract price for many of the arms, indicating that they were substandard.

GOOD—$900   FINE—$2,750

U.S. MODEL 1861 RIFLE-MUSKET, "NEW YORK" CONTRACT, .58 CALIBER, PAPER CARTRIDGE, PERCUSSION

Manufactured by Sarson & Roberts, New York City, ca. 1862–63. Total production: 5,140.
Overall length: 56". Weight: 9 lbs. 2 oz.
Muzzleloader, single shot.
"US / NEW YORK / [year]" stamped below bolster cutout on lock plate; spread eagle at center of lock plate.
On December 26, 1861, John B. Sarson and William S. Roberts' Sarson & Roberts armory in New York City contracted to supply the U.S. government with 25,000 Model 1861 rifle-muskets. However, the firm delivered a total of only 5,140 units. Sarson & Roberts manufactured the barrels, stocks, and sights, but secured all other parts from Alfred Jenks & Son.

GOOD—$900   FINE—$2,750

U.S. MODEL 1861 RIFLE-MUSKET, SAVAGE REVOLVING FIRE ARMS CO. CONTACT, .58 CALIBER, PAPER CARTRIDGE, PERCUSSION

Rock Island Auction Company

Manufactured by Savage Fire Arms Co., Middletown, Connecticut, ca. 1862–64.
Total production: 25,520.
Overall length: 56". Weight: 9 lbs. 2 oz.
Muzzleloader, single shot.
"SAVAGE R.F.A. CO / MIDDLETOWN. CON." below bolster cutout on lock plate; spread eagle over "U.S." at center of lock plate; "1862", "1863", or "1864" ar rear of lock plate.

Rock Island Auction Company

In September 1863 the Savage Revolving Fire Arms Co. was assigned a contract originally held by Parker, Snow, Brooks & Co. to supply 25,000 Model 1861 rifle-muskets to the U.S. government. Savage delivered a total of 13,520 stands under this contract, and subsequently fulfilled another contract dated February 25, 1864, for another 12,000 Model 1861 rifle-muskets. The U.S. government paid well below the stipulated prices for many of these arms, which were apparently substandard.

GOOD—$900   **FINE—$2,750**

U.S. MODEL 1861 RIFLE-MUSKET, SCHUBARTH CONTACT, .58 CALIBER, PAPER CARTRIDGE, PERCUSSION

Manufactured by C. D. Schubarth & Co., Providence, Rhode Island, ca. 1861–63. Total production: 9,500.

Overall length: 56". Weight: 9 lbs. 2 oz.

Muzzleloader, single shot.

"U.S. / C.D. SCHUBARTH / PROVIDENCE" below bolster cutout on lock plate; spread eagle at center of lock plate; year toward rear of lock plate.

C. D. Schubarth & Co. (Caspar D. Schubarth, James M. Ryder, and Frederick Griffin) produced Model 1861 rifle-muskets under contracts of October 11 and November 1, 1861, with deliveries between December 19, 1862, and October 14, 1863. All parts of the rifle-muskets were manufactured by subcontractors (including 3,000 locks made by Alfred Jenks), with assembly taking place at the Schubarth factory.

GOOD—$1,000   **FINE—$3,000**

U.S. MODEL 1861 RIFLE-MUSKET, "SUHL" CONTACT, .58 CALIBER, PAPER CARTRIDGE, PERCUSSION

Manufactured by Christoph Funk Gewehrfabrik, Suhl, Germany, ca. 1861. Total production: several hundred.

Overall length: 56". Weight: 9 lbs. 2 oz.

Muzzleloader, single shot.

"US" or "U.S." toward front of lock plate; spread eagle at center of lock plate; "1861" toward rear of lock plate; "U" and serial number on barrel bands; "G" within a diamond and "SUHL" or "CH FUNK / SUHL" on some barrel bottoms (other barrel bottoms lack markings).

In 1861 the Christoph Funk Gewehrfabrik of Suhl, Germany, produced several hundred Model 1861 rifle-muskets for export to the United States. The weapons were similar to the standard U.S. Model 1861 arm, with variations in certain details, including a maple stock instead of walnut. It is possible that these arms were among the almost 500 Springfield-type muskets imported by William Hahn of New York City in 1862.

GOOD—$1,500   **FINE—$5,000**

U.S. MODEL 1861 RIFLE-MUSKET, "TRENTON" (OR BURT AND HODGE) CONTACT, .58 CALIBER, PAPER CARTRIDGE, PERCUSSION

Manufactured by Addison M. Burt and James T. Hodge, Springfield, Massachusetts, ca. 1862–64. Total production: 21,995 (11,495 by Burt and 10,500 by Hodge).

Overall length: 56". Weight: 9 lbs. 2 oz.

Muzzleloader, single shot.

"U.S. / TRENTON" below bolster cutout on lock plate; spread eagle at center of plate; year to rear of lock plate; "A. M. BURT" or "J. T. HODGE" stamped on flat of stock opposite the lock on some examples.

Amoskeag Auction Company, Inc.

After receiving separate contracts on December 26, 1861, to produce Model 1861 rifle-muskets, Addison M. Burt and James T. Hodge collaborated in manufacturing the arms without entering into a formal partnership. Leasing the Trenton Locomotive and Machine Company in January 1862, they produced a combined total of 21,995 rifle-muskets, considerably less than the total of 100,000 arms they originally contracted for.

GOOD—$900   FINE—$2,750

U.S. MODEL 1861 RIFLE-MUSKET, UNION ARMS CO. CONTACT, .58 CALIBER, PAPER CARTRIDGE, PERCUSSION

Manufactured by Union Arms Co., New York City, ca. 1862–63. Total production: probably fewer than 300.

Overall length: 56". Weight: 9 lbs. 2 oz.

Muzzleloader, single shot.

"U.A.CO. / NEW YORK" below bolster cutout of lock plate; spread eagle over "U.S." at center of lock plate; "1863" toward rear of lock plate.

The U.S. government issued three contracts totaling 65,000 Model 1861 rifle-muskets to the Union Arms Company between August and November 1861. However, apparently the company produced fewer than 300 stands, and there is evidence that the State of New York, instead of the U.S. Ordnance Department, received these arms.

GOOD—$1,500   FINE—$4,500

U.S. MODEL 1861 RIFLE-MUSKET, "WATERTOWN" (OR, HOARD) CONTACT, .58 CALIBER, PAPER CARTRIDGE, PERCUSSION

Manufactured by Charles B. Hoard, Watertown, New York, ca. 1862–65. Total production: 12,800.

Overall length: 56". Weight: 9 lbs. 2 oz.

Muzzleloader, single shot.

"U.S. / WATERTOWN" below bolster cutout of lock plate; spread eagle at center of plate; year toward rear of lock plate.

Charles B. Hoard converted his steam-engine factory in Watertown, New York, into an armory for manufacturing Model 1861 rifle-muskets under contracts of December 24, 1861 (50,000 stands), and December 1, 1863 (20,000 stands). In all, Hoard delivered 12,800. Except for a number of early-production specimens that included a small quantity of parts furnished by subcontractors, these rifle-muskets were entirely manufactured by Hoard.

GOOD—$900   FINE—$2,750

James D. Julia Auctioneers, Fairfield, Maine

U.S. MODEL 1861 RIFLE-MUSKET, WHITNEY, U.S. CONTACT, .58 CALIBER, PAPER CARTRIDGE, PERCUSSION

Amoskeag Auction Company, Inc.

Manufactured by Eli Whitney, Jr., Whitneyville Armory, New Haven, Connecticut, 1863–65. Total production: 15,001.

Overall length: 56". Weight: 9 lbs. 2 oz.

Muzzleloader, single shot.

"WHITNEY-VILLE" in italics below bolster cutout on lock plate; spread eagle over "U.S." at center of lock plate; "1863" or "1864" stamped vertically toward rear of lock plate; "U.S." stamped on butt plate; inspector's initials such as "FCW", "HW", and "JHG" on flat of stock opposite lock. Markings on the barrel: "V-P" over eagle head proof mark; "FCW", "JHG", or "W"; and "1863" or "1864".

After failing to fulfill a contract of December 24, 1861, to supply the U.S. government with 40,000 Model 1861 rifle-muskets, the Whitneyville Armory completed a second contract dated October 17, 1863, by delivering 15,001 of the rifle-muskets between October 20, 1863, and March 1, 1865. Whitney's U.S. contract rifle-muskets featured three-groove rifling.

GOOD—$1,250   FINE—$3,500

U.S. MODEL 1861 RIFLE-MUSKET, WHITNEY, FLUSH LOCK PLATE, .58 CALIBER, PAPER CARTRIDGE, PERCUSSION

Manufactured by Eli Whitney, Jr., Whitneyville Armory, New Haven, Connecticut, ca. 1863. Total production: probably under 100.

Overall length: 56". Weight: 9 lbs. 2 oz.

Muzzleloader, single shot.

Large spread eagle and U.S. flag over "WHITNEYVILLE" at center of non-beveled lock plate; "1863" vertically near rear of lock plate; "V / P" over six-pointed star, and "G.W.Q." on most barrels.

The Whitneyville Armory manufactured a small number of Model 1861 rifle-muskets with a flush lock plate and three-groove rifling around 1863. Most examples had a pewter fore-end cap, but a few were of iron. In addition to the regular version with 40" barrel and three barrel bands, there exist some examples with a 30" barrel with two bands.

GOOD—$2,250   FINE—$5,000

U.S. MODEL 1861 RIFLE-MUSKET, WHITNEY, CONNECTICUT CONTACT, .58 CALIBER, PAPER CARTRIDGE, PERCUSSION

Manufactured by Eli Whitney, Jr., Whitneyville Armory, New Haven, Connecticut, 1863–65. Total production: 14,000.

Overall length: 56". Weight: 9 lbs. 2 oz.

Muzzleloader, single shot.

Two types of lock plate markings exist: 1) "E. WHITNEY / N.HAVEN" at center of beveled lock plate; 2) large spread eagle and U.S. flags over "WHITNEYVILLE" at center of beveled lock plate. "JHS" or "H" inspector's marks on barrel ("G. W.Q." on late-production specimens).

By April of 1863 the Whitneyville Armory delivered 14,000 Model 1861 rifle-muskets to the State of Connecticut under contracts of 1861 and 1862. They were similar to the standard U.S. pattern, with a few exceptions: they featured seven-groove rifling (but late-production examples had three grooves), a pewter fore-end cap, Whitney-type long-range sight dovetailed into the barrel, and a steel ramrod with brass tip (early-production). In addition, the Connecticut Contract rifle-muskets accepted Enfield-type bayonets. The 22nd and 27th Connecticut Volunteer Infantry Regiments were equipped with these arms, most likely along with several other Connecticut regiments.

GOOD—$1,500   FINE—$5,500

Amoskeag Auction Company, Inc.

U.S. MODEL 1861 RIFLE-MUSKET, "WINDSOR LOCKS" CONTACT, .58 CALIBER, PAPER CARTRIDGE, PERCUSSION

Manufacturer unknown; probably William Muir & Co. or Dinslow & Chase, Windsor Locks, Connecticut, ca. 1863. Total production: unknown.

Overall length: 56". Weight: 9 lbs. 2 oz.

Muzzleloader, single shot.

"U.S. / WINDSOR LOCKS" below bolster cutout of lock plate; spread eagle at center of lock plate; year toward rear of lock plate.

The identity of the manufacturer of Model 1861 contract rifle-muskets marked simply "WINDSOR LOCKS" is uncertain, although it was probably either William Muir & Company, owners of an armory in Windsor Locks, Connecticut, or Dinslow & Chase, manufacturers in that town who are known to have produced rifle-musket parts.

GOOD—$1,250   FINE—$4,000

U.S. MODEL 1861 RIFLE-MUSKET, NEW JERSEY CONTACT, .58 CALIBER, PAPER CARTRIDGE, PERCUSSION

Contracted or manufactured by Perkins & Livingston, New York City; Trenton Arms Co., Trenton, New Jersey; and Schuyler, Hartley, & Graham, New York City, ca. 1863–64. Total production: 20,000.

Overall length: 56". Weight: 9 lbs. 2 oz.

Muzzleloader, single shot.

Specific markings as described below. Also, "N.J." on left side of barrel and on stock opposite the lock; no inspector's marks on barrel.

New Jersey issued contracts to three companies in 1863–64 to supply the state with Model 1861 rifle-muskets (prices are for NJ-surcharged examples):

Perkins & Livingston: 2,200 stands delivered, marked the same as Savage Repeating Fire Arm Company Contract examples: "SAVAGE R.F.A. CO / MIDDLETOWN. CON." below bolster cutout on lock plate; spread eagle over "U.S." at center of lock plate; year to rear of lock plate.

GOOD—$1,500   FINE—$3,750

Trenton Arms Company: 5,300 stands delivered, marked: "U.S. / TRENTON" below bolster cutout on lock plate; spread eagle at center of plate; year to rear of lock plate; "A. M. BURT" or "J. T. HODGE" stamped on flat of stock opposite the lock on some examples.

GOOD—$1,500   FINE—$3,750

Schuyler, Hartley, & Graham: 2,500 Colt Special Model 1861 rifle-muskets delivered: "U.S. / COLT'S PT F.A. MFG CO / HARTFORD CT" below bolster cutout on lock plate; year toward rear of lock plate; spread eagle on percussion cap bolster.

GOOD—$1,500   FINE—$3,750

SPECIAL MODEL 1861 RIFLE-MUSKET, .58 CALIBER, PERCUSSION

Made by four different firms, 1862-1865. Total production: approximately 174,000.

Overall length: 56". Weight: 9 lbs. 3 oz.

The U.S. Special Model 1861 Contract Rifle-Musket differed considerably from the regulation U.S. Model 1861 Rifle-Musket. In fact, very few parts interchange, with the exception of a few screws, the fore-tip, side screw ferrules and trigger assembly. The motivation behind the production of this weapon seems to be the availability of Enfield rifle-musket-making machinery in Hartford, Conn., and Windsor, Vermont. Sitting unused since the bankruptcy of Robbins & Lawrence following the cancellation of their British arms contracts, Colt eyed the machinery as an economical and expedient measure to meeting the Government's demands for weapons.

AMOSKEAG SPECIAL MODEL 1861 RIFLE-MUSKET, .58 CALIBER, PERCUSSION

Amoskeag Auction Company, Inc.

Made by Amoskeag Manufacturing Company, Manchester, New Hampshire, 1862-1865, 27,001 delivered.

Face of the cone seat is stamped with a spread eagle. The lock plate is marked forward of the hammer with a spread eagle between "U." and "S." above "AMOSKEAG MFG. CO. / MANCHESTER, N.H." in two lines. The date is stamped behind the hammer. The barrel is marked with the V.P. and eagle proof marks as well as the date.

The U.S. government gave the Amoskeag Manufacturing its first contract for 10,000 rifle-muskets on January 7, 1862. Amoskeag received a second contract dated November 5, 1863 for 15,000 rifles and a third one on January 6, 1865, for 2,000.

GOOD—$1,200   FINE—$3,500

COLT SPECIAL MODEL 1861 RIFLE-MUSKET, .58 CALIBER, PERCUSSION

James D. Julia Auctioneers, Fairfield, Maine

Made by Colt's Patent Firearms Company, Hartford, Connecticut, 1862-1864; 96,505 delivered.

The face of the cone is stamped with a spread eagle. The lockplate is marked in front of the hammer in three lines, "U.S. / COLTS PT F.A. MFG. CO. / HARTFORD CT." The date of manufacture is stamped behind the hammer. Left barrel flat near the breech stamped "STEEL" on some but not all rifles of all three manufacturing years.

At the outbreak of the Civil War, the Colt Company was one of the largest and most modern private arms manufacturing companies in the world. On July 4, 1861, the Chief of Ordnance Lt. Col. James W. Ripley awarded the Colt company the first contract of the war for rifled-muskets. Colt was to deliver 25,000 weapons at the price of 20 each. First contract rifle-muskets featured barrel bands with integral tension screws. Collectors refer to these as "Type I."

The Colt Company received a second contract dated June 5, 1863, for an additional 50,000 rifled muskets at the same unit price. Weapons of the second and third contracts have plain barrel bands secured by inlet spring catches. These weapons are referred to as "Type II."

The company received a third contract on March 19, 1864, for 37,500 weapons. At the end of 1864, after taking delivery of 21,500 rifle-muskets, the Ordnance Department suspended and canceled the contract in anticipation of the war ending.

In July 1863, Colt agreed to sell to the New York weapons and equipment supplier, Schuyler, Hartley & Graham "Second Class U.S. Rifle Muskets" produced up to that time. The second class weapons were those that had failed to pass government inspection. On July 11, 1863, Schuyler, Hartley & Graham sold 2,500 of these second class rifle-muskets to the state of Connecticut. A plain nipple bolster (no eagle stamp) characterizes the second class weapons.

After the cancellation of the third contract, Colt did not immediately suspend manufacturing of the Special Model 1861 Rifle-Musket. From May to September 1865, workers completed at least 8,000 additional rifle-muskets. In 1866, the Colt Company sold 12,100 Model 1861 Special Rifle Muskets to the government of Egypt.

GOOD—$1,500   FINE—$4,000

LAMSON, GOODNOW & YALE SPECIAL MODEL 1861 RIFLE-MUSKET, .58 CALIBER, PERCUSSION

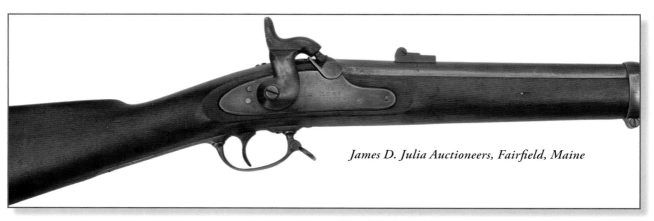

James D. Julia Auctioneers, Fairfield, Maine

Made by Lamson, Goodnow & Yale Company, Windsor, Vermont, and Shelburn Falls, Massachusetts; 1862-1864, 50,000 delivered.

Three different variations of lockplate markings have been encountered. The first is marked in front of the hammer with a spread eagle over "U.S." and beneath the bolster, "L.G. & Y. / WINDSOR-VT" in two lines. The date (1862 being the earliest) is stamped behind the hammer. The second type was marked with a large spread eagle over "U.S." in front of the hammer and "L.G-Y. / WINDSOR- VT" in two lines beneath the bolster. Notice that the second in is italicized on this variant. The date (1863 being the earliest) is stamped behind the hammer. The third version does not have any eagle stamped on the plate and is marked beneath the bolster, "U.S. / L.G-& Y. / WINDSOR-VT." in three lines. The bottom line is in italics. The earliest date to the rear of the hammer on the third version is 1864.

Lamson, Goodnow & Yale Company received their two contracts, each for 25,000 stands at 20 each. The first was awarded on July 11, 1861, followed by the second on October 7, 1861. The company made its first delivery on September 24, 1862, and continued to deliver on the contracts at an average rate of 2,000 rifle-muskets per month until the final delivery on December 10, 1864.

When the terms of the final contract were met, Messrs. Goodnow and Yale left the arms-making business. The company reorganized as E.G. Lamson & Company.

GOOD—$1,200   FINE—$3,500

LAMSON & CO. SPECIAL MODEL 1861 RIFLE MUSKET, .58 CALIBER, PERCUSSION

Made by E.G. Lamson, & Company, Windsor, Vermont, 1865, total quantity estimated at under 500.

Lockplate marked "U.S. / E.G. LAMSON & CO. / WINDSOR VT" in three lines in front of the hammer. Behind the hammer, the plate is marked "1865."

Lamson did not receive a contract to manufacture Special Model 1861 Rifle-Muskets after Goodnow and Yale left the company in 1865. Though Lamson had contracts to produce Palmer and Ball & Lamson carbines, he obviously wanted to take advantage of the surplus parts still in the Windsor manufactory. Though the barrels of known E.G. Lamson & Co. rifle-muskets bear the usual "V / P / [eagle head]" proof marks, none of the completed arms received inspector's initials on the stocks. It has yet to be discovered to whom Lamson sold the rifles.

GOOD—$1,350   FINE—$3,500

U.S. MODEL 1863 RIFLE-MUSKET, TYPE I, .58 CALIBER, PAPER CARTRIDGE, PERCUSSION

Manufactured by Springfield Armory, Springfield, Massachusetts, 1863. Total production: 273,265.
Overall length: 56". Weight: 8 lbs. 12 oz.
Muzzleloader, single shot.

"U.S. / SPRINGFIELD" below bolster cutout on lock plate; spread eagle at center of lock plate and on face of bolster; "1863" near rear of lock plate; "V / P" over eagle head on upper left barrel flat; "1863" on top flat of barrel; "U.S." on tang of butt stock; inspector's initials on left flat of stock opposite lock.

Over a quarter-million stands of the U.S. Model 1863 rifle-musket, Type I, were produced at the Springfield Armory during a production run lasting less than one year. The arm was similar to the U.S. Model 1861 rifle-musket, with certain exceptions, including: The nipple bolster was not as tall as that of the 1861 model, had a small eagle stamped on the face, and lacked a cleanout screw. The barrel bands were of the split oval type and were retained by screws instead of band springs. The hammer was of a noticeably different shape, with beveled edges. And, the hammer and lock plate were casehardened, rather than bright finished. Otherwise, the barrel and all furniture were finished bright.

Good—$950   Fine—$3,000

*James D. Julia
Auctioneers,
Fairfield, Maine*

U.S. MODEL 1863 RIFLE-MUSKET, NORRIS & CLEMENT (OR, MASSACHUSETTS) CONTRACT, TYPE I, .58 CALIBER, PAPER CARTRIDGE, PERCUSSION

Manufactured or assembled by Norris & Clement, Springfield, Massachusetts, 1863. Total production: 13,000.

Overall length: 56". Weight: 8 lbs. 12 oz.

Muzzleloader, single shot.

"S.N. & W.T.C. / FOR / MASSACHUSETTS" and eagle over "U.S." on lock plate forward of the hammer; year toward rear of lock plate; "L.F.R." on left facet of barrel.

The State of Massachusetts bought 13,000 Model 1863 rifle-muskets from Samuel Norris and W. T. Clement of Springfield, Massachusetts, in 1863. They were similar to the standard U.S. Model 1863 rifle-musket except for the markings, as noted above.

Good—$1,200   Fine—$3,500

U.S. MODEL 1863 RIFLE-MUSKET, TYPE II, .58 CALIBER, PAPER CARTRIDGE, PERCUSSION

Manufactured by Springfield Armory, Springfield, Massachusetts, ca. 1864–65. Total production: 255,040.

Overall length: 56". Weight: 8 lbs. 12 oz.

Muzzleloader, single shot.

"U.S. / SPRINGFIELD" below bolster cutout on lock plate; spread eagle at center of lock plate and on face of bolster; "1864" or "1865" near rear of lock plate and on top flat of barrel; "V / P" over eagle head on upper left barrel flat; "U.S." on tang of butt stock; inspector's initials on left flat of stock opposite lock.

The last of the U.S. military breechloading arms, the U.S. Model 1863 rifle-musket, Type II, was similar to the Type I, with a few notable exceptions: The split bands were replaced by solid barrel bands, with band springs mounted on the right side of the stock. Tulip-head ramrods or knurled-and-slotted ramrods of a later design were used. The shoulders of the nipple cone were rounded, instead of the faceted shoulders found on Type I specimens.

Good—$1,000   Fine—$3,000

U.S. MODEL 1863 LINDSAY DOUBLE RIFLE-MUSKET .58 CALIBER PAPER CARTRIDGE, PERCUSSION

Made by J. P. Lindsay, New York, ca. 1863–64. Total production: approximately 1,000. Overall length: 56". Weight: 9 lbs.
Muzzleloading, two concentric shots.

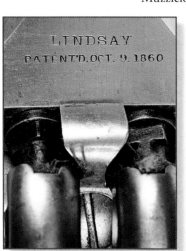

"LINDSAY / PATENT'D. OCT. 9. 1860" on top of breech; inspector's initials "ADK" (A. D. King) and sub-inspector's initials on left flat of stock near breech; "US" on butt plate tang.

This double rifle operated on the principle of two cartridges loaded one in front of the other into a single barrel, with a dual-ignition system that fired the front cartridge first, and then the rear cartridge. Two hammers were mounted side by side along the centerline; the right hammer struck a cap, projecting flame through a channel to the front cartridge. The left hammer and cap directly ignited the rear cartridge. The rifle, which was used in at least one battle near the end of the war, suffered from fouling of the right-hand ignition channel and the occasional ignition of both cartridges. The round, 41-1/8" barrel and all furniture were bright iron. Oval barrel bands were 1/2" wide, with the upper sling swivel on the bottom of the center band. The lower sling swivel was on the front of the trigger guard. The two-leaf rear sight was blued, and an iron blade front sight was mounted atop a stud for a socket bayonet. Oil-finished black walnut stock.

GOOD—$2,500   FINE—$6,750

Rock Island Auction Company

J. P. MOORE-ENFIELD RIFLE-MUSKET, .58 CALIBER, TYPE I, PAPER CARTRIDGE, PERCUSSION

Made by John P. Moore Sons, New York City, 1861–63.
Total production: over 1,080.
Overall length: 55-3/8". Weight: 9 lbs.
Muzzleloader, single shot.

Year engraved on lock plate in front of hammer; eagle over Union shield with letter "M" in field on lock plate to rear of hammer. Markings sometimes found on barrel bands.

Moore, agents for Colt's, assembled these rifle-muskets per a contract to supply 1,080 "American rifles, Enfield Pattern" to the Ordnance Department. They featured a flush, unbeveled lock plate; oil-finished black walnut stock; and 39" round barrel rifled with three wide lands and grooves, and surmounted with a long-range rear sight and iron blade front sight on a bayonet stud. Three barrel bands, split-clamping type, were 1/2" wide, and the upper sling swivel was on the bottom of the forward band. All metal parts were finished bright; furniture was iron, except brass fore-end cap, trigger guard, butt plate, and side screw ferrules.

GOOD—$1,200   FINE—$2,250

J. P. MOORE-ENFIELD RIFLE-MUSKET, .58 CALIBER, TYPE II, PAPER CARTRIDGE, PERCUSSION

Made by John P. Moore Sons, New York City, 1861–63. Total production: Unknown.
Muzzleloader, single shot.

Year engraved on lockplate in front of hammer; eagle over Union shield with letter "M" in field on lockplate to rear of hammer. Proof marks sometimes found on barrels and barrel bands.

J. P. Moore produced a number of Enfield Pattern rifle-muskets with two split-clamping barrel bands and 31-1/2" round barrels (as opposed to the 39" round barrel of Moore's three-band model). They included a stud for a socket bayonet, upper sling swivel on the forward barrel band, and lower swivel on the front of the trigger guard bow.

GOOD—$1,200   FINE—$2,250

BLUNT "ENFIELD" RIFLE-MUSKET, .58 CALIBER PAPER CARTRIDGE, PERCUSSION

Made by Orison Blunt, New York City, 1861–62. Total production: 500.

Overall length: 56". Weight: 10 lbs. 8 oz.

Muzzleloader, single shot.

Stampings "DP / B" within an oval on the upper left side of barrel 1" from breech.

The U.S. Ordnance Department issued a contract to Orison Blunt in September 1861 for 20,000 Enfield-pattern .58-caliber rifle-muskets with 40" barrels. Blunt had completed only 500 by May 1862 but failed to have the weapons proved by an ordnance inspector; thus, the Ordnance Department refused acceptance of the firearms. These rifle-muskets apparently comprised a mix of American and British parts, including an American black walnut stock, blued barrel with long-range rear sight soldered to it, three 1/2"-wide oval clamping bands, brass butt plate, and one-piece trigger guard bow and plate. Both the lock plate and hammer had two engraved lines around their edges.

GOOD—$1,000   **FINE—$2,250**

ROBBINS & LAWRENCE "WINDSOR" RIFLE-MUSKET, .577 CALIBER, PAPER CARTRIDGE, PERCUSSION

Made by Robbins & Lawrence, Windsor, Vermont and Hartford, Connecticut, 1855–58. Total production: approximately 16,000.

Overall Length: 55". Weight: 9 lbs. 2 oz.

Muzzleloader, single shot.

Year / "WINDSOR" on lock plate in front of hammer; royal crown on lock plate behind hammer; British proof marks on barrel near breech.

Robbins & Lawrence produced these copies of the P1853 Rifle-Musket under a contract with the British, originally for use in the Crimean War. It is thought to have been the only Enfield-style longarm made entirely of U.S. components in the United States. Many of the rifles never left the States, or were bought back from England during the Civil War. They included a 39" barrel with rear long-range sight with a 2-1/4" long base soldered 3-1/2" from the breech. The forward of three iron bands held the upper swivel sling, the lower sling being mounted on the front of the trigger guard bow. Furniture was brass with the exception of the bands.

GOOD—$1,200   **FINE—$2,250**

WHITNEY "ENFIELD" RIFLE-MUSKET, .58 CALIBER, PAPER CARTRIDGE, PERCUSSION

Made by Whitneyville Armory, New Haven, Connecticut, ca. 1859-62. Total production: approximately 3,000.

Overall length: 56". Weight: 9 lbs.

Muzzleloader, single shot.

"E. WHITNEY" stamped on lock plate in front of hammer; letter over serial number on barrel near muzzle.

Whitney's version of the Long Enfield .58-caliber rifle-musket had a 40" round barrel with combination bayonet stud and iron blade front sight 1-1/2" from the muzzle and rear sight dovetailed and screwed to the barrel, as described below. The lock plate was flat and unbevelled, while the trigger guard had a brass bow bolted to an iron guard plate. The weapon included a pewter fore-tip, three solid oval iron barrel bands with springs to the front of the bands, and upper sling swivel on the front band. The knurled and slotted ramrod and curved butt plate were typical of Enfield designs. Purchases of the Whitney-Enfield rifle-musket included Georgia in 1860, Mississippi in 1861 (75 examples between the two states), Maryland in 1861 (2,000), and the U.S. government in 1861 (100).

Two basic variants exist:

Type I: Equipped with Whitney long-range tangent rear sight with 2-1/4"-long base, 5-5/8" from breech.

Type II: Single-leaf sight with 300-yard pierced window and 1-1/4"-long base, 2-3/4" from breech.

BOTH TYPES: GOOD—$1,200 FINE—$3,000

J.H. KRIDER .69 CALIBER RIFLE-MUSKET, PAPER CARTRIDGE, PERCUSSION

Manufactured by John H. Krider, Philadelphia, Pennsylvania, ca. 1861. Total production: approximately 200.

Overall length: 56".

Muzzleloader, single shot.

"KRIDER" on lock plate in front of hammer; "PHILADA" on barrel at breech; serial numbers noted on some breeches.

Some Pennsylvania three-months' militia were issued this rifle-musket in the early days of the Civil War. The round, browned barrel, variously reported as 39" and 40" long, was fastened to the walnut stock with three bands. The front sight also served as a lug for a socket bayonet; the rear sight was a folding-ladder type, about 5" from the breech. The furniture was brass, or a mix of brass and iron, and included a two-piece Sharps-style patch box near butt. The lock was casehardened.

GOOD—$2,500   **FINE—$4,750**

James D. Julia Auctioneers, Fairfield, Maine

RICHMOND ARMORY RIFLE-MUSKET, .58 CALIBER, PAPER CARTRIDGE, PERCUSSION

Made by C.S. Armory, Richmond, Virginia, 1861-1865. Total production: Unknown, but the largest number of weapons produced by a single Confederate facility.

Overall length: 56".

Muzzleloader, single shot.

The capture of machinery and parts at Harpers Ferry, Virginia, provided the foundation for the largest weapons manufactory in the Confederacy. Known to collectors as "C.S. Richmond rifle-muskets," the three-band, .58-caliber muzzle-loaders were based on the design and built with pieces of U.S. Model 1855 rifle-muskets. Collectors have broken down the production down into three major types:

Richmond Armory rifle-musket, Type I.

Type I: The earliest rifles assembled at the Richmond Armory (before it was turned over to the control of the Confederacy) incorporated a "high hump" lock plate marked forward of the hammer, "RICHMOND, VA." and behind the hammer, vertically, "1861." Examples exist that even incorporate the iron patch box of the U.S. Model 1855 rifle-musket, though these are very scarce.

Richmond Armory rifle-musket, Type II.

Lock plates of Type II Richmond Armory rifle-muskets are dated 1862.

Type II: The second variant is quite similar to the first except that the letters "CS" are stamped on the lock plate above the word "RICHMOND", reflecting the government takeover of the armory. Type II rifle-muskets will be dated "1862".

Type III: This is the easiest of the three to recognize because it incorporates a "low hump" lock plate. Dates will range from 1862 to 1865 on Type III rifle-muskets.

ALL TYPES: GOOD—$3,750 FINE—$17,500

Richmond Armory rifle-musket, Type III.

"Low-hump" lock plate of a Type III Richmond Armory rifle.

BRITISH PATTERN 1853 RIFLE-MUSKET, .577 CALIBER, PAPER CARTRIDGE, PERCUSSION

Made by various English manufactures, London, England, Liege, Belgium, 1854-1866 Total imported: Unknown but more than 500,000.

Overall length: 55".

Muzzleloader, single shot.

Lock plates vary depending on year of manufacture. Generally, the lock plate will be stamped with a crown over "VR", the British "broad arrow" and the year of manufacture in addition to "Tower", depending on place of manufacture. London Armoury weapons will be marked "LAC" or "LA Co". Liege-manufactured weapons will only have royal monogram and year of manufacture. No imported weapon will have the British broad arrow mark or "Enfield" stamped lock plate. Barrels manufactured for export will have a provisional proof, a gauge mark ("25" for .577 or "24" for .58). Premiums are paid for weapons bearing a "JS / [anchor]" mark, as this is popularly thought to denote certain Confederate use (though no hard evidence can verify the belief).

James D. Julia Auctioneers, Fairfield, Maine

The P53 Rifle-Musket is the best known imported weapon of the Civil War. By the end of July 1863, the U.S. Ordnance Department imported no fewer than 505,000 English-produced weapons, many of which were the P1853 Rifle-Musket. The Confederacy purchased between 300,000 and 400,000. Though there are four distinct "types" of P53 rifle muskets, only the third, manufactured between 1858 and 1864, were imported during the war.

The Type III P53 utilized screw clamping barrel bands, rear sights graduated to 1,000 yards, and a thick, straight ramrod with no swell.

GOOD—$750   FINE—$2,750

AUSTRIAN MODEL 1842 LONG RIFLE, .69/.71 CALIBER, PAPER CARTRIDGE, TUBE-LOCK/PERCUSSION

Made by Austrian National Armory and private gun manufactories, ca. 1842-1849 Total imported: Unknown, probably not more than 10,000.

Overall length: 48-1/2".

Muzzleloader, single shot.

Markings are uncommon. Each lock plate was stamped with a small Austrian eagle and the year of manufacture (with the first digit omitted, e.g., "843"). A few examples have the year of manufacture stamped on the barrel near the breech in addition to "IB" in an oval. Some arms bear the mark of a private manufacturer, "RS Heretta".

Because many of the obsolete Model 1842 and 1849 rifles were sold to Giuseppe Garibaldi's revolutionary Italian forces, these weapons are often called "Garibaldi rifles". The three-band, Model 1842 long rifles were originally fitted with the Augustin-Consol tube-lock ignition system developed in Austria. When they were deemed "obsolete," the Austrians sent the Model 1842 rifles to Liège for conversion. The Belgian gunsmiths used two methods: brazing a small cone seat to the upper right side of the barrel that was then tapped to accept a percussion nipple or the Prussian system (similar to the U.S. patent breech) that required the barrel to be cut and fitted with a new breech and bolster. All iron furniture was left bright. Import records to not differentiate between the Model 1842 and 1849 rifle, however, the former is rarely encountered in the United States whereas the latter is quite common.

GOOD—$375   FINE—$1,250

49

AUSTRIAN MODEL 1849 LONG RIFLE, .71 CALIBER, PAPER CARTRIDGE, TUBE-LOCK/PERCUSSION

Made by Austrian National Armory and private gun manufactories, ca. 1842-1849. Total imported: Unknown, probably not more than 20,000.

Overall length: 48-1/2".

Muzzleloader, single shot.

Markings are uncommon. Each lock plate was stamped with a small Austrian eagle and the year of manufacture (with the first digit omitted, e.g., "843"). Some examples are stamped with an "F" in an oval on the trigger guard.

Because many of the obsolete Model 1842 and 1849 rifles were sold to Giuseppe Garibaldi's revolutionary Italian forces, these weapons are often called "Garibaldi rifles." The three-band, Model 1849 long rifles were originally fitted with the Augustin-Consol tube-lock ignition system developed in Austria. When they were deemed "obsolete," the Austrians sent the Model 1849 rifles to Liège for conversion. The Belgian gunsmiths used two methods: brazing a small cone seat to the upper right side of the barrel that was then tapped to accept a percussion nipple or the Prussian system (similar to the U.S. patent breech) that required the barrel to be cut and fitted with a new breech and bolster. All iron furniture was left bright. The nearly half-length octagonal barrel tapers to round. Import records to not differentiate between the Model 1842 and 1849 rifle, however, the former is rarely encountered in the United States whereas the latter is quite common. U.S. Ordnance Department records show purchases of at least 26,201 "Garibaldi rifles." There are no known Confederate purchases.

GOOD—$375   FINE—$1,250

AUSTRIAN MODEL 1854 LONG RIFLE, .54 CALIBER, PAPER CARTRIDGE, PERCUSSION

Made by Vienna National Armory and private gun manufactories, ca. 1854-? Total imported: Unknown, but more than 300,000.

Overall length: 52-1/2".

Muzzleloader, single shot.

Markings are uncommon. Each lock plate was stamped with a small Austrian eagle and the year of manufacture (with the first digit omitted, e.g., "843"). Various private contractor marks found on the barrel near the breech include "ANN J. OSERLIEN", "PIRKO in WIEN", "CHARL HEISER", "ZEILINGER", and "FRED FRUWIRTH".

Known to Civil War purchasing agents as the "Lorenz," the three-band rifle replaced the earlier Model 1842 and 1849 tube-lock, long rifles. Two types of rear sights are encountered: a simple block sight of the standard infantry weapon and a folding leaf sight graduated to 900 paces for rifle battalions. Finish varied. Some rifles were blued while others were left bright. U.S. Ordnance Department records show purchases of at least 250,000 Lorenz "rifle-muskets". Caleb Huse purchased at least 100,000 for the Confederacy.

GOOD—$1,250   FINE—$4,500

SAXON MODEL 1851 RIFLE-MUSKET, .58 CALIBER, PAPER CARTRIDGE, PERCUSSION

Made by P.J. Malherbe, Liege, Belgium, ca. 1851-ca. 1857 Total imported: Unknown.

Overall length: 53".

Muzzleloader, single shot.

Back-action lock plate stamped "P.J. MALHERBE & Cie. / a LIEGE". In addition, some plates are marked with "[crown] / JH" or "[crown] / HW". A Liege proof mark is usually stamped on the barrel.

Though originally employing a tige system for expanding the bullet, this was quickly abandoned. It is believed that no examples with the tige system were imported to the United States. Rear sight had leaves for 200, 400, and 600 paces. The front barrel band is notched to fit around the brass blade front sight. George Schuyler purchased 27,055 "Dresden Rifles" while in Europe. Marcellus Hartley purchased 1,740 similarly labeled weapons. These numbers probably included the older Model 1844 rifled muskets as well.

GOOD—$375   FINE—$1,250

SAXON MODEL 1857 RIFLE-MUSKET, .58 CALIBER, PAPER CARTRIDGE, PERCUSSION

Made by P.J. Malherbe, Liege, Belgium, ca. 1857-ca. 1861 Total imported: Unknown.

Overall length: 56".

Muzzleloader, single shot.

Back-action lock plate stamped "P.J. MALHERBE & Cie. / a LIEGE". In addition, some plates are marked with "[crown] / JH" or "[crown] / HW". A Liege proof mark is usually stamped on the barrel.

Slightly longer than the Model 1851, the Model 1857 is nearly identical in all other respects. Rear sight had leaves for 200, 400, and 600 paces. The front barrel band is notched to fit around the brass blade front sight. George Schuyler purchased 27,055 "Dresden Rifles" while in Europe. Marcellus Hartley purchased 1,740 similarly labeled weapons. These numbers probably included the older Model 1844 rifled muskets as well. No records of Confederate purchases are known.

GOOD—$375   FINE—$1,250

SUHL ENFIELD RIFLE-MUSKET, .577 CALIBER, PAPER CARTRIDGE, PERCUSSION

Made by private manufacturer, Suhl, Germany, ca. 1861. Total imported: 1,273. Overall length: 55".

Muzzleloader, single shot.

Lock plate stamped "[crown] / SP.&SR." Barrel stamped with Birmingham proof marks.

The "Suhl Enfield" is a faithful copy of the British Pattern 1853 rifle-musket. The New York firm of Schuyler, Hartley and Graham made arrangements for the purchase of 1,500 Enfield rifles to be manufactured in Suhl. Finally deliveries totaled 1,273.

GOOD—$875　　　　**FINE—$1,500**

FRENCH MODEL 1857 RIFLE-MUSKET, .70 CALIBER, PAPER CARTRIDGE, PERCUSSION

Made by French royal and Imperial arsenals and copied by Liege manufacturers, ca. 1857-ca. 1859. Total imported: Unknown, but Union records show over 147,000 French and Belgium long arms were purchased.

Overall length: 55-3/4".

Muzzleloader, single shot.

French lock plates are inscribed with "Mre. Impale. de" followed by the city name. Liege lock plates may be engraved have the maker's name or his crowned initials. The barrel tang is engraved with the model designation, "M 1857" and year of manufacture. Liege-made examples have only the year of manufacture and proof marks. French barrels may also be stamped with caliber in millimeters in addition to the usual proof marks.

In 1857, the French military adopted the Minié bullet as the new standard projectile. The Model 1857 was the first rifle-musket the French adopted as a standard long arm. The arsenals built the new arm using the same barrel bands, retaining springs, trigger guard and other furniture of the Model 1842. All iron was left bright. Each was fitted with a block sight fixed to the barrel tang. Union gun buyers purchased at least 147,000 French and Belgian rifled and smoothbore long arms during the Civil War. However, their records do not indicate model designations making it impossible to know exactly how many Model 1857 rifle-muskets made it to the United States. The U.S. Ordnance Department rated French and Belgian rifled long arms as 2nd class. No record of Confederate purchases is known.

GOOD—$375　　　　**FINE—$1,250**

FRENCH .58 RIFLE-MUSKET, .58 CALIBER, PAPER CARTRIDGE, PERCUSSION

Made by Liege, Belgium manufacturers, ca. 1862-1863. Total imported: Unknown, but Union records show at least 3,241 rifles of unknown caliber were purchased.

Overall length: 55-3/4".

Lock plates marked with a "G" in a circle. The barrel and rear sight are stamped with a "[crown] /GM".

In 1857, the French military adopted the Minié bullet as the new standard projectile. The .58 caliber rifle-musket is nearly identical to the Model 1857 rifle-musket except for the small caliber. It is equipped with rear sight graduated to 800 meters. The rifle uses the same style barrel bands, trigger guard and other furniture found on the Models 1842 and 1857. Concrete evidence of sales to American customers has not been located; however, John Pondir did deliver 3,241 French rifles to the U.S. Ordnance Department in 1863. The Department rated the weapon as 1st class. No record of Confederate purchases is known.

GOOD—$375　　　　**FINE—$1,250**

James D. Julia Auctioneers, Fairfield, Maine

Amoskeag Auction Company, Inc.

Infantry formation of the 18th and 19th century generally designated a small number of troops to carry rifles. To the armies, a "rifle" was a two-banded weapon, somewhat shorter than a rifle-musket, that had a rifled bore and was equipped to support a saber bayonet.

By the turn of the century, flank companies in U.S. Army regiments generally were equipped as riflemen. Though they had weapons capable of sharpshooting, these "flankers'" primary role was not that of marksmen, but rather, as skirmishers. The shorter weapon was seen as an aid to mobility, not a tool of deadly accuracy.

After the War with Mexico concluded in 1848, it became apparent to military planners that the rifle afforded more than simply lightening the load of flankers. The world's armies were rearming with rifled weapons. The United States would be forced to follow suit if it wanted to remain a recognized power.

The Army, however, was not ready to give up on its vision of the well-equipped soldier. Plans were made to provide rifled weapons; however, the bulk of troops would received the full-length rifle-musket. Rifles would still be reserved for the flank companies.

When the southern states seceded and declared war, the delineation between who would receive what weapons became increasingly clouded. Rather than just two companies receiving rifles, entire regiments received issues of the shorter, lighter weapons. In most cases just as accurate as a rifle-musket, rifles became one of the soldiers' favorite weapons.

Today, muzzleloading rifles still receive the same attention. Because they tend to be more ornate then their longer counterparts, rifles are favorites among collectors.

U.S. Model 1817 Contract Rifle (or, "Common Rifle," "Deringer Rifle"), .54 Caliber, Paper Cartridge, Flintlock or Converted to Percussion

James D. Julia Auctioneers, Fairfield, Maine

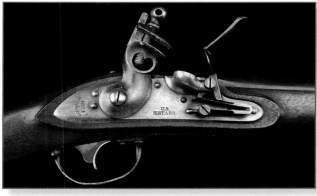

Manufactured by H. Deringer, Philadelphia, Pennsylvania; R. Johnson, R. & J. D. Johnson, S. North, and N. Starr, all of Middletown, Connecticut, ca. 1817–1820s, early 1840s. Total production: approximately 38,200.

Overall length: 51-3/8". Weight: 10 lbs. 4 oz. Muzzleloader, single shot.

Lock plate marked according to manufacturer. H. Deringer: "US / H. DERINGER / PHILADA" at center, year vertically at rear; or, "DERINGER / PHILADELA" at center. R. Johnson: "R. JOHNSON" in arc over large spread eagle flanked on either side by "U" and "S" over MIDDN CONN", year vertically at rear; or, "US / R. JOHNSON / MIDDLETOWN" at center; no year. R. & J. D. Johnson: "US / R. & J.D. JOHNSON" at center; "[year] / MIDDN CONN." vertically at rear; or, "US / [large spread eagle] / R. & J.D. JOHNSON" at center, "[year] / MIDDN. CONN." vertically at rear. S. North: "U.S. / S. NORTH" at center, "MIDLTN / CONN / [year]" vertically at rear. N. Starr: "U.S. / N. STARR" at center, "[year] / MIDN CON." vertically at rear; or, "N. STARR & SON" in a 3/4 circle over a sunburst, over "U.S." at center, "MIDDTN / CONN / [year]" vertically at rear. Other markings: "US / P" on left side of barrel near breech; year on barrel tang; "US" on tang of butt plate.

Model 1817 rifle with the cone-in-breech percussion conversion.
James D. Julia Auctioneers, Fairfield, Maine

With the exception of a number of pattern rifles made at Harpers Ferry Armory, the U.S. Model 1817 flintlock rifle was manufactured solely by private contracts. Many of these rifles were in state armories at the beginning of the Civil War, and it is likely that they saw some service in that conflict. The Model 1817 rifle featured a browned, round, 36-1/2" barrel rifled with seven narrow grooves. All furniture was browned iron, and included three flat bands and a large, oval patch box. The trigger guard plate was distinctive, with the rear end curving outward from the butt stock to form a sort of pistol grip.

Quantities of Model 1817 rifles by all of the contractors were later converted from flintlock to percussion. In addition, H. Deringer produced a small number of Model 1817 rifles originally as percussion, in .58 caliber. These were stamped "US / H. DERINGER / PHILADA" on the lock plate and only "P" (no "US") on the barrel.

Values for converted rifles: Good—$900   Fine—$2,250

*James D. Julia
Auctioneers,
Fairfield, Maine*

U.S. Model 1841 Rifle, .54 Caliber, Paper Cartridge, Percussion

Made by Harpers Ferry Armory (it is believed that only model pieces were made at the Springfield Armory in 1849), 1846-1855. Total production: 25,296.

Overall length: 48-1/2". Weight: 9 lbs. 12 oz.

Lock plate marked forward of the hammer, (eagle) / US and vertically behind the hammer, HARPERS / FERRY / (date). Harpers Ferry barrels are marked with V/P and an eagle head near the breech as well as PM, WW, AW or WW over P, all in small letters. The date is stamped on the breech plug tang. A small "S" forward of the bolster on rifles made after 1851 denote a steel barrel. No stock cartouches, but the left side of the stock stamped with inspector initials "JHK" or "J.L.R." in block letters.

The Model 1841 percussion rifle was also known as the "Mississippi rifle," "Windsor rifle," "Harpers Ferry rifle," "Whitney rifle," "Remington rifle" and "Yaeger rifle." The Model 1841 rifle remained in production at the federal armory until 1855, when the Secretary of War ordered that the .58 caliber Minié cartridge be adopted for all U.S. shoulder arms. The Model 1841 had been designed for use with a .54 caliber ball and loose powder. The Secretary of War made the Model 1841 obsolete, at the same time, giving rise to a large conversion aftermarket that would convert the Model 1841 to current specifications.

As originally produced, the Model 1841 rifle was equipped with a brass blade front sight and a simple V-notch rear sight. They were produced without any provision for a bayonet. During 1854-55, the last year of production, Harpers Ferry did attempt to bring Model 1841 rifles up to current specifications by equipping each with more precise sights provisions to accept a bayonet.

Good—$1,250   **Fine—$4,500**

1841 CONTRACT MODELS

U.S. MODEL 1841 PERCUSSION RIFLE, .54 CALIBER, REMINGTON CONTRACT

Rock Island Auction Company

Made by E. Remington, Herkimer, New York, ca. 1846-1854. Three contracts totaling 20,000 rifles.

Lock plate marked forward of the hammer, "REMINGTON'S / HERKIMER / N.Y." and "U.S. / (date) behind it

GOOD–$1,250   FINE–$4,500

U.S. MODEL 1841 PERCUSSION RIFLE, .54 CALIBER, ROBBINS, KENDALL & LAWRENCE CONTRACT

Rock Island Auction Company

On February 18, 1845, the firm jointly owned by Samuel E. Robbins, Nicanor Kendall and Richard S. Lawrence received a contract for 10,000 Model 1841 rifles. The Windsor, Vermont, firm was to deliver the rifles at the rate of 2,000 a year at a price of $11.90 each. The contract was complete 18 months early.

The lock plate is marked forward of the hammer in four lines, "ROBBINS / KENDALL & / LAWRENCE / U.S. Behind the hammer, the lock plate is marked vertically, in two lines, "WINDSOR VT / (date).

GOOD–$1,250   FINE–$4,500

U.S. MODEL 1841 PERCUSSION RIFLE, .54 CALIBER, ROBBINS & LAWRENCE CONTRACT

Rock Island Auction Company

Samuel Robbins and Richard Lawrence of Windsor, Vermont (successors to the manufactory, Robbins, Kendall & Lawrence), received a contract on January 5, 1848, to produce 15,000 Model 1841 rifles at the rate of 3,000 a year.

The lock plates of these rifles are marked forward of the hammer in four lines, "ROBBINS / & / LAWRENCE / US". Behind the hammer, each plate is marked vertically, "WINDSOR VT / (date)".

GOOD–$1,250   FINE–$4,500

James D. Julia Auctioneers, Fairfield, Maine

U.S. MODEL 1841 PERCUSSION RIFLE, .54 CALIBER, TRYON & SON CONTRACT

On April 22, 1848, Philadelphian George W. Tryon received a contract to produce 5,000 rifles priced at $12.87½ each.

The lock plates of Tryon contract rifles are marked in two lines forward of the hammer, "TRYON / US" and in behind the hammer, "PHILADA / PA / (date)".

GOOD–$1,250   FINE–$4,500

U.S. MODEL 1841 PERCUSSION RIFLE, .54 CALIBER, WHITNEY CONTRACT, TYPE I

Overall length, 48-1/2". Weight 9 lbs. 12 oz.

Made at New Haven, Connecticut, 1843-1854. Total production: 25,900.

Lock plate marked forward of the hammer, E. WHITNEY / U.S. The rear of the plate is vertically marked N. HAVEN / (date). Butt plate tang marked U.S. Whitney barrels are marked US over SK, SM, GW, JAG, JH, JCB, JPC or ADK and P or V over P. After 1848, breech also marked STEEL. Breech tang dated the same as the lock.

Each of Whitney's contract rifles featured a "V" notch open type rear sight and a brass tipped ramrod. They were not equipped to accept a bayonet.

GOOD–$1,250   FINE–$4,500

U.S. MODEL 1841 PERCUSSION RIFLE, .54 CALIBER, WHITNEY CONTRACT, TYPE II

Overall length, 48-1/2". Weight 9 lbs. 12 oz.

Made at New Haven, Connecticut, 1855. Total production: 600.

Lock plate marked forward of the hammer, E. WHITNEY / U.S. The rear of the plate is vertically marked N. HAVEN / 1855. Butt plate tang marked U.S. Whitney barrels are marked US over SK and SM, GW, JH, JCB, JPC or ADK over VP. After 1848, breech also marked STEEL. Breech tang dated the same as the lock. Breech tang marked 1855.

The 600 rifles of Whitney's 1855 delivery were altered to conform with Harpers Ferry's second style of alteration. Before this last shipment was made, the stock of each rifle was shortened slightly. Whitney replaced the brass-tipped ramrods with a steel-tipped version cupped for use with Minié bullets. Furthermore, each of the 600 was fitted a with a bayonet stud that incorporated a 1" guide brazed to the right side of the barrel. Like the Harpers Ferry altered rifles, Whitney's featured shortened front double-strap barrel bands.

GOOD–$1,250   FINE–$4,500

U.S. MODEL 1841 PERCUSSION RIFLE, .54 CALIBER, WHITNEY SOUTH CAROLINA CONTRACT

Overall length, 48-1/2". Weight 9 lbs. 12 oz.

Made by Whitney Arms Company, New Haven, Connecticut, ca. 1849. Total production: estimated at 274.

Lock plate marked forward of the hammer, E. WHITNEY / SC The rear of the plate is vertically marked N. HAVEN / 1849.

Though only two contracts to supply rifles to the State of South Carolina are known, it is possible that Whitney made sales to other state governments. The South Carolina Whitney rifles were probably guns that failed government inspection so probably will not have inspector markings. Flaydermann reports that South Carolina rifles featured a blade-type front sight affixed to the upper strap of the front barrel band and a bayonet lug on the underside of the barrel near the muzzle to accept a socket bayonet.

GOOD–$3,000   FINE–$6,500

U.S. MODEL 1841 PERCUSSION RIFLE, .54 CALIBER, WHITNEY MISSISSIPPI CONTRACT

Overall length, 48-1/2". Weight 9 lbs. 12 oz.

On June 6, 1860, Eli Whitney agreed to supply the state of Mississippi with 1,500 Model 1841 rifles with bayonets. By October 15, 1860, he had sent 60 to Mississippi Adjutant General W.L. Sykes for inspection. Sykes reported that the "arms were received and examined and proved to be old guns fixed up." With the exception of the 60 sample rifles, no others were delivered under the terms of the contract.

GOOD—$3,000   **FINE—$6,500**

U.S. MODEL 1841 PERCUSSION RIFLE, .54 CALIBER, PALMETTO ARMORY, SOUTH CAROLINA CONTRACT

Overall length, 49". Weight 9 lbs. 12 oz.

Made by Palmetto Armory, Boatwright & Glaze, proprietors, Columbia, South Carolina, 1852-1853. Total production: 1,000.

Lock plate marked forward of the hammer, PALMETTO ARMORY / S*C in a circle around a palmetto tree The rear of the plate is vertically marked Columbia / S.C. (date). Barrel marked P / V with a palmetto tree. Left flat marked either W.G. & Co or WM. GLAZE & CO. near the breech. Tang marked (date). Butt plate tang marked SC. The patch box does not have a specific location inlet for a spare nipple.

William Glaze and James Boatwright formed the Palmetto Armory in 1850. William Glaze entered into an agreement with Benjamin Flagg, owner of B. Flagg & Co. and signed a contract with the State of South Carolina on April 15, 1851 to produce a number of arms—including 1,000 rifles—all of which were "to be made with in the confines of the State of South Carolina. The contract stipulated that the first 350 rifles be ready for inspection by January 1852. U.S. General William Sherman's forces reported that 500 Palmetto rifles were destroyed at the Citadel College in Columbia on February 17, 1865.

(Reilly reports that these were not fitted for a bayonet, but it appears he studied a sample that had a replaced barrel. Madaus and Richard Taylor Hill report that the rifle had a bayonet lug on the top of the barrel to accept a triangular bayonet).

GOOD—7,500   **FINE—25,000**

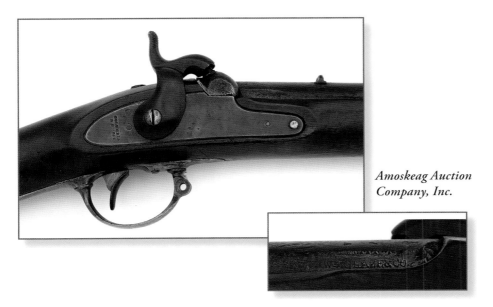

Amoskeag Auction Company, Inc.

Amoskeag Auction Company, Inc.

ALTERATIONS TO THE U.S. MODEL 1841 RIFLE

The following section, a photographic guide, is intended to take the confusion out of deciphering the many variations of the Model 1841 rifle. This would not have been possible without the generous cooperation of Rock Island Auction Company. In 2006, the firm conducted the largest sale of Model 1841 rifles since the Civil War. The efforts Rock Island made to accurately catalog and categorize the rifles was a major contribution to the field of collecting and studying these stunning rifles.

U.S. MODEL 1841 PERCUSSION RIFLE, .54 CALIBER, HARPERS FERRY FIRST ("SNELL") ALTERATION, 1854-1855

Rock Island Auction Company

During 1854-1855, the Harpers Ferry Armory altered 590 Model 1841 rifles from its own inventory and 1,041 Harpers Ferry manufactured rifles stored at the Washington Arsenal. The armory fitted the rifles with a new long-range rear sight consisting of a single-standing ladder with a screw adjustable range setting on a 1/2"-long base dovetailed 2-15/16" from the breech (this style of sight was found to be unsatisfactory and many were replaced with simple open "V" block sights). In addition, the armory modified the barrels to accept the 27-1/4"-long Snell-pattern saber bayonet. The modification required two ½" horizontal slot milled on the right side of the muzzle and a ½" elliptical cut milled perpendicular to (but not intersecting) the horizontal slot. Harpers Ferry produced 1,646 bayonets for these altered rifles in 1855. The first style Harpers Ferry alteration were left in .54 caliber.

GOOD—$1,250   FINE—$4,500

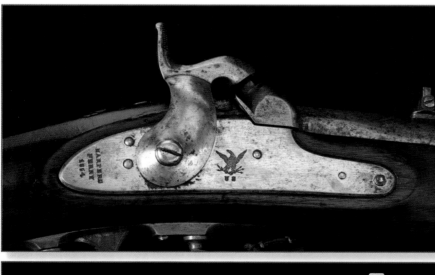

Rock Island Auction Company

U.S. MODEL 1841 PERCUSSION RIFLE, .54 CALIBER, HARPERS FERRY SECOND ALTERATION, 1854-1855

In addition to the first "Snell" alterations, 449 rifles of Harpers Ferry's production and 1,200 rifles stored at the Washington Arsenal (all Harpers Ferry-produced) were adapted to accept a second style of saber bayonet that did not incorporate a ring on the handle like the Snell pattern. The Armory brazed a bayonet lug with a 1" guide key on the right side of each barrel to accept this new bayonet. A stamped letter/number code on the face of each barrel mated it to a bayonet marked with the same code on the quillion. Between 1855-1857, Harpers Ferry produced 10,286 bayonets of this type. To accommodate this style of bayonet, the double-strap front barrel band was replaced with a new, shorter double-strap band and the forestock was slightly shortened.

These rifles were fitted with long-range sights (a copy of the English P1853 rifle-musket sight) soldered 2-7/8" from the breech. The 2-3/16"-long side wall of each sight was marked with "2", "3" and "4" 100-yard gradients. The folding adjustable ladder was marked from 500-1,000 yards.

GOOD—$1,250　　　**FINE—$4,500**

Rock Island Auction Company

Rock Island Auction Company

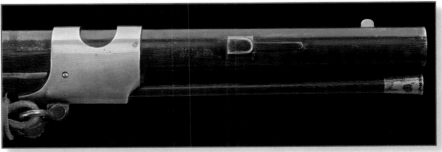

*Rock Island
Auction
Company*

U.S. MODEL 1841 PERCUSSION RIFLE, .54 CALIBER, HARPERS FERRY THIRD ALTERATION, 1855-1856

During 1855-1856, Harpers Ferry altered 250 rifles to accept the second style saber bayonet. Instead of using the ladder-style rear sight used during the second alteration of 1854-55, a new sight was added to these rifles. The new sight had a side wall with gradients denoted with "200", "3" and "4" and intermediate 50-yard steps.

GOOD—$1,250   FINE—$4,500

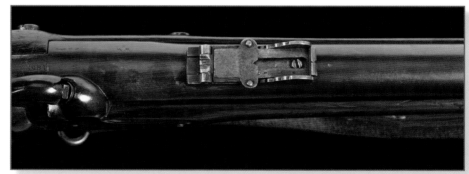

Rock Island Auction Company

U.S. MODEL 1841 PERCUSSION RIFLE, HARPERS FERRY FOURTH ALTERATION, 1857-1859

Marked "W.C.K." on the barrel forward of the bolster and in the wood opposite the lock plate.

The introduction of the Model 1855 rifle led to changes to existing Model 1841 rifles. The 803 Model 1841 rifles that were converted to .58 caliber during 1856-1857 and the 1,663 rifles altered during 1857-1858 (presumably left in .54 caliber) as well as the 842 .58 caliber rifles altered during 1858-1859 at Harpers Ferry were all modified to take the saber bayonet and sights of the Model 1855 rifle. This alteration added a bayonet lug with no guide to each barrel. The Armory added an iron block/blade front sight and a rear site with a 2-7/16" base. The side walls of the rear sight were graduated in 100 yard increments and denoted with "2", "3" and "5". All of these arms went through an inspection after the alteration. Those that passed were marked "W.C.K." on the barrel and in the wood opposite the lock plate.

GOOD—$1,250   FINE—$4,500

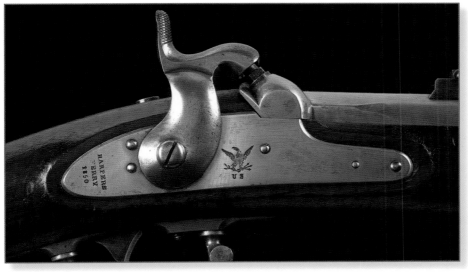

Rock Island Auction Company

Rock Island Auction Company

Rock Island Auction Company

U.S. Model 1841 Percussion Rifle, .58 Caliber, Harpers Ferry Fifth Alteration, 1859-1860

When a new sight was adopted for the Model 1855 rifle in 1858, it was applied to the Model 1841 rifles still undergoing alteration at Harpers Ferry as well. The new pattern rear sight, which did not become available until 1859, consisted of a 1-3/16" long stepped block and two folding leaves for 300 and 500 yards (marked "3" and "5"). It was dovetailed and screwed to the barrel 2-15/16" from the breech. These rifles retained same guideless bayonet lug and front sight as prescribed for the fourth alteration. All of the 2,133 rifles that underwent this fifth alteration were rebored to .58 caliber (three grooves equal to the width of the lands) and received a full steel, trumpet head ramrod without a brass tip.

Good—$1,250   Fine—$4,500

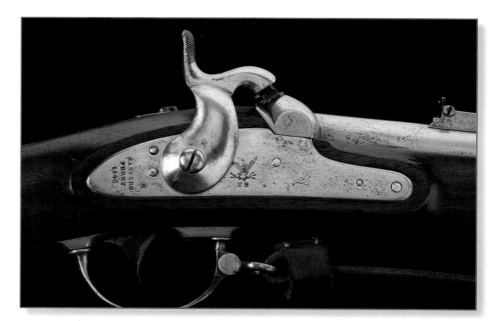

Rock Island Auction Company

U.S. MODEL 1841 PERCUSSION RIFLE, .58 CALIBER, COLT ALTERATION, 1861-1862

In the summer of 1861, the Colt's Patent Fire Arms Manufacturing Company of Hartford, Connecticut, purchased 11,368 U.S. Model 1841 rifles from the Federal government for $10 each. His intent was to rebore the rifles to .58 caliber, equip each with a saber bayonet and sell them back to the Ordnance Department for $18.50 per unit. Apart from 468 rifles in .54 caliber that Colt sold to Connecticut (with saber bayonets), all were rebored with 7-groove rifling to .58 caliber. Colt resighted each with the Colt New Model 1855 revolving rifle pattern rear sight and affixed a slip ring clamp with a guide stud to the muzzle to accept a Collins & Company saber bayonet. Both the clamp, bayonet and the lower right side of the barrel near the muzzle were stamped with matching serial numbers. In addition to the inspector's initials, "CC" stamped on the left side of the barrel and either side of the butt stock or comb, an oval cartouche encompassing the initials CGC, WAT, or GTB in script marks each of Colt's altered rifles. By May 1862, Colt had sold 10,200 of the altered rifles back to the Federal government.

GOOD—$1,250   **FINE—$4,500**

Rock Island Auction Company

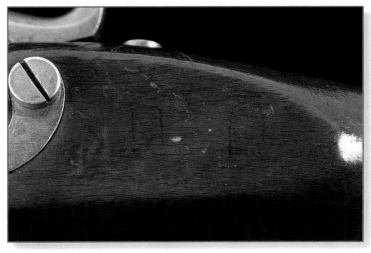

Rock Island Auction Company

Rock Island Auction Company

U.S. MODEL 1841 PERCUSSION RIFLE, .54 CALIBER, NEW YORK (REMINGTON) ALTERATION, 1861

In 1861, New York took delivery of 5,000 Remington U.S. Model 1841 rifles from Watervliet Arsenal. On May 30 of that year, the state contracted E. Remington & Sons to equip each rifle to accept a Collins, Hartford brass hilted saber bayonet without shortening the stock or front barrel band. Remington brazed a slightly longer than ½" stud 4-1/2" from the muzzle on the right side of the barrel. By September 1861, Remington was only able to acquire enough bayonets to deliver 3,286 altered rifles (see Grosz alteration for the balance of the 5,000). The Remington altered rifles remained .54 caliber.

GOOD—$1,250   **FINE—$4,500**

Rock Island Auction Company

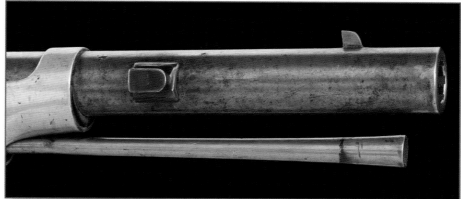

Rock Island Auction Company

U.S. MODEL 1841 PERCUSSION RIFLE, .54 CALIBER, NEW YORK (GROSZ) ALTERATION, 1861

When E. Remington & Sons was unable to complete the modification of 5,000 U.S. Model 1841 rifles to accept a saber bayonet, 1,600 old U.S. Model 1842 musket socket bayonets were procured from the Springfield Armory. New York City gunsmith Frederick H. Grosz received the contract to alter the rifles that E. Remington & Sons was unable to equip with saber bayonets. Grosz turned town the barrel of the each rifle to the inner diameter of the Model 1842 socket bayonets from the muzzle for 2-11/16". He moved the brass blade front sight behind the turning. Finally, he brazed a square bayonet stud on the underside of the turned town section to act as the bayonet's retainer. Grosz delivered all of the rifles by December 1861. All of these rifles remained in .54 caliber.

GOOD—$1,250   **FINE—$4,500**

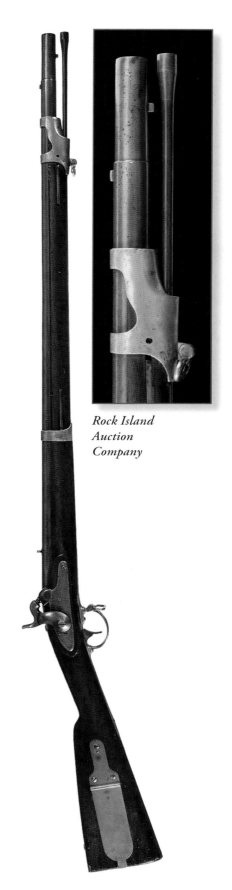

Rock Island Auction Company

Rock Island Auction Company

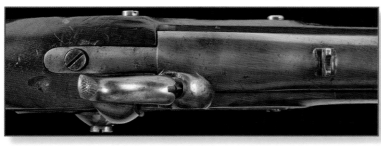

U.S. MODEL 1841 PERCUSSION RIFLE, .58 CALIBER, PENNSYLVANIA (LEMAN) ALTERATION, 1861

In 1861, the Commonwealth of Pennsylvania contracted gunsmith Henry E. Leman of Lancaster to convert 2,352 U.S. Model 1841 rifles to .58 caliber and modify them to accept the triangular U.S. Model 1842 socket bayonet. Leman bored and rifled each barrel with three wide grooves equal in width to the lands. He then turned down barrel from the muzzle to 2-11/16" to accept a socket bayonet. He brazed a bayonet stud on the underside of the barrel to lock the bayonet in place. Finally, the front sight which had to be removed to turn down the barrel was replaced with a new, triangular brass blade behind the turning. A three-digit serial number stamped on the left side of the barrel and on the butt plate tang completed the alteration.

GOOD—$1,250   **FINE—$4,500**

Rock Island Auction Company

U.S. MODEL 1841 PERCUSSION RIFLE, .54 CALIBER, MASSACHUSETTS (DRAKE) ALTERATION, 1862

In 1862, the Commonwealth of Massachusetts contracted A.J. Drake of Boston to alter 1,839 Windsor rifles (most likely U.S. Model 1841 rifles made by Robbins, Kendall & Lawrence of Windsor, Vermont). On each rifle, Drake replaced the front blade sight with a block base site suitable for mounting a socket bayonet and added a three-leaf rear sight. All of the Drake-altered rifles remained in .54 caliber. The barrels were stripped of their browning. The majority of the Drake altered rifles were issue to either the 46th or 51st Massachusetts Infantry and bear additional markings appropriate for either regiment. Less than 75 of the Drake rifles were left in the brown. These "brown Drakes" do not have show any regimental markings.

GOOD—2,750 FINE—12,500

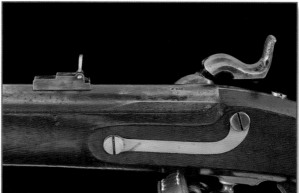

Rock Island Auction Company

U.S. Model 1841 Percussion Rifle, .54 Caliber, Maine Alteration

The so-called "Maine alteration" is thought to number less than 1,000 rifles (according to George Moller, *Long Arms of Massachusetts*). Characterized by a bayonet lug attached to the left side of the barrel with one large pin and two small pins. the top of the bayonet lug is convex ("crowned") as opposed to the normal flat top profile of other saber bayonet lugs. No alteration to the sights.

Good—$1,250   Fine—$4,500

Rock Island Auction Company

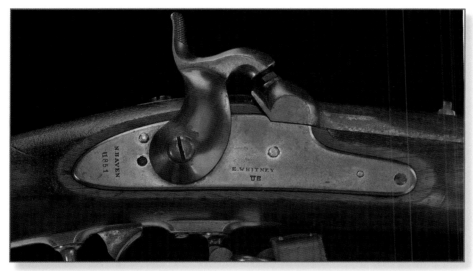

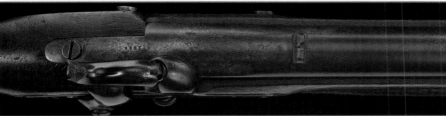

Rock Island Auction Company

U.S. Model 1841 Percussion Rifle, .54 Caliber, New Hampshire Alteration

The bayonet lug is attached by two screws.

Good—$1,250   Fine—$4,500

Rock Island Auction Company

U.S. Model 1841 Percussion Rifle, .54 Caliber, Vermont Alteration

The bayonet lug accepts a New Hampshire Collins style saber bayonet and differs from the New Hampshire alteration in that it is attached without screws and has clipped corners at the front.

Good—$1,250   Fine—$4,500

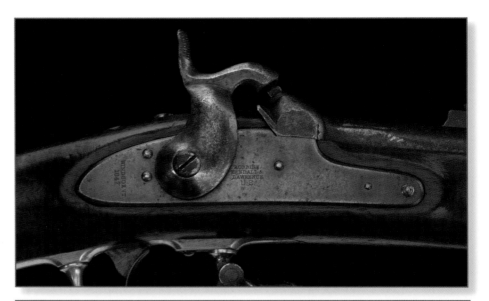

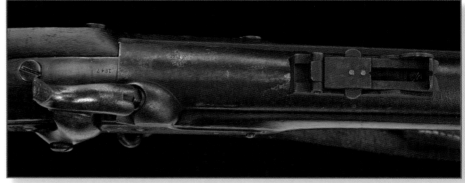

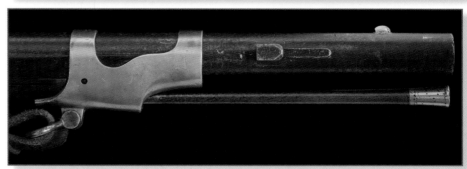

Rock Island Auction Company

U.S. MODEL 1841 PERCUSSION RIFLE, .54 CALIBER, NEW JERSEY ALTERATION, TYPE I

Front sight is mortised into the socket of the imported Belgian or Austrian bayonet rather than on the muzzle of the barrel. The front 2-3/4" of the barrel was turned to 13/16" inches and a round stud fastened to the bottom of the barrel to accept and hold a bayonet in place. Barrel is stamped "N.J." on the left flat side of the breech. Type Is are Tryon-assembled rifles.

GOOD—$1,500　　　**FINE—$5,000**

Rock Island Auction Company

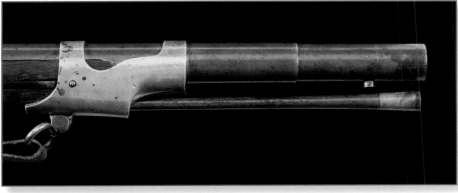

Rock Island Auction Company

69

U.S. MODEL 1841 PERCUSSION RIFLE, .54 CALIBER, NEW JERSEY ALTERATION, TYPE II

Rock Island Auction Company

Front sight is mortised into the socket of the imported Belgian or Austrian bayonet rather than on the muzzle of the barrel. The front 2-3/4" of the barrel was turned to 13/16" inches and a round stud fastened to the bottom of the barrel to accept and hold a bayonet in place. Barrel is stamped "N.J." on the left flat side of the breech. Type IIs are Whitney-assembled rifles.

GOOD—$1,500   FINE—$5,000

U.S. MODEL 1841 PERCUSSION RIFLE, .54 CALIBER, NEW JERSEY ALTERATION, TYPE III

Rock Island Auction Company

Front sight is mortised into the socket of the imported Belgian or Austrian bayonet rather than on the muzzle of the barrel. The front 2-3/4" of the barrel was turned to 13/16" inches and a round stud fastened to the bottom of the barrel to accept and hold a bayonet in place. Barrel is stamped "N.J." on the left flat side of the breech. Type IIIs are composites of Whitney barrels and Tryon locks or vice versa.

GOOD—$1,500   FINE—$5,000

LINDER ALTERATION OF U.S. MODEL 1841 CONTRACT RIFLES, .54 CALIBER COMBUSTIBLE CARTRIDGE, PERCUSSION

Allen & Morse of Boston contracted with the State of Massachusetts in late 1861 to convert 100 U.S. Model 1841 Contract Rifles to the breechloading system patented by Edward Lindner in 1859. All of these rifles were contract weapons manufactured by Robbins & Lawrence, Windsor, Vermont. Three additional rifles had been altered by Amoskeag Manufacturing Company at an earlier date. All 103 examples were held in storage during the Civil War. The barrel was cut off 4-1/2" from the breech and a new action installed. When the shooter flipped the bolt of a sleeve to the left, the spring-operated breech popped up, allowing the chamber to be loaded from the front with a .54-caliber combustible cartridge. After pressing the breech unit back down and flipping the sleeve back to the right, the rifle was ready for firing. Other alterations included a new rear sight and combination bayonet stud / blade front sight.

GOOD—$5,500   **FINE—$10,500**

Rock Island Auction Company

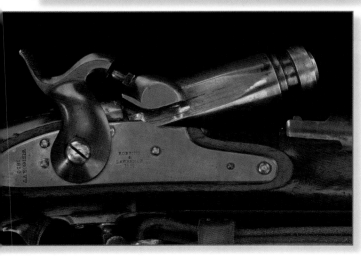

Rock Island Auction Company

MERRILL ALTERATION OF U.S. MODEL 1841 RIFLE .58 CALIBER, PERCUSSION, COMBUSTIBLE CARTRIDGE

Early in the Civil War a few U.S. Model 1841 Rifles were altered with the addition of the Merrill breech apparatus. This device incorporated a lever which, when raised, opened a chamber where the cartridge could be inserted. Lowering the lever activated a breech plunger that seated cartridge into the breech.

GOOD—$6,500   FINE—$15,000

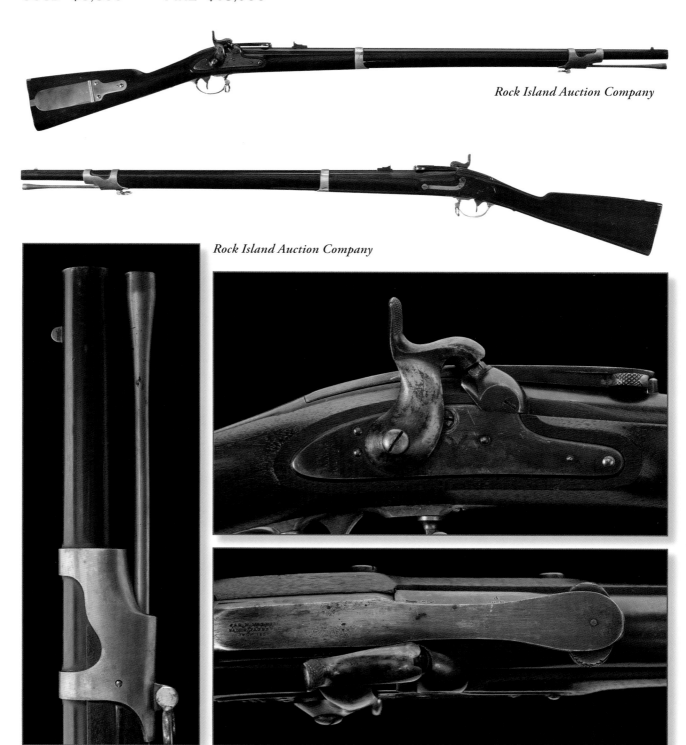

Rock Island Auction Company

Rock Island Auction Company

POST-MODEL 1841 RIFLES

U.S. MODEL 1855 "HARPERS FERRY" RIFLE, .58 CALIBER, PAPER CARTRIDGE, PERCUSSION

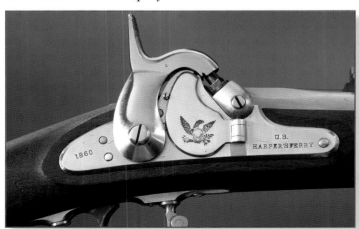

Rock Island Auction Company

Manufactured by Harpers Ferry Armory, Harpers Ferry, Virginia (now West Virginia), ca. 1857–61. Total production: approximately 8,700.

Overall length: 49-3/8". Weight: 10 lbs.

Muzzleloader, single shot.

"U.S. / HARPERS FERRY" to front of lock plate; year to rear of lock plate; spread eagle on primer door; "V / P" over eagle head on breech; year on top of barrel near breech.

The U.S. Model 1855 Percussion Rifle, commonly known as the Harpers Ferry Rifle, was the final model of muzzleloading rifle to be manufactured in a U.S. armory. It featured a Maynard tape priming mechanism, a 33" round barrel rifled with three wide grooves, oil-finished black walnut stock, a patch box on the right side of the butt, two flat barrel bands (with a sling swivel on the upper band), and a lug for a saber-type bayonet on the right side of the barrel.

Two basic types of the rifle existed:

Type I, Brass-Mounted: Rifles manufactured before 1860, approximately half of the total production run, had brass furniture, as well as a long-range rear sight graduated to 500 yards, and (on early-production specimens of this type) a double-ring crosshair fixture that could be attached to the front sight.

GOOD—$3,750   **FINE—$10,000**

Rock Island Auction Company

Type II, Iron-Mounted: Rifles made from 1860 on had iron furniture. They lacked the detachable crosshair fixture, and the rear sight was smaller and graduated to 400 yards.

GOOD—$2,500   **FINE—$6,500**

*James D. Julia
Auctioneers,
Fairfield, Maine*

WHITNEY MODEL 1861 PERCUSSION NAVY (OR "PLYMOUTH") RIFLE, .69 CALIBER, PAPER CARTRIDGE, PERCUSSION

Made by Whitneyville Arms Company, New Haven, Connecticut, ca. 1861–64. Total production: 10,000.

Overall Length: 50". Weight: 9 lbs. 10 oz.

Muzzleloader, single shot.

Early production examples: "U.S. / WHITNEY-VILLE" below bolster cutout on lock plate; large spread eagle with U.S. flag at center of lock plate; "1863" vertically near rear of lock plate. Late production: "WHITNEY-VILLE" below bolster cutout; smaller spread eagle over "U.S." at center of lock plate; "1863" or "1864" vertically near rear of lock plate. Also, "V / P / [eagle head]" and "1863" or "1864" on barrel near breech.

The Whitney Model 1861 Percussion Navy Rifle is also referred to as the "Plymouth Rifle" because the design was developed on the USS Plymouth while the personnel of that ship were experimenting with new naval weapons in the late 1850s. The rifle shared the same lock plate as the regulation U.S. .58-caliber rifle-musket. It had a 34" bright-finished rifle, rifled with four deep grooves, and with an unusually large rear sight. On the left side of the barrel near the muzzle was a lug for a saber-type bayonet. The 45" black walnut stock was fastened to the barrel with two bands (the upper of which was a unique, single-strap design), which in turn were secured by band springs. The head of the ramrod had a pronounced, cylindrical shape, with a hole drilled through it, and the end cupped to fit a Minié bullet. All furniture was iron, either blued or bright. There were two variations in the markings of the lock plate, as described above.

GOOD—$1,500   FINE—$4,000

WHITNEY MODEL 1855-DERIVATIVE .58 CALIBER RIFLE FOR MILITIA, PAPER CARTRIDGE, PERCUSSION

Made by Whitneyville Armory, New Haven, Connecticut, ca. 1859. Total production: probably very low.

Overall Length: 49".

Muzzleloader, single shot.

"E. WHITNEY" on lock plate in front of hammer; "V", "P", and eagle head on upper left flat of barrel; year on top of barrel near breech.

This rifle, designed for the militia trade, featured unmilled locks of the U.S. Model 1855 Maynard tape-primer type with the hump ground off. They combined a cut-down rifle-musket stock fastened with two brass bands to a browned 33" barrel rifled with three grooves. A lug for a saber bayonet on the right side near the muzzle. The barrels probably were rejected Harper's Ferry U.S. Model 1855 rifle barrels. All furniture but the barrel bands were iron. The rear sight was a Whitney Model 1855 tangent sight mounted 3" from the breech, and the front sight was an iron block-and-blade type.

GOOD—$1,250   FINE—$4,500

REMINGTON MODEL 1863 CONTRACT RIFLE, .58 CALIBER, PAPER CARTRIDGE, PERCUSSION

Made by E. Remington & Sons, Ilion, New York, ca. 1863–65. Total production: 12,501.

Overall Length: 49-1/8". Weight: 9 lbs. 6oz.

Muzzleloader, single shot.

"REMINGTON'S / ILION, N.Y." below bolster cutout on lock plate; spread eagle over "U.S." at center of lock plate; year to rear of lock plate; year, "STEEL," inspector's initials, and "V / P / [eagle head] on barrel near breech; "U.S." on butt plate tang; "U" on right side of each barrel band.

The Remington Model 1863 Contract Rifle was a very well manufactured firearm. It had a 33" round, blued barrel rifled with three or, most commonly, seven grooves (or also, according to arms expert Robert M. Reilly, five grooves). The barrel was fitted near the muzzle with a large lug for a saber-type bayonet, and the rifle came with a tulip-head ramrod. The lock plate was casehardened, and all furniture was bright brass, including the fore-tip and two solid, oval bands. According to the original Ordnance Department contract for this rifle, dated July 30, 1861, it was to be of the Harpers Ferry pattern of 1855. It is not known how the arm came to be referred to as "Zouave Rifle." Because of the excellent condition of many of the surviving specimens, it is thought that a large proportion of them never saw service.

GOOD—$2,750   FINE—$4,500

James D. Julia Auctioneers, Fairfield, Maine

ASHEVILLE ARMORY RIFLE, .58 (TYPES I AND II) AND .577 (TYPE III) CALIBER, PAPER CARTRIDGE, PERCUSSION

Made by Asheville Armory, Asheville, North Carolina, 1862-63. Total production: approximately 875.

Overall length: 48-5/8" (Type I); 49" (Type II).

Muzzleloader, single shot.

Marked forward of the hammer in two lines, "ASHEVILLE / N.C." Type II and III rifles will often have an inspector's mark (usually "A.W.K.") and a script "Asheville N.C." on the left side of the stock, both in oval cartouches.

It is presumed that the Asheville Armory used salvaged parts of U.S. Model 1841 rifles to construct the Asheville rifles. Early examples have flat butt plates while Type III rifles have curved butt plates.

GOOD—$17,500   FINE—$37,500

C. CHAPMAN RIFLE, .58 CALIBER, PAPER CARTRIDGE, PERCUSSION

Manufacturer unknown, ca. 1862-1863. Total production: About 60.

Overall length: 48-3/4".

Muzzleloader, single shot.

Lock plate stamped forward of the hammer, "C. CHAPMAN."

Patterned after the U.S. Model 1841 rifle with brass barrel bands, side plate and butt plate, the C. Chapman rifle remains a collector's enigma. "C. Chapman" has not been identified, though speculation is that the maker may have resided in Tennessee. Recent scholarship points to similarities to another unknown rifle stamped "SUMNER / ARMORY". For now, though, "C. Chapman" remains unknown to collectors.

GOOD—$20,000   FINE—$40,000

Collection Of Frank Reile, photo by Alya Alberico

CLAPP, GATES & COMPANY RIFLE, .50-.58 CALIBERS, PAPER CARTRIDGE, PERCUSSION

Made by Clapp, Gates & Company, Cedar Hill Foundry, Alamanee Creek, North Carolina, 1862-63. Total production: 1,031.

Dimensions vary—see below.

Muzzleloader, single shot.

Type I: 52" overall; .50 caliber with "inside-lock" firing mechanisms with a centrally mounted hammer. Mountings are brass with a spring-retained rear barrel band. Front barrel band serves as a nose cap.

Type II: 52" overall; .50 caliber with a flat-faced hammer mounted on the outside of the lock, one-piece trigger guard, iron barrel bands, and a separate brass nose cap.

Type III: Approximately 50" overall; .50 caliber with brass lock washers, longer nose cap, U.S. Model 1855-type bayonet lug, and a rounded-contour hammer.

Type IV: .577 caliber. Production of Type IV rifles began in March 1863.

ALL TYPES: GOOD—$10,000   FINE—$30,000

M. CODY & SON RIFLE, .54 CALIBER, PAPER CARTRIDGE, PERCUSSION

Made by Michael Cody & Son, Nashville, Tennessee, 1862-63. Total production: Fewer than 800.

Overall length: 48-5/8" - 49".

Muzzleloader, single shot.

Large script number on barrel tang is the only marking.

Made in the style of the U.S. Model 1841 rifle with very minor variations. Brass furniture with pin-fastened barrel bands.

GOOD—$7,500   FINE—$25,500

Collection Of Frank Reile, photo by Alya Alberico

COOK & BROTHER RIFLE, ATHENS. .58 CALIBER, PAPER CARTRIDGE, PERCUSSION

Made by Cook and Brother, Athens, Georgia, 1862-1864. Total production: Approximately 3,000.

Overall length: 48-3/4".

Muzzleloader, single shot.

Lock plate stamped forward of the hammer, "COOK & BROTHER, ATHENS GA" with the date in two lines. A Confederate "Stars and Bars" flag is stamped at the rear of the lock plate. Top of barrel stamped behind the rear sight with the serial number, "COOK & BROTHER, N.O./ATHENS GA." and the date over the serial number. Some barrels marked "PROVED" at the breech.

Athens-made Cook rifles have one-piece brass trigger guards with the rear swivel as an integral part of the trigger guard tang.

GOOD—$15,500   FINE—$35,500

*James D. Julia
Auctioneers,
Fairfield,
Maine*

James D. Julia Auctioneers, Fairfield, Maine

James D. Julia Auctioneers, Fairfield, Maine

COOK & BROTHER RIFLE, NEW ORLEANS. .58 CALIBER, PAPER CARTRIDGE, PERCUSSION

Made by Cook and Brother, New Orleans, Louisiana, 1861-1862. Total production: Approximately 500.
Overall length: 48-3/4".

Muzzleloader, single shot.

Lock plate stamped forward of the hammer, "COOK & BROTHER, N.O." along with the date and serial number in one line. A Confederate "Stars and Bars" flag is stamped at the rear of the lock plate. Top of barrel stamped behind the rear sight with the serial number, "COOK & BROTHER, N.O." and the date

New Orleans-made Cook rifles have two-piece brass trigger guards.

GOOD—$17,500   FINE—$37,500

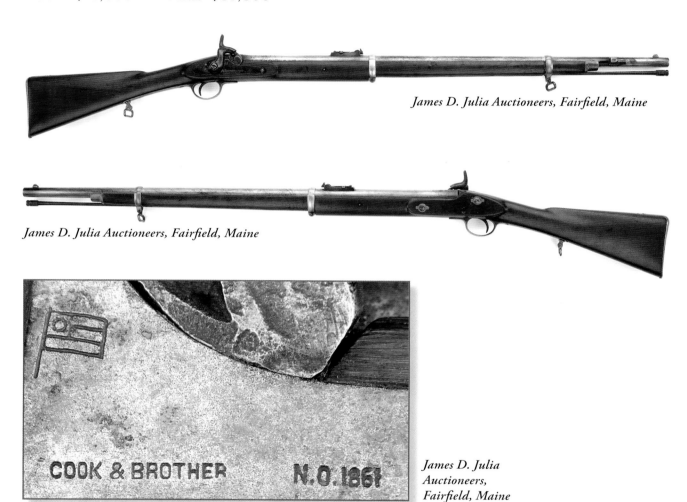

James D. Julia Auctioneers, Fairfield, Maine

James D. Julia Auctioneers, Fairfield, Maine

*James D. Julia
Auctioneers,
Fairfield, Maine*

DAVIS & BOZEMAN RIFLE, .577 CALIBER, PAPER CARTRIDGE, PERCUSSION

Made by Henry J. Davis and David W. Bozeman, Equality, Alabama, 1863-1865. Total production: Approximately 900. Overall length: 49".

Muzzleloader, single shot.

Lock plate stamped forward of the hammer, "D.&B." along with the date. The serial number is stamped behind the hammer. "ALA. and the date stamped on barrel breech.

Styled after the U.S. Model 1841 rifle without a patch box.

GOOD—$15,000   FINE—$40,000

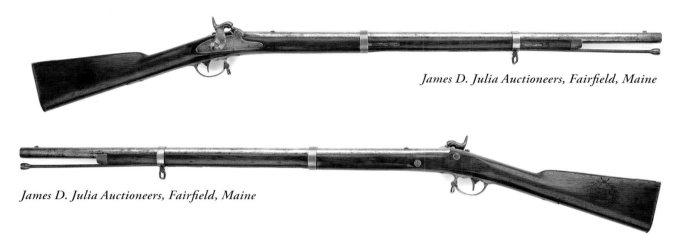

James D. Julia Auctioneers, Fairfield, Maine

James D. Julia Auctioneers, Fairfield, Maine

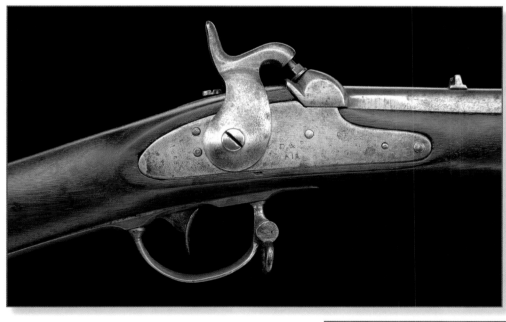

James D. Julia Auctioneers, Fairfield, Maine

DICKSON, NELSON RIFLE, .58 CALIBER, PAPER CARTRIDGE, PERCUSSION

Made by Dickson, Nelson & Company, Adairsville, Georgia, (1862); Macon, Georgia, (1863-1864); and Dawson, Georgia, (1864-1865). Total production: Approximately 3,500.

Overall length: 48".

Muzzleloader, single shot.

Lock plate stamped forward of the hammer, "DICKSON / NELSON & CO. / C.S." Stamped behind the hammer is "ALA. / [date]". Barrel stamped "ALA. [date]" in one line. Some stocks are known to be stamped "F. ZUNDT".

Styled after the U.S. Model 1841 rifle without a patch box, the mountings are usually brass.

GOOD—$12,500   FINE—$37,500

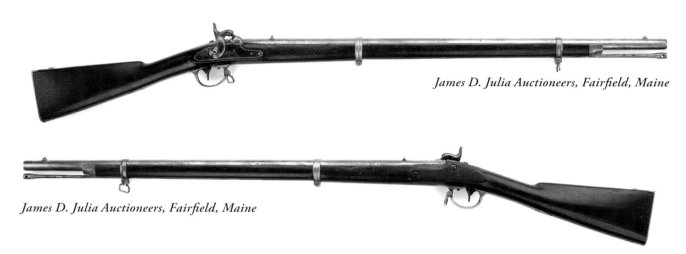

James D. Julia Auctioneers, Fairfield, Maine

James D. Julia Auctioneers, Fairfield, Maine

*James D. Julia
Auctioneers,
Fairfield, Maine*

FAYETTEVILLE ARMORY RIFLE, .58 CALIBER, PAPER CARTRIDGE, PERCUSSION

Made by Fayetteville Armory, Fayetteville, North Carolina, 1861-1865. Total production: Approximately 9,000.

James D. Julia Auctioneers, Fairfield, Maine

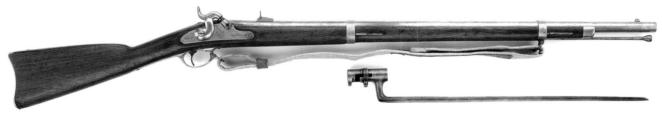

Overall length: 49".

Muzzleloader, single shot.

Type I: High-hump lock plate stamped forward of the hammer, "C.S.A. / FAYETTEVILLE, N.C." Made with or without a brass patch box. Produced ca. 1861-1862.

GOOD—$10,000   FINE—$30,000

Type II: Low hump lock plate marked forward of the hammer with an eagle over "C.S.A." and "FAYETTEVILLE". The date is stamped behind the hammer. Some brass butt plates marked "C.S.A." on Type II rifles.

GOOD—$10,000   FINE—$35,000

Type III: No hump on lock plate. Markings as found on Type II.

Hammer has a distinctive "S" shape. Saber bayonet lug on right side of barrel near muzzle.

GOOD—$8,500   FINE—$25,000

Type IV: Markings as with Type II and Type III except with later years of 1864 or 1865. No saber bayonet lug. Rather,

James D. Julia Auctioneers, Fairfield, Maine

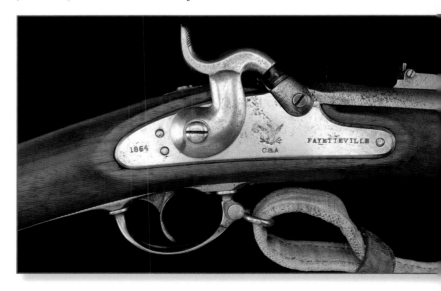

accepts a socket-type bayonet that locks over the front sight.

GOOD—$8,000   FINE—$22,500

FLORENCE ARMORY RIFLE, .50 CALIBER, PAPER CARTRIDGE, PERCUSSION

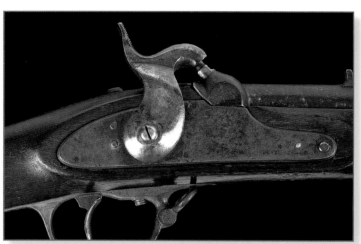

Made by Florence Armory, Florence, North Carolina, 1861-1864. Total production: Unknown.

Overall length: 48-1/16".

Muzzleloader, single shot.

Assembled from a variety of parts of different Federal and Confederate weapons, the Florence rifle is difficult to pin down into a set description. Examples are know to be built with parts from H.C. Lamb & Co. rifles, U.S. Model 1841 rifles, and even Austrian rifles. Because of this, extreme care should be exercised whenever considering a weapon represented as a "Florence Armory rifle."

GOOD–N/A   **FINE–N/A**

Rock Island Auction Company

GILLAM & MILLER CONTRACT RIFLE, .577 CALIBER, PAPER CARTRIDGE, PERCUSSION

Made by D.L. Gillam and James Miller, Jamestown, North Carolina, 1862-1863. Total production: Fewer than 1,000.

Overall length: 48-3/4".

Muzzleloader, single shot.

Top of barrel stamped "P". Top of butt stock comb marked "GILLAM & / MILLER".

Based on the U.S. Model 1841 Rifle, Gillam & Miller rifles are configured with two-bands and separate nose cap. They do not have brass patch boxes.

GOOD–$7,500   **FINE–$12,500**

P. S. JUSTICE RIFLE, .58 CALIBER, PAPER CARTRIDGE, PERCUSSION

Made by Philip S. Justice, Philadelphia, ca. 1861. Total production: Approximately 2,469.

Overall length: 51". Weight: 9 lbs. 2 oz.

Muzzleloader, single shot.

"P.S. JUSTICE / PHILADA" and eagle on lock plate to front of hammer; "P.S. JUSTICE / PHILADA" on barrel; on some examples, serial number near rear of trigger guard plate.

The U.S. government purchased 2,469 of these rifles for distribution to Pennsylvania volunteers in the first months of the Civil War. Hastily produced, the weapons were shoddy. The round, 35" barrel was browned and rifled with three shallow grooves. A lug for a saber bayonet was 3-1/2" from the muzzle on the right side of the barrel. Furniture, which included a patch box in the butt stock, was usually brass, but some examples were of iron. The brass-furniture rifles had distinctively shaped trigger-guard bows, with a reverse-curve on the bottom of the bow. Barrel bands were oval, split clamping type, although a few of these rifles were issued as rifle-muskets with pin-fastened barrels.

GOOD–$950   **FINE–$2,000**

HENRY C. LAMB RIFLE, VARIOUS CALIBERS, PAPER CARTRIDGE, PERCUSSION

Made by H.C. Lamb & Co., Jamestown, North Carolina, 1861-1864. Total production: ?Unknown.

Overall length: 48-3/8" to 49-1/2".

Muzzleloader, single shot.

Type I: Made in .50 caliber with iron washers on the lock plate bolts.

Type II: Also .50 caliber but a Type II will have a brass side plate opposite the lock .

Type III: .577 caliber and 49" overall. Stock opposite lock plate stamped "H.C. LAMB & CO. / N.C."

ALL TYPES: GOOD—$8,500 FINE—$17,500

Mendenhall, Jones & Gardner Contract Rifle, Various Calibers, Paper Cartridge, Percussion

Type III Mendenhall, Jones & Gardner North Carolina contract rifle. Rock Island Auction Company

Rock Island Auction Company

Made by Mendenhall, Jones & Gardner, Alamance, North Carolina, 1862-1864. Total production: Fewer than 2,500.

Overall length: 49-1/8".

Muzzleloader, single shot.

Based on the U.S. Model 1841 Rifle, Mendenhall, Jones & Gardner rifles are broken into four types:

Type I: .50 caliber. Has elongated bayonet lug on side of muzzle. Marked "N.C. / P" on barrel behind rear sight. Lock plated stamped forward of hammer, "MJ & G / N.C." Vertically stamped behind the hammer is "C.S. / 1862". Type I rifles have curved butt plates.

Type II: Same as above except .577 caliber with a shorter bayonet lug and a straight, iron butt plate. Some lock plates of Type II rifles are stamped "GUILFORD" between "MJ & G" and "N.C.". Some stocks also marked opposite the lock with an oval cartouche containing "MJ&G".

Type III: Similar to Type II except that the brass escutcheons on the bolts securing the lock plate are of the Enfield pattern. Type III rifles will be dated 1863 or 1864.

Type IV: Type IV rifles will have a two-leaf rear sight and an Enfield-style hammer and lock plate bolt escutcheons.

Top of barrel stamped "P". Top of butt stock comb marked "GILLAM & / MILLER".

ALL TYPES:
GOOD—$12,500   FINE—$30,000

Type II-IV rifles have a short-style bayonet lug. Rock Island Auction Company

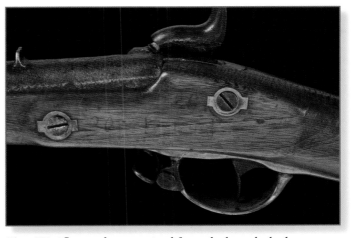

Type III rifles can be recognized from the brass lock plate screw escutcheons. Rock Island Auction Company

*James D. Julia
Auctioneers,
Fairfield, Maine*

J. P. MOORE-ENFIELD RIFLE, .58 CALIBER, PAPER CARTRIDGE, PERCUSSION

Made by John P. Moore Sons, New York City, 1861–63. Total production: Unknown.

Muzzleloader, single shot.

Year engraved on lock plate in front of hammer; eagle over Union shield with letter "M" in field on lock plate to rear of hammer. Proof marks sometimes found on barrels and barrel bands.

J. P. Moore manufactured a quantity of .58-caliber Enfield Pattern rifles with American black walnut stocks and a mix of imported and domestic parts. This rifle was fitted with a lug for a saber bayonet on the right side of the barrel near the muzzle. It had a 34-1/2" round barrel, unbeveled lock plate flush with the stock, and long-range ladder-type rear sight. Two barrel bands, split-clamping type, with upper sling swivel on forward band; lower swivel on trigger guard bow. Some examples reported with brass furniture.

GOOD—$1,000   **FINE—$1,500**

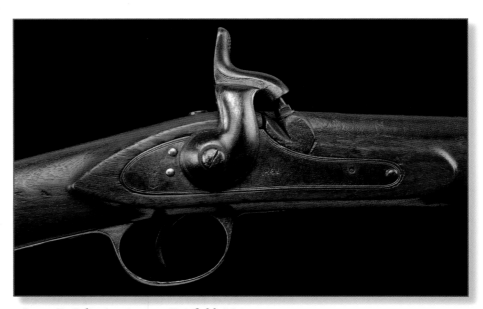

James D. Julia Auctioneers, Fairfield, Maine

MORSE "INSIDE LOCK" RIFLE, .54 CALIBER, PAPER CARTRIDGE, PERCUSSION

Made by George W. Morse, Greenville, South Carolina, ca. 1863-1864. Total production: Fewer than 200.

Overall length: 41-3/4".

Muzzleloader, single shot.

The only external marking is "1842" stamped horizontally on the barrel tang.

The two-band, muzzle-loading rifle incorporated a centrally located lock mechanism inside the stock. A shaft runs horizontally through the lock, terminating at an oval brass plate on the left side of the stock and attached to the hammer on the right. Variations exist that appear to be Morse conversions of U.S. Model 1841 rifles.

GOOD—$25,000   **FINE—$65,000**

J.P. MURRAY RIFLE, .577 CALIBER, PAPER CARTRIDGE, PERCUSSION

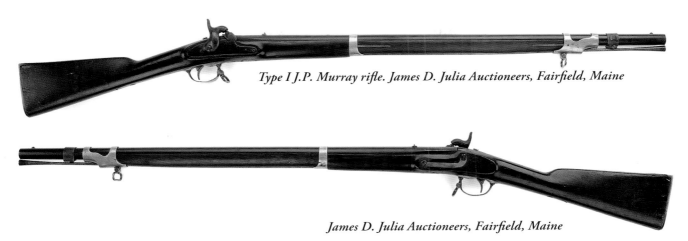

Type I J.P. Murray rifle. James D. Julia Auctioneers, Fairfield, Maine

James D. Julia Auctioneers, Fairfield, Maine

Made by Greenwood & Gray, Columbus, Georgia, 1862-1864. Total production: Fewer than 300.

Overall length: 48-1/2" - 49".

Muzzleloader, single shot.

Based on the U.S. Model 1841 Rifle, J.P. Murray rifles are broken into three types. Based on the U.S. Model 1841 Rifle, all are 48-1/2" - 49" long and .58 caliber. Lock plates are found both marked and unmarked. Those that are marked, are stamped on the lock plate forward of the hammer, "J.P. MURRAY / COLUMBUS GA".

Type I: Fitted with a Boyle, Gamble, and MacFee bayonet adaptor. Upper surface of barrel stamped with a number (assumed to correspond with a bayonet). Type I has the Model 1841-style, one-piece front barrel band and nose cap as well as a brass side plate..

Type II: Two flat brass barrel bands, screw-fastened brass nose cap, Model 1855-style round brass washers on lock plate bolts.

Type III: Type III rifles were produced for the State of Alabama and will usually show a "ALA" acceptance stamp on the left side of the barrel near the breech. Type III rifles were produced without bayonet adaptors.

ALL TYPES: GOOD—$10,000   FINE—$30,000

PULASKI ARMORY RIFLE, .54 CALIBER, PAPER CARTRIDGE, PERCUSSION

Made by Pulaski Armory, Pulaski, Tennessee, 1861. Total production: Unknown, but presumed to be fewer than 500.

Overall length: 49".

Muzzleloader, single shot.

The upper left surface of the barrel is stamped "PULASKI. T. C.S.A." in one line. An example is known be marked on the side of the barrel, "FIELD. ARROWSMITH, C.S.A. 1861" in one line. Because sporting locks were used, a variety of manufacture marks may be found. One such is stamped "JAMES & SON / G___" within a scroll.

Patterned on the U.S. Model 1841 Rifle, Pulaski rifles seemed to have been assembled using a variety of sporting locks. Distinctive features include the small, iron block front sight, rear "rabbit-ear" iron sight; and single lock plate screw with a brass, diamond-shape escutcheon.

GOOD—$10,000   FINE—$25,000

READ & WATSON RIFLE, FIRST MODEL, .54 CALIBER, PAPER CARTRIDGE, PERCUSSION

Made J.B. Barrett, Wytheville, Virginia, 1861. Total production: Unknown, but presumed to be fewer than 300.
Overall length: 48-1/2".
Muzzleloader, single shot.
Breech stamped "NTR".

The "Barrett" rifle was the result of the only known contract awarded during the Civil War for the conversion of breech-loading weapons to muzzle-loading configurations. J.B. Barrett utilized parts from Hall breech loading rifles to create a new center-hung hammer arrangement. Barrett employed a brass breech piece in the conversion. The First Model rifles have a small narrow insert that extends along the top of the stock's wrist. There is a wide variation of stocks and styles, including carbines, but all were made in .58 caliber. The iron front sight doubled as a bayonet lug for a socket bayonet.

GOOD—$12,500   **FINE—$20,000**

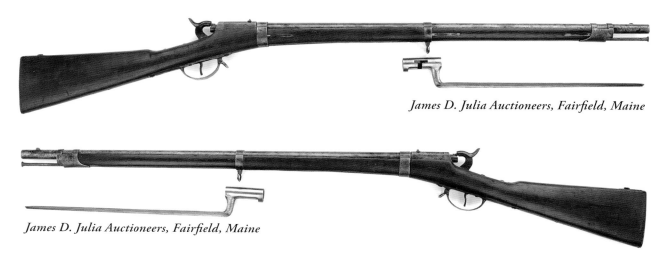

James D. Julia Auctioneers, Fairfield, Maine

James D. Julia Auctioneers, Fairfield, Maine

*James D. Julia
Auctioneers,
Fairfield, Maine*

READ & WATSON RIFLE, SECOND MODEL, .54 CALIBER, PAPER CARTRIDGE, PERCUSSION

Made J.B. Barrett, Wytheville, Virginia, 1861. Total production: Unknown, but presumed to be fewer than 300.
Overall length: 48".
Muzzleloader, single shot.
Breech stamped "NTR".

The "Barrett" rifle was the result of the only known contract awarded during the Civil War for the conversion of breech-loading weapons to muzzle-loading configurations. J.B. Barrett utilized parts from Hall breech loading rifles to create a new center-hung hammer arrangement. Barrett employed a brass breech piece in the conversion. A Second Model rifle has a large, one-piece bass breech casting that extends the length of the wrist to the comb.

GOOD—$12,500   FINE—$20,000

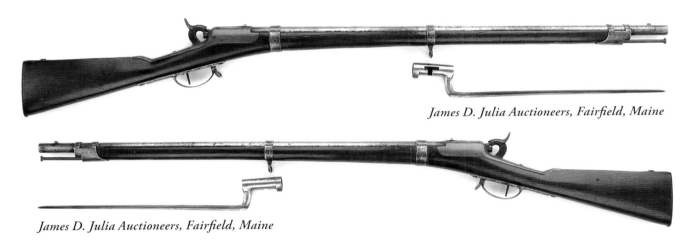

James D. Julia Auctioneers, Fairfield, Maine

James D. Julia Auctioneers, Fairfield, Maine

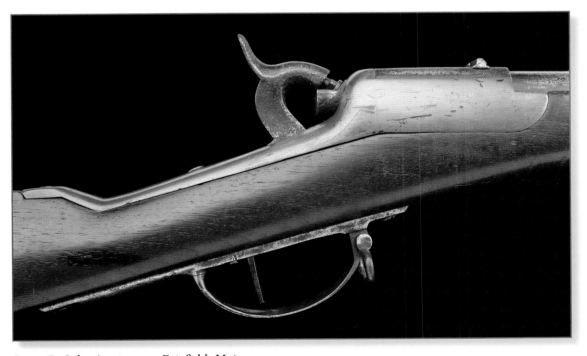

James D. Julia Auctioneers, Fairfield, Maine

RICHMOND ARMORY RIFLE, .58 CALIBER, PAPER CARTRIDGE, PERCUSSION

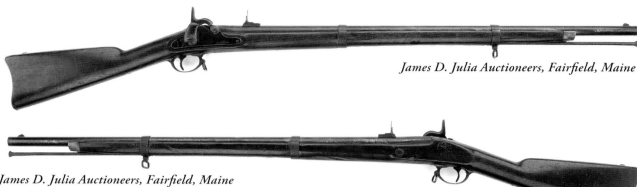

James D. Julia Auctioneers, Fairfield, Maine

James D. Julia Auctioneers, Fairfield, Maine

Made C.S. Richmond Armory, Richmond, Virginia, 1862-1864. Total production: Unknown, but presumed to be fewer than 1,000.

Overall length: 49".

Muzzleloader, single shot.

The Richmond Armory made rifles using both U.S. Model 1855 and Model 1861 stocks with either iron or brass fittings. The nose cap and butt plate are brass. Lock plates are the Richmond Type III low-hump pattern. Markings are identical to those on the longer rifle-muskets.

GOOD—$5,000 FINE—$17,500

BRITISH PATTERN 1837 "BRUNSWICK" RIFLE, .70-.75 CALIBER, PAPER CARTRIDGE, PERCUSSION

Made by various English manufactures, London, England, 1837-1845. Total imported: 2,020.
Overall length: 46".
Muzzleloader, single shot.

Because many of the Pattern 1837 were made by private London manufacturers, lock plate markings vary. Enfield produced weaons are stamped "R. Manufactory Enfield" or "Enfield." Birmingham-manufactured rifles are marked "Tower". In addition, lock plates are stamped with the a crown over "VR" and the year of manufacture. Barrel markings also vary.

The only documented sale of Brunswick rifles during the Civil War were to the Confederate purchasing agent, Caleb Huse. The sale does not mention the Pattern 1837 rifles specifically. It is assumed that the surplus weapons would have been of this older pattern and not the newer Pattern 1845, since the British considered the Brunswick rifle a serviceable reserve arm.

GOOD—$900 FINE—$1,500

BRITISH PATTERN 1856 RIFLE, .577 CALIBER, PAPER CARTRIDGE, PERCUSSION

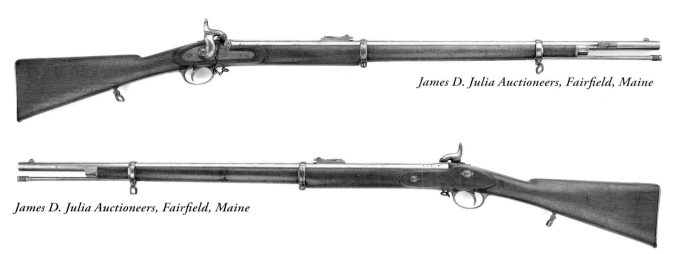

James D. Julia Auctioneers, Fairfield, Maine

James D. Julia Auctioneers, Fairfield, Maine

Made by various English manufactures, London, England, Liege, Belgium, 18541866. Total imported: Unknown but more than 50,000.

Overall length: 55".

Muzzleloader, single shot.

Lock plates vary depending on year of manufacture. Generally, the lock plate will be stamped with a crown over "VR", the British "broad arrow" and the year of manufacture in addition to "Tower", depending on place of manufacture. London Armoury weapons will be marked "LAC" or "LA Co". Liege-manufactured weapons will only have royal monogram and year of manufacture. No imported weapon will have the British broad arrow mark or "Enfield" stamped lock plate. Premiums are paid for weapons bearing a "JS / [anchor]" mark, as this is popularly thought to denote certain Confederate use (though know hard evidence can verify the belief).

U.S. and northern states purchased at 13,000 P56 two-band rifles. The Confederate-purchased quantity is unknown though likely to number in the tens of thousands. Only weapons made by private manufacturers were imported.

GOOD—$900 FINE—$2,000

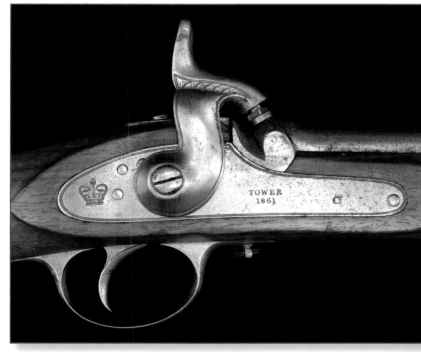

James D. Julia Auctioneers, Fairfield, Maine

WHITWORTH RIFLE, .45 CALIBER, PAPER CARTRIDGE, PERCUSSION

James D. Julia Auctioneers, Fairfield, Maine

Made by Manchester Ordnance and Rifle Company, Manchester, England, ca. 1862-1865 Total imported: Unknown.
Overall length: 52".
Muzzleloader, single shot.

Lock plates stamped either "Whitworth Rifle Co." or "Manchester Ordnance & Rifle Co." along with either the Whitworth crest or royal crown. Some trigger guards stamped "2d quality." Serial numbers are stamped on the underside of the barrel.

Though the British Ordnance Board adopted the Whitworth rifle as the Pattern 1862 rifle, none of these were available for export. However, non-contracted weapons produced at the Manchester Ordnance and Rifle Company, generally in the 33" barrel length (52" overall) found their way into American hands. Most Confederate purchased weapons were produced in 1862 and are numbered between C1-C999 and D1-D999. A typical import Whitworth have checkered stocks that extend to within a short distance of the muzzle. Whitworth rifles fitted with 14-1/2" long Davidson telescopic sights command premium prices.

GOOD—$4,500   **FINE—$12,000**

AUSTRIAN MODEL 1854 SHORT RIFLE, .54

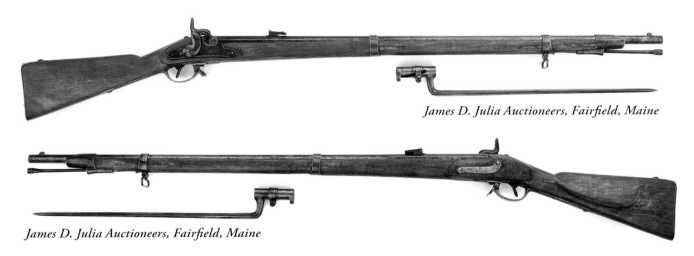

James D. Julia Auctioneers, Fairfield, Maine

James D. Julia Auctioneers, Fairfield, Maine

CALIBER, PAPER CARTRIDGE, PERCUSSION

Made by Vienna National Armory and private gun manufactories, ca. 1854-? Total imported: Unknown, but more than 300,000.
Overall length: 43-1/4".
Muzzleloader, single shot.

Markings are uncommon. Each lock plate was stamped with a small Austrian eagle and the year of manufacture (with the first digit omitted, e.g., "843"). Various private contractor marks found on the barrel near the breech.

Extended rear leaf sight of Austrian Model 1854 rifle. James D. Julia Auctioneers, Fairfield, Maine

Known to Civil War purchasing agents as the "Jaeger" or "Yaeger," the two-band rifle replaced the earlier Model 1842 tube-lock, rifles. The ramrod was not originally carried under the barrel. Rather, Austrian soldiers affixed the ramrod to a cross-the-shoulder strap. Weapons purchased for import to the United States were altered by inletting a ramrod channel, boring the stock, and adding a thimble. The ramrod was simply a shortened version of the type used on the Lorenz long rifle. U.S. Ordnance Department records show purchases of at least 7,292 Lorenz short rifles which it classified as a second class weapon. Many of these were rebored to .58 caliber. Although Caleb Huse purchased at least 100,000 Austrian Lorenz rifles for the Confederacy, none are thought to have been the short rifle pattern.

GOOD—$1,200   FINE—$3,000

FRENCH MODEL 1840 RIFLE, .71 CALIBER, PAPER CARTRIDGE, PERCUSSION

Made by French royal and Imperial arsenals and copied by Liege manufacturers, ca. 1840-ca. 1842. Total imported: Unknown but Union records show approximately 36,000 French and Belgium rifles were purchased.

Overall length: 55-3/4".

Muzzleloader, single shot.

French lock plates are inscribed with various manufacturers' marks. Liege lock plates may be engraved have the maker's name or his crowned initials. The barrel tang is engraved with the model designation, "M 1840" and

year of manufacture. Liege-made examples have only the year of manufacture and proof marks. French barrels may also be stamped with caliber in millimeters in addition to the usual proof marks.

The Model 1840 was the first mass-produced rifle adopted by the French army. It was fitted with a Delvigne chambered breech that expanded the projectile when fired. Barrel bands and butt plates are found in either brass or iron. The saber bayonet attaches to a lug on the right side of the barrel. Union gun buyers purchased approximately 36,000 French and Belgian rifles during the Civil War. However, their records do not indicate model designations making it impossible to know exactly how many Model 1840 rifles made it to the United States. The U.S. Ordnance Department rated French and Belgian rifled long arms as 2nd class. No record of Confederate purchases is known.

GOOD—$400 FINE—$1,200

FRENCH MODEL 1842 RIFLE, .71 CALIBER, PAPER CARTRIDGE, PERCUSSION

Made by French royal and Imperial arsenals and copied by Liege manufacturers, ca. 1842-ca. 1846. Total imported: Unknown but Union records show approximately 36,000 French and Belgium rifles were purchased, of which 8,689 were either the Model 1840 or 1842 rifle.

Overall length: 55-3/4".

Muzzleloader, single shot.

French lock plates are inscribed with various manufacturers' marks. Liege lock plates may be engraved have the maker's name or his crowned initials. The barrel tang is engraved with the model designation, "M 1842" and year of manufacture. Liege-made examples have only the year of manufacture and proof marks. French barrels may also be stamped with caliber in millimeters in addition to the usual proof marks.

The Model 1842 was fitted with a Delvigne chambered breech that expanded the projectile when fired. The bolster was brazed to the side of the barrel. Barrel bands and butt plates are found in either brass or iron. A two-leaf rear sight is fitted to the barrel. The saber bayonet attaches to a lug on the right side of the barrel. Union gun buyers purchased approximately 36,000 French and Belgian rifles during the Civil War. However, their records do not indicate model designations making it impossible to know exactly how many Model 1842 rifles made it to the United States. Herman Boker supplied 8,689 rifles, either of the Model 1840 or 1842 pattern, to the U.S. government. The U.S. Ordnance Department rated French and Belgian rifled long arms as 2nd class. No record of Confederate purchases is known.

GOOD—$400 FINE—$1,200

FRENCH MODEL 1846 RIFLE, .71 CALIBER, PAPER CARTRIDGE, PERCUSSION

Made by French royal and Imperial arsenals and copied by Liege manufacturers, ca. 1846-ca. 1853. Total imported: Unknown but Union records show approximately 36,000 French and Belgium rifles were purchased.

Overall length: 55-3/4".

Muzzleloader, single shot.

French lock plates are inscribed with various manufacturers' marks. Liege lock plates may be engraved have the maker's name or his crowned initials. The barrel tang is engraved with the model designation, "M 1846" and year of manufacture. Liege-made examples have only the year of manufacture and proof marks. French barrels may also be stamped with caliber in millimeters in addition to the usual proof marks.

The Model 1846 was fitted with a Thouvenin chambered breech. Because it used a metal column called à tige that extended from the breech plug in the bore, the French referred to the rifle as the Carbine à tige. The barrel flats extended a bit farther than those on the Model 1842. The bolster was brazed to the side of the barrel. Barrel bands and butt plates are found in either brass or iron. A rear sight is graduated to 1,000 meters. The saber bayonet attaches to a lug and slide on the right side of the barrel. Union gun buyers purchased approximately 36,000 French and Belgian rifles during the Civil War. However, their records do not indicate model designations making it impossible to know exactly how many Model 1846 rifles made it to the United States. The U.S. Ordnance Department rated French and Belgian rifled long arms as 2nd class. There is some indication that Confederate agents purchased either Model 1846 or 1853 rifles, but the quantity is unknown.

GOOD—$400 FINE—$1,200

FRENCH MODEL 1853 RIFLE, .71 CALIBER, PAPER CARTRIDGE, PERCUSSION

Made by French royal and Imperial arsenals and copied by Liege manufacturers, ca. 1853-ca. 1859. Total imported: Unknown but Union records show approximately 36,000 French and Belgium rifles were purchased.

Overall length: 55-3/4".

Muzzleloader, single shot.

French arsenal-produced weapons have lock plates are marked "Mre. Impale. de" followed by the city name. The barrel tang is engraved with the model designation, "M 1843" and year of manufacture. Liege-made examples have only the year of manufacture proof marks. French barrels may also be stamped with the date of alteration and caliber in millimeters in addition to the usual proof marks.

The Model 1846 and Model rifles were fitted with the Thouvenin chambered breech. Because it used a metal column called à tige that extended from the breech plug in the bore, the French referred to the rifle as the Carbine à tige. The Model 1853 has a somewhat heavier breech than the Model 1846. Barrel bands and butt plates are found in either brass or iron. A rear sight is graduated to 1,000 meters. The saber bayonet attaches to a lug and slide on the right side of the barrel. Union gun buyers purchased approximately 36,000 French and Belgian rifles during the Civil War. However, their records do not indicate model designations making it impossible to know exactly how many Model 1853 rifles made it to the United States. The U.S. Ordnance Department rated French and Belgian rifled long arms as 2nd class. There is some indication that Confederate agents purchased either Model 1846 or 1853 rifles, but the quantity is unknown.

GOOD—$400 FINE—$1,200

FRENCH MODEL 1859 BRASS-MOUNTED LIGHT MINIÉ RIFLE, .58 CALIBER, PAPER CARTRIDGE, PERCUSSION

Made by Liege, Belgium manufacturers, ca. 1862-1863. Total imported: Unknown.

Overall length: 48-1/2".

French-style back action lock plates marked Liege manufacture name and a crown over the manufacturer's initials. The latter is also stamped on the barrel bands. Bayonet lug stamped with a number (presumably to match to a bayonet with the same number.

This weapon is actually a Liege-produced copy of the French Model 1859 Light Minié Rifle. The barrel bands, trigger guard, butt plate, rear swivel log and the lock screw plate are brass. It is fitted with a British style rear sight with an elevating leaf graduated up to 900 meters. The muzzle of the barrel is fitted with a long slide and lug to accept a copy of the French Model 1842/59 22-4/5" yataghan-blade saber bayonet. Concrete evidence of sales to American customers has not been located, however, John Pondir and John Hoey delivered quantities of "French Minié Rifles." It is likely that these Belgian copies were part of those purchases. No record of Confederate purchases is known.

GOOD—$400 FINE—$1,200

FRENCH MODEL 1859 SHORT RIFLE, .58 CALIBER, PAPER CARTRIDGE, PERCUSSION

Made by Liege, Belgium manufacturers, 1861-1862. Total imported: Unknown but Union records show at least 10,000 were purchased.

Overall length: 49-1/4".

Muzzleloader, single shot.

Back-action lock is generally unmarked but a few have been observed with a small, stamped "L". Breech is stamped with a small crown and a Liege proof mark.

The U.S. Ordnance Department contracted with John Pondir on July 26, 1861 for "10,000 .58 caliber Minié Rifles with sabre bayonets." To fill the contract, Pondir turned to Belgian manufacturers to produce a copy of the French Light Minié Rifle. The result was a rifle with blued furniture (though some lock plates and hammers were case-hardened), French-style folding rear sight graduated to 700 yards, and fitted to carry a copy of the French Model 1846/59 22-4/5" yataghan bayonet. The entire order was completed as of October 4, 1862. The U.S. Ordnance Department rated the rifle as 1st class (though its lists its caliber as .577). No records of Confederate purchases are known.

GOOD—$400 FINE—$1,200

BRAZILIAN LIGHT MINIÈ RIFLE, .577 CALIBER, PAPER CARTRIDGE, PERCUSSION

Made by O.P. Drissen & Cie., Liege, Belgium, ca. 1862. Total imported: Unknown.

Overall length: 48-1/4".

Muzzleloader, single shot.

An anchor flanked by the initials "D" and "C" appear on several parts. The barrel is marked with Liege proof marks. Some examples are known to have "OHIO" stamped on the stock. A small brass plate with an embossed eagle is affixed to the stock's wrist.

The Brazilian Light Miniè Rifle is a combination of characteristics of the English Pattern of 1856 rifle and the French Light Minié Rifle. The butt plate, trigger guard and lock plate screw side cups are brass while the barrel bands are steel The right side of the barrel near the muzzle features a bayonet lug and slide bar. The U.S. Ordnance Department rated the rifle as 1st class, but purchasing data is not known. Likewise, there is no known record of Confederate purchase.

GOOD—$700 FINE—$1,250

*James D. Julia
Auctioneers,
Fairfield, Maine*

During the first half of the nineteenth century, military planners regarded breech-loading weapons with skepticism. They reasoned that if a soldier were given the opportunity to use a breech-loading weapon, the system of coordinated, linear tactics would fall apart. Furthermore, they postulated, breechloaders would lead to an inordinate amount of ammunition waste.

Despite the out-of-touch view of some, the U.S. Army continued to explore the advantages of breechloaders during the first half of the nineteeth century. Most notably, it adopted the breech-loading rifle designed by J.H. Hall as early as 1817, although numbers issued were far from significant.

It was not until the end of the Civil War that the Army fully accepted the potential of equipping each soldier in the line with a breech-loading weapon. However, it would not have been a decision so easily reached had they not witnessed the breechloader's destructiveness first-hand.

MODEL 1819 HALL BREECH-LOADING RIFLE, .52 CALIBER, FLINTLOCK

James D. Julia Auctioneers, Fairfield, Maine

Made at Harpers Ferry Armory, ca. 1817, 1819, 1823-24, and 1827-1840. Total production estimated at 19,780.

Overall length: 52-3/4". Weight: 10 lbs. 4 oz.

First production rifles are marked on the breech in four lines: J.H. HALL / H. FERRY / 1824 / U.S.

Second production rifles, dated 1826-1838, are marked on the breech in four lines, J.H. HALL / H. FERRY / US / (date).

Third production rifles, dated 1837-1840, are marked on the breech in three lines, J.H. HALL / US / (date).

At least 13,940 of the total combined production of Hall and Contract Model 1819 rifles were distributed to various states in lieu of contract arms through the Militia Act of 1808. By 1855, states that reported the possession of Hall rifles included, Alabama, 639; Arkansas, 7; Delaware, 143; Florida, 300; Illinois, 220; Indiana, 788; Kentucky, 420; Maine, 1,071; Maryland, 295; Massachusetts, 400; Michigan, 40; Mississippi, 313; Missouri, 100; New Hampshire, 1,095; New York, 500; North Carolina, 700; Pennsylvania, 871; Tennessee, 180, and Virginia, 1,000.

In 1860, Federal arsenals in Alabama, Arkansas, Virginia, South Carolina, Georgia and Louisiana reported 10,229 Hall rifles on hand. The bulk of these were seized by the Confederacy. After a transfer of 1,000 from Baton Rouge, the State of Mississippi had more than 1,300 Hall rifles at the outbreak of the war. Confederate troops from Mississippi, Arkansas and Tennessee are known to have carried flintlock Hall rifles as late as April 1862. The federal Washington Arsenal still reported 677 flintlock Hall rifles on hand in 1864.

FIRST PRODUCTION: GOOD—$4,000   FINE—$8,750
SECOND PRODUCTION: GOOD—$1,750   FINE—$3,750
THIRD PRODUCTION: GOOD—$1,750   FINE—$3,750

CONTRACT MODEL 1819 BREECH-LOADING RIFLE, .52 CALIBER, FLINTLOCK

James D. Julia Auctioneers, Fairfield, Maine

Made by Simeon North, Middletown, Conn., ca. 1830-1836. Total produced: 5,700.

Overall length: 52-3/4". Weight: 10 lbs. 4 oz.

The Contract Model 1819 rifle is virtually identical to the Model 1819 Hall Rifle. Breechblock marked in four lines, U.S. / S. NORTH / MIDLTN / CONN. / (date).

GOOD—$2,000   FINE—$4,000

MODEL 1819 HALL BREECH-LOADING RIFLE, .52 CALIBER, CONVERSION

Rock Island Auction Company

Overall length: 52-3/4". Weight: varies from 9 lbs 12 oz. to 10 lbs. 4 oz.

With the exception of a single Hall rifle converted to percussion at the Mount Vernon (Alabama) Arsenal in 1856, there were no other Hall rifles converted in federal arsenals prior to 1861. Ultimately, federal workers converted at least 5,000 rifles. Since these were considered fourth-class arms, though, few were issued. Anecdotal information indicates that Berdan's U.S. Sharpshooters possessed a few Hall rifles while stationed in Washington, D.C., during the fall of 1861. The unit turned these in, however, before departing for the front. The Ordnance Department did purchase an additional 1,575 privately-converted percussion Hall rifles during 1861. All of these were sent to the Washington Arsenal but were never issued. In both the 1862 and 1864 inventory, Washington Arsenal recorded 1,620 percussion Hall rifles still in its racks.

Some states, both north and south, did embark on their programs of conversion. New Hampshire, for example, issued 200 converted Hall rifles to its 3rd Infantry Regiment. The State of Mississippi converted 1,000 Hall rifles during July 1861. Towards the end of the same year, the State of North Carolina converted 448 Hall rifles to percussion and shortened the barrels which it then issued to cavalry troopers. An additional 70 rifles were converted but not shortened.

GOOD—$950   FINE—$1,750

MODEL 1841 HALL BREECH-LOADING RIFLE, .52 CALIBER, PERCUSSION

James D. Julia Auctioneers, Fairfield, Maine

Overall length: 52-3/4". Weight: 9 lbs. 12 oz.

Made at Harpers Ferry Armory. Total produced: Estimated from 2,700 to 4,213.

For years, collectors regarded all percussion Hall rifles as conversions of the original flintlocks. However, in May 1841, 1,500 percussion breechblocks for rifles had been produced. Pre-assembly projections had estimated that enough stocks, barrels and breechblocks were on hand to complete 3,000 rifles. By June 30, 1844, the Harpers Ferry Arsenal had completed 2,700 Model 1841 rifles. An 1860 Harpers Ferry inventory recorded 3,239 Hall rifles. Unfortunately, it is impossible to know how many were converted Model 1819 rifles or Model 1841 rifles. A notation to the 1860 inventory recommends selling 10,491 of the 12,563 Hall rifles in all of the U.S. arsenals. Most likely, this recommendation was made with the intent to sell the vast majority of unconverted Hall rifles while retaining the percussion examples.

GOOD—$1,750   FINE—$4,250

HENRY REPEATING RIFLE, TYPES I, II, AND III, .44 CALIBER, RIMFIRE CARTRIDGE

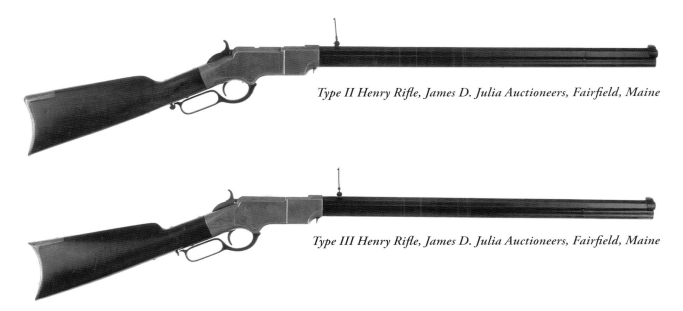

Type II Henry Rifle, James D. Julia Auctioneers, Fairfield, Maine

Type III Henry Rifle, James D. Julia Auctioneers, Fairfield, Maine

Manufactured by the New Haven Arms Co., New Haven, Connecticut, 1860–66. Total production: approximately 14,000.

Overall length: 43-1/8" (Type I) or 43-1/2" (Type III). Weight: approximately 9 lbs. 4 oz.

Breechloader, sliding breech block, 15 shot.

"HENRY'S PATENT. OCT. 16, 1860 / MANUFACT'D BY THE NEW HAVEN ARMS. CO. NEW HAVEN, CT." on top of barrel to front of rear sight; serial number on top of barrel near breech; inspector's initials over "H" on right barrel flat, and inspector's initials over "C" on bottom of butt stock of government-purchased specimens.

Judged by some authorities as the most sophisticated firearm of the Civil War, the Henry Repeating Rifle featured a cylindrical, 15-round magazine underneath and integral to the barrel, and a sliding-breech-block loading mechanism actuated by lowering and raising the operating lever/trigger guard. Although there were several variants of the Henry, all had a 24" blued, octagonal barrel and oil-finished black walnut butt stock.

There were three principal types:

Type I: The frame and furniture were iron, the side profile of the butt plate had a gentle curve, and there was no operating lever latch. About 275 were manufactured, in the 1–400 serial number range.

Type II: The frame and furniture were brass, there was an iron sling swivel on the left side of martial examples, and examples are found with or without operating lever latches. Serial numbers overlapped the Type I serial range, and some 1,500 units were manufactured.

Type III: Features were similar to those of the Type II, but most, if not all, examples had operating lever latches. Starting at around serial number 4000, a different butt plate was introduced with a more pronounced curve, like that of a sporting model firearm. The serial number range had some overlap with early-production Winchester Model 1866 Rifles.

TYPE I: GOOD—$30,000   FINE—$100,000

TYPE II: GOOD—$15,000   FINE—$35,000

TYPE III: GOOD—$10,000   FINE—$30,000

GOVERNMENT SURCHARGED EXAMPLES:
        GOOD—$20,000   FINE—$70,000

*James D. Julia
Auctioneers,
Fairfield, Maine*

JENKS BREECH-LOADING RIFLE, .54 CALIBER PAPER CARTRIDGE PERCUSSION RIFLE

Made by N. P. Ames, Springfield, Massachusetts, 1841–ca. 1842. Total production: 1,000

Overall length: 52-1/4". Weight: 6 lbs. 12 oz.

Breech-loading, lever action, sliding bolt, single-shot.

"N. P. AMES/SPRINGFIELD/MASS" and "Wm. Jenks" stamped on lock plate. "Wm. Jenks". "W JENKS / USN / [inspector's initials] / P / [year]" stamped at breech. Inspector's initials stamped on left side of stock near breech.

Also called the Jenks Navy Rifle, this long arm was produced per a U.S. Navy contract of August 31, 1841; all weapons were delivered by 1844. Operation was by raising a lever above the breech, which moved the sliding breech-bolt to the rear. Powder and ball were placed in the chamber and the lever lowered, sending the charge into the breech. The side hammer (nicknamed the "mule ear") was cocked, exposing the nipple for capping. The round barrel was browned, 30", with six grooves. Stock was black walnut, full-length, 49-1/2" long. No ramrod or sling swivels. All furniture is polished brass. The lock is case-hardened.

GOOD—$1,850   FINE—$4,250

MODEL 1855 JOSLYN .58 CALIBER PAPER CARTRIDGE PERCUSSION RIFLE

Made by A. H. Waters & Co., Milbury, Massachusetts, ca. 1855–1860. Total production: Fewer than 200.

Overall length: 45-3/4". Weight: 7 lbs. 14 oz.

Breechloader, single shot.

Marked on the lock plate forward of the hammer: "A.H. WATERS & CO/ MILBURY MASS". Serial number on left side of lever. Some examples are marked on top of the lever "PATD BY / B. F. JOSLYN / AUG. 28, 1855".

The Navy Department ordered 500 of these rifles, sometimes called the Joslyn Model 1855 Percussion Rifle, but it is estimated that fewer than 200 were delivered. Loading was accomplished by lifting a breech lever which incorporated a breech block, then loading the paper cartridge into the open breech. The 30" barrel was usually browned, although some were blued; a bayonet lug was on the right side of the barrel. The forward sight was a blade type, while the rear sight was a folding leaf with a sliding bar. The stock was of black walnut; all furniture was polished brass.

GOOD—$3,750   FINE—$8,000

LINDER ALTERATION OF U.S. MODEL 1841 CONTRACT RIFLES, .54 CALIBER COMBUSTIBLE CARTRIDGE, PERCUSSION

Rock Island Auction Company

Made by Robbins & Lawrence, Windsor, Vermont; alterations by Allen & Morse, Boston, Massachusetts, 1861. Total production: 103.

Overall length: 48-1/2". Weight: 9 lbs., 12 oz.

Breech-loading, rising breech, single shot.

"PATENTED / MAR. 29, 1859" on top of locking sleeve of breech mechanism; serial number beneath locking sleeve; original proof marks on barrel near breech.

Allen & Morse of Boston contracted with the State of Massachusetts in late 1861 to convert 100 U.S. Model 1841 Contract Rifles to the breech-loading system patented by Edward Lindner in 1859. All of these rifles were contract weapons manufactured by Robbins & Lawrence, Windsor, Vermont. Three additional rifles had been altered by Amoskeag Manufacturing Company at an earlier date. All 103 examples were held in storage during the Civil War. The barrel was cut off 4-1/2" from the breech and a new action installed. When the shooter flipped the bolt of a sleeve to the left, the spring-operated breech popped up, allowing the chamber to be loaded from the front with a .54-caliber combustible cartridge. After pressing the breech unit back down and flipping the sleeve back to the right, the rifle was ready for firing. Other alterations included a new rear sight and combination bayonet stud / blade front sight.

Rock Island Auction Company

GOOD—$5,500   FINE—$10,500

MERRILL ALTERATION OF U.S. MODEL 1842 RIFLED MUSKET .69 CALIBER, PERCUSSION, COMBUSTIBLE CARTRIDGE

Made by Springfield and Harper's Ferry Arsenals, conversion by James H. Merrill, Baltimore, Maryland, ca. 1861–62. Total production: Approximately 100.

Overall Length: 57-13/16".

Breech-loading, sliding breech block, single shot.

"SPRING / FIELD" or "HARPERS / FERRY" over year, vertically, on lock plate behind hammer; eagle and "US" on lock plate in front of hammer; Merrill name and patent dates on lever.

The Merrill alteration of the U.S. Model 1842 Musket entailed rifling the barrel, fitting it with a long-range rear sight, and installing the 6"-long Merrill breech apparatus, patented between July 20, 1858, and October 22, 1861. Operation was by pulling the lever up and to the rear, opening the chamber for insertion of a paper-cartridge Minié bullet. Closing the lever actuated a pivoted breech plunger, sending the cartridge into the breech.

GOOD—$2,750   FINE—$5,000

MERRILL BREECH-LOADING RIFLE, .54 CALIBER PAPER CARTRIDGE PERCUSSION RIFLE

Type I Merrill Rifle. Rock Island Action Company

Made by James H. Merrill, Baltimore, Maryland, ca. 1861-1865. Total production: estimated at 800.

Overall length: 48-1/2". Weight: 9 lbs. 2 oz.

Breech lever marked "J.H. MERRILL BALTO. / PAT. JULY 1858." Lock plate marked forward of the hammer, "J.H. MERRILL BALTO. / PAT. JULY 1858 / APL. 9 MAY 21-28-61." Later production rifles were marked "1863" on the lock plate rear of the hammer.

Union soldiers used two types of the breech-loading Merrill rifle: the earlier type with a knurled-lever latch and a later design that incorporated a button-lever latch. Collectors refer to these as the "Type I" and "Type II", respectively. In all, the U.S. Government purchased a total of 770 rifles of both types.

Rock Island Action Company

Though some Union regiments purchased their own Merrill rifles in 1861, it was not until March 1862 that the Ordnance Department placed its first order for 566 rifles at a cost of $45 each. This order was destined for the 21st Indiana Infantry, three companies of which had already purchased their own Merrill rifles. Other units known to have used the Merrill rifle include the 6th Michigan Infantry (who borrowed the rifles from the 21st Indiana after it was converted into a heavy artillery regiment) and the 1st Company Massachusetts (Andrews) Sharpshooters. In addition, soldiers assigned as

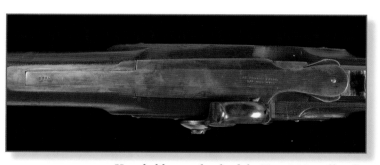

Knurled button latch of the Type I Merrill Rifle. Rock Island Action Company

sharpshooters from the 7th Michigan Infantry, 10th Michigan Infantry, 4th Arkansas Infantry, and the 8th Ohio Infantry were given Merrill rifles. Merrill rifles are reported to have been issued to some Wisconsin and Maryland troops as well. Interestingly, an 1863 ordnance report for Virginia Military Institute records 2 Merrill rifles.

TYPE I: GOOD—$1,550   **FINE—$3,750**
TYPE II: GOOD—$1,250   **FINE—$2,000**

Type II Merrill Rifle. James D. Julia Auctioneers, Fairfield, Maine

MERRILL ALTERATION OF U.S. MODEL 1841 RIFLE .58 CALIBER, PERCUSSION, COMBUSTIBLE CARTRIDGE

Original manufacturer(s) not determined; conversion by James H. Merrill, Baltimore, Maryland, ca. 1861–62. Total production: Unknown, small number.

Overall Length: 48-1/2".

Maker's marks on lock plate; Merrill name and patent dates on lever.

Early in the Civil War a few U.S. Model 1841 Rifles were altered with the addition of the Merrill breech apparatus. This device incorporated a lever which, when raised, opened a chamber where the cartridge could be inserted. Lowering the lever activated a breech plunger that seated cartridge into the breech.

GOOD—$6,500   FINE—$15,000

Rock Island Auction Company

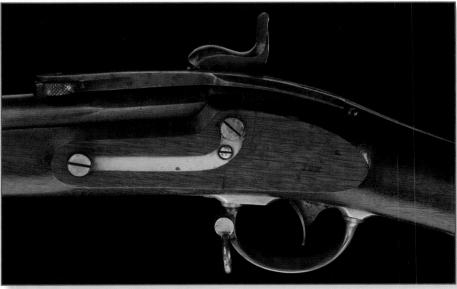

Rock Island Auction Company

*James D. Julia
Auctioneers,
Fairfield, Maine*

MORSE ALTERATION OF U.S. MODEL 1816 RIFLED MUSKET, .69 CALIBER CENTERFIRE CARTRIDGE

Made by Springfield Armory, ca. 1859–60. Total production: 55.
Overall length: 57-11/16". Weight: approximately 10 lbs.
Breechloader, sliding breech block, single shot.
Maker marks on lock plate.

The Morse Alteration of the U.S. Model 1816 rifled musket is historically significant as the first breech-loading cartridge firearm manufactured by a U.S. arsenal. During fiscal year 1859–60, the Springfield Armory altered 55 of these muskets (previously altered to rifled, percussion) to incorporate the George W. Morse breech-loading apparatus patented in 1856 and 1858. The conversion entailed cutting out the upper part of the barrel at the breech and installing a new, rear-pivoting breech apparatus. The original hammer, modified by removal of the cap striker at the front, now functioned as a locking mechanism for the breechblock. Half-cocking the hammer enabled the breechblock swing upward manually. Firing of the centerfire cartridge was accomplished by an internal locking lever striking the firing pin.

GOOD—$5,500   **FINE—$18,000**

SHARPS MODEL 1853 RIFLE, .52 CALIBER, PAPER OR LINEN CARTRIDGE

Rock Island Auction Company

Manufactured by Sharps Rifle Manufacturing Co., Hartford, Connecticut, ca. 1855. Total production unknown; probably very few.

Overall length: 43-3/8". Weight: approximately 8 lbs. 12 oz.

Breechloader, falling breech block, single shot.

"SHARP'S / PATENT / 1852" on lock plate to rear of hammer; "SHARPS / PATENT / 1848" and serial number on breech tang; "SHARP'S RIFLE / MANUFG CO. / HARTFORD, CONN." on barrel.

The Sharps Model 1853 Rifle was produced per a special order of the U.S. Navy, with few examples having been delivered. It featured the Sharps' patented primer-pellet mechanism and the slanted breech arrangement. The 27-3/8" round, blued barrel was rifled with six grooves and was fitted on the underside with a lug for a saber bayonet. The receiver was casehardened. Furniture was brass, including curved butt plate, patch box, and 1/2" wide barrel band. The rear sight was the patented R. S. Lawrence single-leaf model and was located 4-3/4" from the breech.

GOOD—N/A   **FINE—N/A**

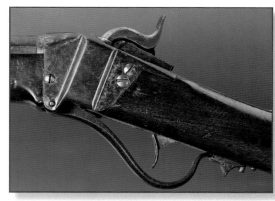

*Rock Island
Auction Company*

SHARPS MODEL 1855 RIFLE, TYPE I, .52 CALIBER, PAPER OR LINEN CARTRIDGE

James D. Julia Auctioneers, Fairfield, Maine

Manufactured by the Sharps Rifle Manufacturing Co., Hartford, Connecticut, ca. 1856. Total production: Approximately 200.

Overall length: 44-1/4". Weight: Approximately 9 lbs.

Breechloader, falling breech block, single shot.

"EDWARD MAYNARD / PATENTEE 1845" on tape primer door; "SHARPS RIFLE / MANUFG. CO. / HARTFORD CONN." on barrel; "SHARPS / PATENT / 1848" on breech tang, with serial number (range of approximately 20000 to 21000) to the rear of it; small anchor stamped on barrel at breech on some specimens.

The Sharps Model 1855 Rifle, Type I, was delivered in small numbers—probably 200 or fewer—to the Navy Department in 1856. It bore similarities to the Sharps Model 1855 Carbine, including the slanting breech and Maynard tape-priming mechanism, but with a lengthened barrel with a bore of 28-1/4" (27" to the frame) with a lug for a saber bayonet on the underside near the muzzle; a flat barrel band without the forward-projecting lower tip; and a fore stock that was two inches longer that that of the carbine. It included all-brass furniture and a casehardened frame.

GOOD—$5,750   **FINE—$25,750**

SHARPS MODEL 1855 RIFLE, TYPE II, .52 CALIBER, PAPER OR LINEN CARTRIDGE

Rock Island Auction Company

Manufactured by the Sharps Rifle Manufacturing Co., Hartford, Connecticut, ca. 1856. Total production: 50.

Overall length: 44-1/4". Weight: approximately 9 lbs.

Breechloader, falling breech block, single shot.

"R. WHITE'S / PATENT / 1855" to rear of hammer on lock plate; "EDWARD MAYNARD / PATENTEE 1845" on tape primer door; "SHARPS RIFLE / MANUFG. CO. / HARTFORD CONN." on barrel; "SHARPS / PATENT / 1848" on breech tang, with serial number (range of approximately 20000 to 21000) to the rear of it; small anchor stamped on barrel at breech on some specimens.

Fifty Sharps Model 1855 Rifles were fitted with Rollin White's self-cocking device, which cocked the hammer when the operating lever was actuated. After the mechanism was found to be unreliable, all but a few were converted back to the standard mechanism.

GOOD—$5,750   **FINE—$27,750**

James D. Julia Auctioneers, Fairfield, Maine

Rock Island Auction Company

*Rock Island
Auction
Company*

*Rock Island
Auction
Company*

SHARPS MODEL 1855 RIFLE, TYPE III, .52 CALIBER, PAPER OR LINEN CARTRIDGE

Manufactured by the Sharps Rifle Manufacturing Co., Hartford, Connecticut, ca. 1856. Total production: 12.

Overall length: 56".

Breechloader, falling breech block, single shot.

"EDWARD MAYNARD / PATENTEE 1845" on tape primer door; "SHARPS RIFLE / MANUFG. CO. / HARTFORD CONN." on barrel; "SHARPS / PATENT / 1848" on breech tang, with serial number to the rear of it.

In the mid- to late 1850s, the U.S. Army reportedly contracted for twelve examples of the Sharps Model 1855 Rifle altered with a greatly lengthened, 39" barrel and full fore stock secured to the barrel with three bands, instead of one. Rather than the brass furniture of the standard Sharps Model 1855 Rifle, this type had iron furniture and lacked the lug for a saber-type bayonet.

GOOD—$5,750   FINE—$25,750

SHARPS "NEW MODEL" 1859 RIFLE, .52 CALIBER, PAPER OR LINEN CARTRIDGE

James D. Julia Auctioneers, Fairfield, Maine

Manufactured by Sharps Rifle Manufacturing Co., Hartford, Connecticut, ca. 1859–62. Total production: Approximately 7,900.

Overall length: 47-1/8" (with 30" barrel) or 53-1/8" (36" barrel). Weight: 8 lbs. 12 oz. (30" barrel).

Breechloader, falling breech block, single shot.

"C. SHARPS' PAT. / OCT 5TH 1852" on lock plate to rear of hammer; "R. S. LAWRENCE' PAT / APRIL 12TH 1859" on lock plate to rear of hammer; "C. SHARPS' PAT. / SEPT. 12TH 1848" on left side of receiver; "SHARPS RIFLE / MANUFG. CO. / HARTFORD CONN" on barrel to front of rear sight; "NEW MODEL 1859" on barrel to rear of rear sight; "R. S. LAWRENCE / PATENTED FEB 15TH 1859" on base of rear sight; "R.S. LAWRENCE / PATENT / DEC. 20, 1859" AND "H. CONANT. / PATENT. / APR.1ST 1856" on rear face of breech block; inspector's initials on bottom of fore stock near the breech; serial number on tang of receiver.

The Sharps 1859 rifle introduced the so-called "straight" breech, as opposed to the "slanted" breeches of previous Sharps rifles and carbines. They had round, blued barrels, the Sharps patented pellet primer mechanism, and two-piece black walnut stocks. The receiver and all furniture, including three barrel bands, patch box, and fore cap, were casehardened iron. Occasionally, examples are found with double-set triggers.

There were four basic variants of this rifle:

Type I: 1,500 U.S. Army-contract and 2,800 U.S. Navy-contract examples were manufactured with 30" barrels and a lug for a saber-type bayonet on the underside of the barrel near the muzzle

Type II: 100 U.S. Army-contract examples with 30" barrels were fitted to accept a socket bayonet.

Type III: 600 made with 36" barrel with bayonet lug; most specimens are within serial number range 36,000 and 37,000 and had blued receivers.

Type IV: 2,000 units issued to Col. Hiram Berdan's 1st and 2nd Regiments, U.S. Sharpshooters, around 1862, had 30" barrels, serial number range approximately 54,374–57,567 (and possibly lower), most with double-set triggers, and fitted with either socket bayonet stud or saber bayonet lug.

Rifles issued to the Hiram Berdan's U.S. Sharpshooters will often be stamped on the barrel, "U.S.S.S." James D. Julia Auctioneers, Fairfield, Maine

Detail of single trigger on New Model 1859 Sharps rifle. James D. Julia Auctioneers, Fairfield, Maine

TYPE I: GOOD—$4,750	FINE—$10,750	
TYPE II: GOOD—$4,750	FINE—$10,750	
TYPE III: GOOD—$4,000	FINE—$10,750	
TYPE IV: GOOD—$5,000	FINE—$15,000	

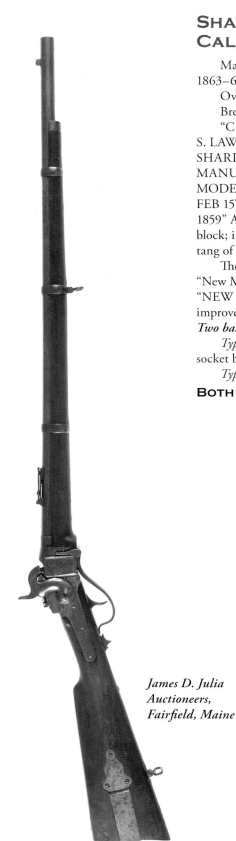

SHARPS "NEW MODEL" 1863 RIFLE, .52 CALIBER, PAPER OR LINEN CARTRIDGE

Manufactured by Sharps Rifle Manufacturing Co., Hartford, Connecticut, ca. 1863–65. Total production: Approximately 7,150.

Overall length: 47-1/8". Weight: 8 lbs. 12 oz..

Breechloader, falling breech block, single shot.

"C. SHARPS' PAT. / OCT 5TH 1852" on lock plate to rear of hammer; "R. S. LAWRENCE' PAT / APRIL 12TH 1859" on lock plate to rear of hammer; "C. SHARPS' PAT. / SEPT. 12TH 1848" on left side of receiver; "SHARPS RIFLE / MANUFG. CO. / HARTFORD CONN" on barrel to front of rear sight; "NEW MODEL 1863" on barrel to rear of rear sight; "R. S. LAWRENCE / PATENTED FEB 15TH 1859" on base of rear sight; "R.S. LAWRENCE / PATENT / DEC. 20, 1859" AND "H. CONANT. / PATENT. / APR.1ST 1856" on rear face of breech block; inspector's initials on bottom of fore stock near the breech; serial number on tang of receiver.

The Sharps 1863 "New Model" rifle was virtually identical to the Sharps 1859 "New Model" rifle with the 30" barrel, with the exception of the addition of the "NEW MODEL 1863" marking on the barrel near the breech, and a few other, minor improvements.

Two basic types existed:

Type I: Some 6,150 units in the C30,000 to C40,000 serial number range had socket bayonet studs.

Type II: About 1,000 units had saber bayonet lugs.

BOTH TYPES: GOOD—$3,750   FINE—$9,750

James D. Julia
Auctioneers,
Fairfield, Maine

SHARPS & HANKINS MODEL 1861 NAVY MODEL BREECH-LOADING RIFLE, .52 CALIBER, RIMFIRE CARTRIDGE

Rock Island Auction Company

Manufactured by Sharps & Hankins, Philadelphia, Pennsylvania, 1861–62. Total production: approximately 700.

Overall length: 47-5/8". Weight: 8 lbs.

Breechloader, sliding barrel, single shot.

"SHARPS / & / HANKINS / PHILADA." on right side of frame; "SHARPS / PATENT / 1859" on left side of frame; serial numbered.

The Sharps & Hankins Model 1861 Navy Rifle fired a .52-56 Sharps & Hankins rimfire cartridge. Upon lowering the operating lever/trigger guard, the 32-3/4" round, browned barrel slid forward, exposing the breech for loading. Rifling was six-groove, and there was a lug for a saber-type bayonet on the underside of the barrel. The butt plate was brass, while the receiver, hammer, lever, and lower and upper tangs were casehardened. The black walnut fore stock was secured to the barrel with three oval bands, with band springs on the underside of the fore stock for the upper and middle bands, and the lower band screwed to the stock. Serial numbers were in the 1–700 range. Most examples were issued to marines stationed on ships, and at least one example has been reported with original leather protective cover on the barrel.

Rock Island Auction Company

GOOD—$1,400   FINE—$5,000

SHARPS & HANKINS MODEL 1862 ARMY MODEL BREECH-LOADING RIFLE, .52 CALIBER, RIMFIRE CARTRIDGE

Manufactured by Sharps & Hankins, Philadelphia, Pennsylvania, ca. 1862. Total production: Unknown; probably very few made.

Overall length: 42-1/8". Weight: 8 lbs.

Breechloader, sliding barrel, single shot.

"SHARPS / & / HANKINS / PHILADA." on right side of frame; "SHARPS / PATENT / 1859" on left side of frame; serial numbered.

Sharps & Hankins Model 1862 Army Rifle was similar to that company's 1861 Navy Model, except that it had a 27" barrel rather than 32-3/4" and lacked the fore stock, barrel bands, and the bayonet lug. The barrel was blued, and, unlike the 1861 Navy Model, it had a lubricating aperture below the markings on each side of the frame, and a firing pin inside of the receiver, instead of on the front of the hammer.

GOOD—$1,400   FINE—$5,000

*James D. Julia
Auctioneers,
Fairfield, Maine*

MODEL 1860 SPENCER ARMY RIFLE, .52 CALIBER RIMFIRE CARTRIDGE

Made by Spencer Repeating Rifle Company, Boston, Massachusetts, ca. 1861–ca. 1865.
Total production: Between 11,000 and 20,000.
Overall length: 47". Weight: 10 lbs.
Breech-loading, falling block, seven shot.
"SPENCER REPEATING / RIFLE CO BOSTON MASS / PAT'D MARCH 6, 1860" on top of the receiver; serial number to rear of ejection port; some specimens lack serial number.

Dubbed the "most successful of all Civil War weapons" by firearms expert Robert M. Reilly, the Model 1860 Spencer Army Rifle featured the repeater apparatus invented by Christopher M. Spencer. When the shooter pushed the lever/trigger guard forward, lowering the breech block, a cylindrical magazine in the butt stock, fitted with a coil spring and holding seven Spencer No. 56 .52-Caliber copper rimfire cartridges, fed rounds into the open breech. After firing, repeating the process ejected the spent round and drove a fresh cartridge into the chamber. The blued barrel was 30" long and was fastened to the black walnut fore-stock by three blued iron barrel bands. The receiver was case hardened. Atop a stud for a socket bayonet was the front blade sight (brass). The rear sight was a single-leaf, folding type.

GOOD—$2,500   FINE—$4,000

MODEL 1860 SPENCER NAVY RIFLE, .52 CALIBER RIMFIRE CARTRIDGE

Made by Spencer Repeating Rifle Company, Boston, Massachusetts, ca. 1861–ca. 1865.
Total production: Between 11,000 and 20,000.
Overall length: 47". Weight: 10 lbs.
Breech-loading, falling block, 7 shot.
"SPENCER REPEATING / RIFLE CO BOSTON MASS / PAT'D MARCH 6, 1860" on top of the receiver; serial number to rear of ejection port; some specimens lack serial number.

The U.S. Navy submitted an order for Model 1860 Spencer .52-caliber rifles in June 1861 and began receiving shipments of them around end of 1862. In most respects, this rifle was similar to the Model 1860 Spencer Army Rifle, with the exception that the Navy version was fitted with a lug on the underside of the barrel, 3-1/2" from the muzzle, to accept a saber bayonet. Although the stock Navy version had a blued barrel and furniture, reportedly, the metal surfaces of some Navy Spencers were tinned or varnished.

GOOD—$2,500   FINE—$5,000

MODEL 1860 SPENCER RIFLE-MUSKET, .52 CALIBER, RIMFIRE CARTRIDGE

Made by Spencer Repeating Rifle Company, Boston, Massachusetts, ca. 1861–ca. 1865.
Total production: over 2,000.
Overall length: 55-7/8"
Breech-loading, falling block, 7 shot.
"SPENCER REPEATING / RIFLE CO BOSTON MASS / PAT'D MARCH 6, 1860" on top of receiver; serial number to rear of ejection port.

The Model 1860 Spencer Rifle-musket, .52 Caliber, was similar in design and appearance to the Model 1860 Spencer Army Rifle, .52 Caliber, with the exception that the rifle-musket had a longer barrel, yielding an overall length of 55-7/8", or 8-7/8" longer than the Army Rifle version. The U.S. government bought approximately 2,000 of these rifle-muskets from 1862 to 1864, from a consignment originally ordered by Massachusetts.

GOOD—$2,500   FINE—$4,750

SPRINGFIELD JOSLYN .56-50 RIMFIRE CARTRIDGE RIFLE

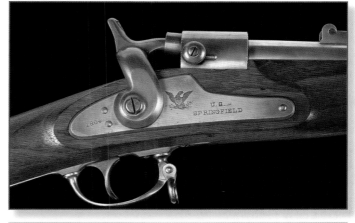

Rock Island Auction Company

Made by Springfield Armory, Springfield, Massachusetts, 1865. Total production: 3,007.

Breech-loading, hinged lever/breech block, single shot.

"U.S. / SPRINGFIELD" and eagle on lock plate forward of hammer and "1864" to rear of hammer; "B. F. JOSLYN'S PATENT / OCT 8th 1861 / JUNE 24th 1862" on breech block; serial number.

The Springfield Armory manufactured this, the first genuine breech-loading cartridge firearm to be made in numbers by a U.S. armory, in early 1865. Actions and breeches furnished by the Joslyn Firearms Company were installed on factory-new rifles made especially for the purpose. It is possible that some rifles were distributed to U.S. troops before the end of the Civil War. The Springfield Joslyn had a 35-1/2" round barrel attached to the walnut stock by three bands. The lock was probably a modified 1863 type. The rifle fired a .50-60-540 Joslyn rimfire cartridge.

GOOD—$900   FINE—$2,250

TRIPLETT & SCOTT REPEATING RIFLE, .50 CALIBER RIMFIRE CARTRIDGE

Rock Island Auction Company

Made by Meriden Manufacturing Co., Meriden, Connecticut, ca. 1864–65. Total production: approximately 3,000.

Overall length: 46-1/8".

Breech-loading, rotating chamber, 7 shots.

"MERIDEN MANFG. CO. / MERIDEN, CONN." on left side of receiver; "TRIPLETT & SCOTT / PATENT DEC. 6, 1864" on upper receiver strap; "KENTUCKY" on left side of receiver; serial number on right side of frame.

This repeating rifle, based on a design by Louis Triplett of Columbia, Kentucky, featured a chamber that rotated 120 degrees to the right to align with a tubular, coil spring–operated, 7-shot magazine housed in the butt stock. Kentucky bought 3,000 of the rifles around 1865 and began disposing of them by 1868. The round barrel, 27-1/2" to receiver, was blued, with three-groove rifling; furniture, including a single barrel band, was blued iron. The front sight was an iron blade; rear sight was folding leaf with slide, mounted on a base 1-5/16" long.

GOOD—$1,500   FINE—$3,000

The role of mounted troops in the late 18th and early 19th centuries was to ride their horse to a location needed, dismount, and function as infantry soldiers, generally in screening or skirmishing operations. Carrying a full-length shoulder arm on horseback, however, proved impractical. Therefore, they carried "musketoons" or muzzle-loading carbines that had barrels no longer than approximately 26-1/2".

Very few northern regiments carried muzzle-loading musketoons or carbines long into the war. Whereas the Army was slow to adopt breechloaders for its infantry, there never seemed to be the same prejudice regarding cavalry. In fact, several U.S. Dragoon formations received breech-loading carbines in the early 1830s By the outbreak of hostilities in April 1861, breechloaders were commonplace in the hands of Union cavalry troopers.

The same would have been true of Confederate troopers if stocks of breech-loading carbines were available. But they were not. Therefore, Confederate cavalrymen had to rely primarily on muzzle-loading carbines and musketoons, many of which were created from damaged long arms.

This last point should cause some alarm to today's collectors. Creating a muzzle-loading carbine from a longer muzzloader is as easy as shortening the barrel, stock, and ramrod. It is very tempting for the unscrupulous to make a carbine "used by Confederates" out of an otherwise worthless weapon. Before purchasing muzzle-loading carbines, a collector needs to fully understand the variety of purpose-built weapons that were available during the Civil War.

U.S. Model 1847 Artillery Musketoon, .69 Caliber, Paper Cartridge, Percussion

Manufactured by Springfield Armory, Springfield, Massachusetts, 1848–59. Total production: 3,359 (in addition, an unknown number of U.S. Model 1847 cavalry musketoons were converted to artillery musketoons beginning in 1858).

Overall length: 41". Weight: 6 lbs. 8 oz.

Muzzleloader, single shot.

Eagle over "US" at center of lock plate; "SPRING / FIELD / [year]" vertically on lock plate to rear of hammer; "V / P / [eagle head]" proof mark on left barrel flat; year on breech plug tang; "US" on tang of butt plate; inspector's mark on left flat of stock, opposite lock.

The U.S. Model 1847 artillery musketoon had a 26" round, smoothbore barrel fastened to a 38" black walnut stock by two bands, the upper of which was double-strapped. All furniture was iron, and all hardware was finished bright. The ramrod had a trumpet head. The standard version of this musketoon lacked a bayonet stud and had sling swivels under the lower barrel band and on the bottom of the stock near the butt. Beginning in 1858, a number of U.S. Model 1847 cavalry musketoons were altered to artillery musketoons, in part by removing the ramrod swivel and mounting a bayonet stud on the bottom of the barrel near the muzzle to accommodate a Model 1842 musket bayonet. Some examples evidently were rifled later. Similarly, 228 U.S. Model 1847 sappers musketoons were converted to artillery musketoons in the late 1850s.

STANDARD MODEL:
GOOD—$1,500   FINE—$4,750

ALTERED FROM CAVALRY MUSKETOON:
GOOD—$1,250   FINE—$4,000

ALTERED FROM SAPPERS MUSKETOON:
GOOD—$1,250   FINE—$3,750

Model 1847 Artillery Musketoon adapted from a Model 1847 Cavalry Musketoon—note the lack of sling swivels on the rear barrel band and butt stock. James D. Julia Auctioneers, Fairfield, Maine

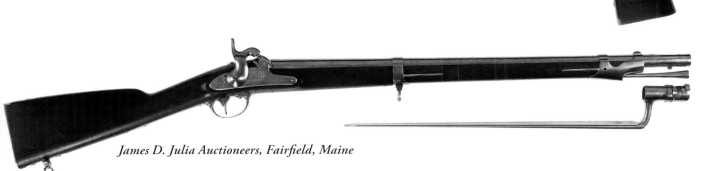

James D. Julia Auctioneers, Fairfield, Maine

U.S. MODEL 1847 CAVALRY MUSKETOON, .69 CALIBER, PAPER CARTRIDGE, PERCUSSION

James D. Julia Auctioneers, Fairfield, Maine

Manufactured by Springfield Armory, Springfield, Massachusetts, 1847–59. Total production: Approximately 6,700. Overall length: 41". Weight: 7 lbs. 4 oz.

Muzzleloader, single shot.

Eagle over "US" at center of lock plate; "SPRING / FIELD / [year]" vertically on lock plate to rear of hammer; "V / P / [eagle head]" proof mark on left barrel flat; year on tang of breech plug; "US" on tang of butt plate; inspector's mark on left flat of stock, opposite lock.

The U.S. Model 1847 cavalry musketoon was similar to the U.S. Model 1847 artillery musketoon, with these differences: The Type I cavalry version had all brass furniture, finished bright; a 9-1/4" ring bar and sling ring on the left side; a button-head ramrod secured to the underside of the muzzle with an iron swivel; and a shortened upper barrel band. Variants include rifled barrels and two-leaf rear sights. Beginning in 1852, the Type II cavalry musketoons were fitted with a slightly lengthened ramrod and a new ramrod retainer consisting of a sliding band on the ramrod, secured by a short chain to a stud on the underside of the muzzle, in lieu of the iron swivel.

TYPE I: GOOD—$2,250   FINE—$4,750
TYPE II: GOOD—$2,750   FINE—$6,500

U.S. MODEL 1847 SAPPERS MUSKETOON, .69 CALIBER, PAPER CARTRIDGE, PERCUSSION

James D. Julia Auctioneers, Fairfield, Maine

Manufactured by Springfield Armory, Springfield, Massachusetts, 1847–48, 1855, and 1856. Total production: 830. Overall length: 41". Weight: 6 lbs. 10 oz.

Muzzleloader, single shot.

Eagle over "US" at center of lock plate; "SPRING / FIELD / [year]" vertically on lock plate to rear of hammer; "V / P / [eagle head]" proof mark on left barrel flat; year on breech plug tang; "US" on tang of butt plate; inspector's mark on left flat of stock, opposite lock.

The U.S. Model 1847 sappers (or, sappers and miners) musketoon was very similar to the U.S. Model 1847 artillery musketoon, except the sappers version was fitted with a lug for a brass-hilted sword bayonet on the right side of the muzzle, and had sling swivels at the toe of the butt stock and on the lower barrel band. The Springfield armory produced 250 sappers musketoons in 1847–48, with additional production runs of 80 in 1855 (for New York State) and 500 in 1856. In the late 1850s, 228 Model 1847 sappers musketoons were converted to artillery musketoons.

GOOD—$2,500   FINE—$6,750

U.S. MODEL 1847 "NAVY" MUSKETOON, .69 CALIBER, PAPER CARTRIDGE, PERCUSSION

Manufactured by Springfield Armory, Springfield, Massachusetts, ca. 1851. Total production: Unknown.

Overall length: 41". Weight: 6 lbs. 8 oz.

Muzzleloader, single shot.

Eagle over "US" at center of lock plate; "SPRING / FIELD / [year]" vertically on lock plate to rear of hammer; "V / P / [eagle head]" proof mark on left barrel flat; year on breech plug tang; "US" on tang of butt plate; inspector's mark on left flat of stock, opposite lock.

The U.S. Model 1847 "navy" musketoon was virtually identical to the U.S. Model 1847 artillery musketoon, but with a shortened upper barrel band (with the front sight on the lower strap instead of on the upper strap, as the artillery version was configured); a heavier and thicker lower band, and shorter band springs.

GOOD—$2,050   FINE—$5,000

U.S. MODEL 1855 RIFLED CARBINE, .54 CALIBER, PAPER CARTRIDGE, PERCUSSION

Rock Island Auction Company

Manufactured by Springfield Armory, Springfield, Massachusetts, ca. 1855–56. Total production: 1,020.

Overall length: 36-3/4". Weight: 6 lbs.

Muzzleloader, single shot.

Eagle over "US" at center of lock plate; "SPRING / FIELD / [year]" vertically on lock plate to rear of hammer; "V / P / [eagle head]" proof mark on left barrel flat; year on tang of breech plug; "US" on tang of butt plate.

This carbine had a 22" round barrel, rifled with three broad lands and grooves. It had the same lock as the U.S. Model 1847 artillery musketoon. The black walnut stock was three-quarter length, with one barrel band and a brass fore tip; all other furniture was bright iron. A sling ring 1" in diameter was attached to the rear of the trigger guard bow. The shaft of the button-head ramrod was exposed from where it exited the stock at the barrel band. Retaining the ramrod was an iron swivel mounted on the underside of the muzzle.

GOOD—$4,500   FINE—$25,000

BILHARZ, HALL & CO. CARBINE, .58 CALIBER, PAPER CARTRIDGE, PERCUSSION

Made by Bilharz, Hall & Co., Pittsylvania Courthouse, Virginia, 1863-1864. Total production: Approximately 700.

Overall length: 37-1/2".

Muzzleloader, single shot.

Barrel breech marked "CS / P" ("CSA / P" also reported).

James D. Julia Auctioneers, Fairfield, Maine

Closely copying the U.S. Model 1855 carbine, the Bilharz incorporates iron mountings with a brass or pewter nose cap. The ramrod is attached to the barrel with an iron swivel. A sling ring is mounted on the rear of the trigger guard bow. Previous works referred to this carbine as the "D.C. Hodgkins & Sons carbine," though current scholarship points to Billharz, Hall & Co. actually being the manufacturer.

GOOD—$10,000   FINE—$25,000

C. CHAPMAN CARBINE, .54 CALIBER, PAPER CARTRIDGE, PERCUSSION

Manufacturer unknown, ca. 1862-1863. Total production: About 60.

Overall length: 39-1/2".

Muzzleloader, single shot.

Lock plate stamped forward of the hammer, "C. CHAPMAN."

Patterned after the U.S. Model 1841 rifle with brass barrel bands, side plate and butt plate, the C. Chapman rifle remains a collector's enigma. "C. Chapman" has not been identified, though speculation is that the maker may have resided in Tennessee. Recent scholarship points to similarities to another unknown lock plate stamped "SUMNER / ARMORY". For now, though, "C. Chapman" carbine remains unknown to collectors.

GOOD—$20,000   FINE—$40,000

James D. Julia Auctioneers, Fairfield, Maine

COLUMBUS ARMORY CARBINE, .54 CALIBER, PAPER CARTRIDGE, PERCUSSION

James D. Julia Auctioneers, Fairfield, Maine

James D. Julia Auctioneers, Fairfield, Maine

Made by Columbus Armory, Columbus, Georgia, ca. 1863-1865. Total production: About 100.

Overall length: 39-1/4".

Muzzleloader, single shot.

Lock plate stamped "COLUMBUS ARMORY" forward of the hammer. Proof marks "PRO. / F.C.H." on the top of the barrel near the breech.

Closely resembling the carbines made by J.P. Murray, recent scholarship confirms that Columbus Armory rifled carbines were produced under the direction of John D. Gray. At some time in 1863, the Confederate government leased the Columbus Armory. It remained in operation until burned in April 1865.

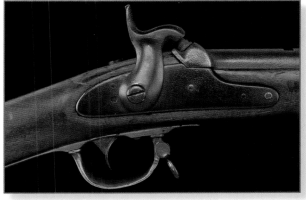

James D. Julia Auctioneers, Fairfield, Maine

Good—$20,000   Fine—$40,000

COOK & BROTHER ARTILLERY MUSKETOON, .58 CALIBER, PAPER CARTRIDGE, PERCUSSION

Cook & Brother type II artillery musketoon produced at Athens, Georgia. Collection Of Frank Reile, photo by Alya Alberico

Made by Cook and Brother, New Orleans, Louisiana, (Type I) and Athens, Georgia, (Type II), 1862-1864. Total production: Unknown.

Overall length: 39-3/4" - 40".

Muzzleloader, single shot.

Lockplate stamped forward of the hammer, "COOK & BROTHER" and either "N.O [date]" or "ATHENS GA" with the date in two lines along with serial number. A Confederate "Stars and Bars" flag is stamped at the rear of the lock plate. Top of barrel stamped "COOK & BROTHER" and/or "PROVED" at the breech.

The artillery carbine is most easily recognized by the use of iron sling swivels. Type I artillery carbines have and long iron block with brass inset blade front sights whereas Type II carbine sights are simple iron block and blade.

BOTH TYPES: GOOD—$10,000 FINE—$25,000

Collection Of Frank Reile, photo by Alya Alberico

COOK & BROTHER CAVALRY CARBINE, .58 CALIBER, PAPER CARTRIDGE, PERCUSSION

Sling swivels are a identifying characteristics of Type I Cook & Brother cavalry carbines. James D. Julia Auctioneers, Fairfield, Maine

James D. Julia Auctioneers, Fairfield, Maine

James D. Julia Auctioneers, Fairfield, Maine

Made by Cook and Brother, Athens, Georgia, 1864. Total production: unknown

Overall length: 37"-37-1/8".

Muzzleloader, single shot.

Lock plate stamped forward of the hammer, "COOK & BROTHER" and "ATHENS GA" with the date in two lines along with serial number. A Confederate "Stars and Bars" flag is stamped at the rear of the lock plate. Top of barrel stamped "COOK & BROTHER" and/or "PROVED" at the breech.

Patterned after the English P1856 cavalry carbine, the Type I has brass enlarged ferrules and iron sling swivels. The Type II has a ring bar attached to ferrules and a ramrod swivel lug at the muzzle

BOTH TYPES:

GOOD–$12,500   FINE–$30,000

James D. Julia Auctioneers, Fairfield, Maine

DAVIS & BOZEMAN
CARBINE, .577 CALIBER, PAPER CARTRIDGE, PERCUSSION

Made by Henry J. Davis and David W. Bozeman, Equality, Alabama, 1864-1865. Total production: Approximately 90.

Overall length: 39-5/8".

Muzzleloader, single shot.

Lock plate stamped forward of the hammer, "D.&B." along with the date. The serial number is stamped behind the hammer. "ALA. and the date stamped on barrel breech.

Type I carbines have tapered barrels. Type II have cut-down rifle barrels.

BOTH TYPES: GOOD–$15,000   FINE–$40,000

DICKSON, NELSON CARBINE, .58 CALIBER,
PAPER CARTRIDGE, PERCUSSION

Made by Dickson, Nelson & Company, Adairsville, Georgia, (1862); Macon, Georgia, (1863-1864); and Dawson, Georgia, (1864-1865). Total production: unknown, though thought to be fewer than 100.

Overall length: 40-1/2".

Muzzleloader, single shot.

Lock plate stamped forward of the hammer, "DICKSON / NELSON & CO. / C.S." "ALA. / [date]" stamped behind the hammer Barrel stamped "ALA. [date]" in one line. Some stocks are known to be stamped "F. ZUNDT".

Using many components based on those of the U.S. Model 1841 rifle, the shorter carbine has a single barrel band, nose cap, and swivel-style ramrod.

GOOD–$12,500   FINE–$35,000

J.P. MURRAY CARBINE, .577, PAPER CARTRIDGE, PERCUSSION

Made by Greenwood & Gray, Columbus, Georgia, 1862-1864. Total production: Fewer than 300.

Overall length: 39-3/4".

Muzzleloader, single shot.

Based on the U.S. Model 1841 Rifle, J.P. Murray carbines have been observed in two styles. Lock plates are found both marked and unmarked. Those that are marked, are stamped on the lock plate forward of the hammer, "J.P. MURRAY / COLUMBUS GA".

Type I: Has two spring-retained barrel bands, the front incorporating a nose cap similar to that on a U.S. Model 1841 rifle.

Type II: Two flat brass barrel bands, screw-fastened brass nose cap, Model 1855-style round brass washers on lock plate bolts.

BOTH TYPES: GOOD–$10,000   FINE–$27,500

J.P. Murray Cavalry Carbine, .58, Paper Cartridge, Percussion

Made by Greenwood & Gray, Columbus, Georgia, 1864. Total production: unknown
Overall length: 38".
Muzzleloader, single shot.
Produced for the State of Alabama, the cavalry carbine is bored to .58 caliber. Those with marked lock plates are stamped forward of the hammer, "J.P. MURRAY / COLUMBUS GA". The upper left surface of the breech is stamped "ALA 1864". The cavalry carbine is recognizable from its swivel ramrod, single barrel band and brass nose cap.

Good—$10,000   Fine—$30,000

Read & Watson Carbine, First Model, .54 Caliber, Paper Cartridge, Percussion

Made J.B. Barrett, Wytheville, Virginia, 1861. Total production: Unknown but presumed to be less than 300 carbines and rifles.
Overall length: 38-1/2".
Muzzleloader, single shot.
Breech stamped "NTR".
The "Barrett" carbine was the result of the only known contract awarded during the Civil War for the conversion of breech-loading weapons to muzzle-loading configurations. J.B. Barrett utilized parts from Hall breech loading rifles to create a new center-hung hammer arrangement. Barrett employed a brass breech piece in the conversion. The First Model rifles have a small narrow insert that extends along the top of the stock's wrist. There is a wide variation of stocks and styles, most are configured with two flat brass barrel bands.

Good—$12,500   Fine—$22,000

Read & Watson Rifle, Second Model, .54 Caliber, Paper Cartridge, Percussion

Made J.B. Barrett, Wytheville, Virginia, 1861. Total production: Unknown, but presumed to be less than 300 carbines and rifles.
Overall length: 42-1/8".
Muzzleloader, single shot.
Breech stamped "NTR".
The "Barrett" rifle was the result of the only known contract awarded during the Civil War for the conversion of breech-loading weapons to muzzle-loading configurations. J.B. Barrett utilized parts from Hall breech loading rifles to create a new center-hung hammer arrangement. Barrett employed a brass breech piece in the conversion. The Second Model carbine has a large, one-piece bass breech casting that extends the length of the wrist to the comb.

Good—$12,500   Fine—$20,000

C.S. Armory Musketoon, .69 Caliber, Paper Cartridge, Percussion

Made by C.S. Armory, Richmond, Virginia, 1862. Total production: More than 5,400.
Overall length: 39-1/2" - 39-3/4".
Muzzleloader, single shot.
Assembled from captured components, lock plate markings observed include "SPRING/FIELD/ 1845", "PALMETTO ARMORY", and "PALMETTO ARMORY. S.*C."
Made as smoothbores from U.S. Model 1842 muskets, the C.S. Armory musketoons have shortened stocks with rounded fore ends with no nose caps but two barrel bands on each. All furniture, including the three sling swivels, is iron.

Good—$4,000   Fine—$10,000

RICHMOND ARMORY CARBINE, .58 CALIBER, PAPER CARTRIDGE, PERCUSSION

James D. Julia Auctioneers, Fairfield, Maine

Made by C.S. Armory, Richmond, Virginia, 1861-1865. Total production: More than 5,400.

Overall length: 40-1/2".

Muzzleloader, single shot.

The capture of machinery and parts at Harpers Ferry, Virginia, provided the foundation for the largest weapons manufactory in the Confederacy. Known to collectors as "C.S. Richmond rifle-muskets," the three-band, .58 muzzle-loaders were based on the design and built with pieces of U.S. Model 1855 rifle-muskets. Collectors have broken down the production down into three major types:

Type I: The earliest rifles assembled at the Richmond Armory (before it was turned over to the control of the Confederacy) incorporated a "high hump" lock plate marked forward of the hammer, "RICHMOND, VA." and behind the hammer, vertically, "1861."

Type II: The second variant is quite similar to the first except that the letters "CS" are stamped on the lock plate above the word "RICHMOND", reflecting the government takeover of the armory. Type II carbines will be dated "1862".

Type III: This is the easiest of the three to recognize because it incorporates a "low hump" lock plate. Dates will range from 1862 to 1865 on Type III carbines.

ALL TYPES: GOOD—$5,500 FINE—$20,000

Type II lock plates are dated 1862. Generally they will be "full-hump" style, though several 1862-dated examples have been observed with the lower humped lock plate. James D. Julia Auctioneers, Fairfield, Maine

Type III Richmond carbines are recognizable from the low-hump lock plate. James D. Julia Auctioneers, Fairfield, Maine

TALLASSEE ARMORY CARBINE .58 CALIBER, PAPER CARTRIDGE, PERCUSSION

Made by Tallassee Armory, Tallassee, Alabama, ca. 1864-1865. Total production: Approximately 500.

Overall length: 40-1/2".

Muzzleloader, single shot.

Lock plated stamped forward of the hammer in two lines, "Tallassee / Ala." The four-digit year is stamped vertically behind the hammer.

Nothing survives to reveal the fate of the 500 carbines ordered and presumably produced at the Tallassee Armory. Patterned after the English P1853 carbine, Tallassee carbines were finished in bright metal with a U.S. Model 1858-type, two-leaf, rear sight. All furniture is brass, though the swivel slings are made of iron.

GOOD—$44,000   FINE—$100,000

BRITISH PATTERN 1853 ARTILLERY CARBINE, .577 CALIBER, PAPER CARTRIDGE, PERCUSSION

James D. Julia Auctioneers, Fairfield, Maine

Made by various English manufactures, London, England, Liege, Belgium, 1854-1866 Total imported: Approximately 8,500.
Overall length: 37".
Muzzleloader, single shot.
Lock plates vary depending on year of manufacture. Generally, the lock plate will be stamped with a crown over "VR", the British "broad arrow" and the year of manufacture in addition to "Tower", depending on place of manufacture. London Armoury weapons will be marked "LAC" or "LA Co". Liege-manufactured weapons will

The "JS-Anchor" mark that many collectors like to associate with the Confederacy. In fact, no research has conclusively linked this mark with weapons exclusively delivered to the Confederate government or its agents. James D. Julia Auctioneers, Fairfield, Maine

only have royal monogram and year of manufacture. No imported weapon will have the British broad arrow mark or "Enfield" stamped lock plate. Barrels manufactured for export will have a provisional proof, a gauge mark ("25" for .577 or "24" for .58). Premiums are paid for weapons bearing a "JS / [anchor]" mark, as this is popularly thought to denote certain Confederate use (though know hard evidence can verify the belief).

The artillery carbine went through three distinct changes. Only examples of the later two made it into hands of northern or southern soldiers:

Type II: Three-groove rifling Does not have a 1.5" key forward of the bayonet lug of the first type. Has a straight ramrod held in place by a spring in the forearm.

Type III: Five-groove rifling and an improved rear sight that resembles the sight found on the rifle-musket.

U.S. Ordnance Department purchased 4800 English carbines imported during the war. It is unknown how many the Confederacy purchased, though it is likely to have been as many as 8,000.

Bayonet lug without a forward key typical of Type II and III carbines. James D. Julia Auctioneers, Fairfield, Maine

ALL TYPES:
GOOD—$1,850   **FINE—$6,500**

PATTERN 1856 CAVALRY CARBINE, .577 CALIBER, PAPER CARTRIDGE, PERCUSSION

Made by various English manufactures, London, England, Liege, Belgium, 1856-1866 Total imported: Unknown.

Overall length: 37".

Muzzleloader, single shot.

Lock plates vary dependant on year of manufacture. Generally, the lock plate will be stamped with a crown over "VR", the British "broad arrow" and the year of manufacture in addition to "Tower", depending on place of manufacture. London Armoury weapons will be marked "LAC" or "LA Co". Liege-manufactured weapons will only have royal monogram and year of manufacture. No imported weapon will have the British broad arrow mark or "Enfield" stamped lock plate. Barrels manufactured for export will have a provisional proof, a gauge mark ("25" for .577 or "24" for .58). Premiums are paid for weapons bearing a "JS / [anchor]" mark, as this is popularly thought to denote certain Confederate use (though know hard evidence can verify the belief).

U.S. records show only 200 English carbines imported during the war. However, the short muzzle-loading carbine was a favorite of Confederate troopers. It is likely that several thousand made their way into Southern hands.

ALL TYPES: GOOD—$1,850   FINE—$6,500

James D. Julia Auctioneers, Fairfield, Maine

AUSTRIAN MODEL 1842 CARBINE, .71 CALIBER, PAPER CARTRIDGE, TUBE-LOCK/PERCUSSION

Made by Austrian National Armory and private gun manufactories, ca. 1842-1849 Total imported: Unknown, but at least 10,000.

Muzzleloader, single shot.

Markings are uncommon. Each lock plate was stamped forward of the hammer with a small Austrian eagle and the year of manufacture (with the first digit omitted, e.g., "843").

Originally fitted with a tube-lock ignition system developed in Austria, Model 1842 carbine is sometimes referred to as the "Früwirth carbine" in reference to the private gun manufacturers, Johann and Ferdinand Früwirth. The smoothbores were originally fitted with tube-lock ignitions but most were converted to percussion by brazing a bolster or cone seat on the upper right side of the barrel and adapting the lock. Examples exist with bolsters welded to the side of the barrel as well. A double sling ring is attached to a bar inletted on the left side of the stock. All iron furniture was left bright. Later, many were rifled to fire a conical bullet. George Schuyler purchased 10,000 Model 1842 carbines in 1861. After the weapons arrived in the United States in 1862, they were issued to General John Frémont for his western command.

ALL TYPES: GOOD—$350   FINE—$1,200

CARBINES, BREECHLOADING

The carbine, a shorter-than-normal shoulder arm, was the essential weapon of the Civil War cavalry trooper. Never in large supply before the Civil War, manufacturers rushed to meet the demand of both the Northern and Southern force. By the war's end, no fewer than 17 different makes had been adopted by U.S. troops. Only a handful of southern manufacturers, on the other hand, successfully produced breechloading carbines for the Confederacy.

One should not be intimidated by the wide variety and price range of these weapons. Carbine collectors have a variety of areas on which they can concentrate their efforts. For example, one could collect just breechloaders, metal cartridge weapons, Southern-produced, imports, or even variations of one specific make like the Sharps or Spencer.

BALL REPEATING CARBINE, .50 CALIBER RIMFIRE CARTRIDGE

 Made by E. G. Lamson & Company, Windsor, Vermont, 1864–65. Total production: 1,002.
Overall length: 37-1/2". Weight: 10 lbs.

Breechloading, 7 shot.

"E. G. LAMSON & CO / WINDSOR, VT. / U.S. / BALL'S PATENT / JUNE 23, 1863 /. MAR. 15, 1864" on left side of receiver; inspector marks, left top of wrist of butt stock near receiver.

The U.S. government contracted for Ball Repeating Carbines in 1864 and received them in May 1865. They had blued iron furniture, including a sling bar and ring on the left side of the receiver. The round, blued barrel was 20-1/2" to the frame. The trigger guard doubled as the breech-operating lever. The stock was two-piece, walnut; in the 3/4-length fore stock was a tubular, 7-shot magazine. The .56-50 rimfire cartridges were loaded through a port which also acted as the ejection port.

GOOD–$2,000   FINE–$3,500

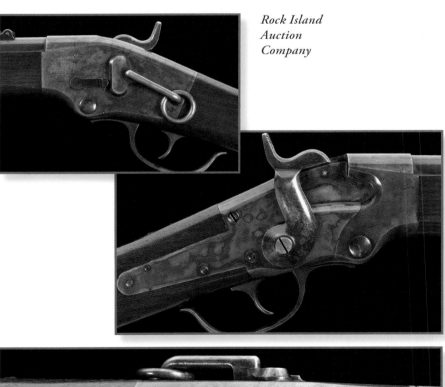

*Rock Island
Auction
Company*

Rock Island Auction Company

BALLARD (DWIGHT & CHAPIN; BALL & WILLIAMS) CARBINE .56-56 CALIBER "OLD MODEL," RIMFIRE CARTRIDGE

Made by Dwight & Chapin, Bridgeport, Connecticut, 1863. Total production: approximately 1,800.

Overall length: 37-3/4" to 38". Weight: 7 lbs.

Breechloader, falling breech block, single shot.

"BALLARD'S PATENT / NOV. 5, 1861" on right side of receiver; "MERWIN & BRAY / AGT'S. N.Y. / [serial number] on left side of receiver; "DWIGHT & CHAPIN / BRIDGEPORT, CONN." over the Merwin & Bray mark; U.S. inspector's mark "D" on most parts; "EMD" on butt stock comb near butt plate.

Based on a patent by Charles S. Ballard, this carbine incorporated a falling breech lock actuated by a lever/trigger guard. The breech block also contained the hammer and trigger. The casehardened receiver was rounded on top. The single iron barrel band included the upper sling swivel; the other swivel was mounted on the butt stock. There were variations in the length of the barrel to the frame; the rear, folding-leaf sight was 1" from the frame. Dwight & Chapin delivered 115 units to Kentucky by September 1863, following which the firm went bankrupt, and Ball & Williams, of Worcester, Massachusetts, took up assembly of the carbine from existing parts. The Ball & Williams–assembled units did not include stampings of their name or Dwight & Chapin's.

DWIGHT & CHAPIN: GOOD—$3,500 FINE—$10,000

BALL & WILLIAMS: GOOD—$950   FINE—$2,500

BALLARD CARBINE, U.S. CONTRACT, TYPE I, .44 CALIBER, SOLID BREECH BLOCK, RIMFIRE CARTRIDGE

Made by Ball & Williams, Worcester, Massachusetts, ca. 1863–64. Total production: Over 1,500.

Overall length: 37-3/8".

Breechloader, falling breech block, single shot.

"BALLARD'S PATENT / NOV. 5, 1861" on right side of receiver; "BALL & WILLIAMS . Worcester, Mass." over "MERWIN & BRAY AGTS. / NEW YORK" on left side of receiver; serial number on top of receiver, inspector's marks on left side of barrel, left side of breech block, butt plate tang, left side of stock, and top of butt stock comb. "KENTUCKY" stamped on top of the receiver of some examples. On U.S. contract examples: "MM" in script in oval cartouche on left side of stock on some units; in subsequent units, "MM" in block letters stamped on major parts and comb of butt stock.

Ball & Williams produced a .44-caliber version of the Ballard Carbine, delivering 1,500 to the U.S. Ordnance Department between March 1864 and August 1864 and furnishing units to Kentucky. The carbine had iron furniture and a blued barrel, part round and part octagonal, 20-5/16" to the frame. There were sling swivels on the underside of the butt stock and on the single barrel band. The rear sight was a pierced "L" leaf 1" from the frame, and the front sight a dovetailed iron blade.

GOOD—$2,750   FINE—$4,750

Rock Island Auction Company

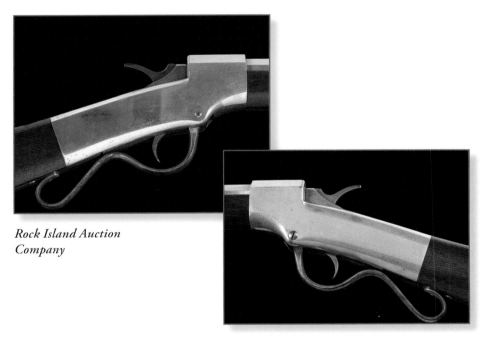

Rock Island Auction Company

BALLARD CARBINE, U.S. CONTRACT, TYPE II, .44 CALIBER, SPLIT BREECH BLOCK, RIMFIRE OR PAPER CARTRIDGE

James D. Julia Auctioneers, Fairfield, Maine

Made by Ball & Williams, Worcester, Massachusetts,1864. Total production: Undetermined
Overall length: 37-1/4".
Breechloader, falling breech block, single shot.
"BALLARD'S PATENT / NOV. 5, 1861" on right side of receiver; "BALL & WILLIAMS . Worcester, Mass." over "MERWIN & BRAY AGTS. / NEW YORK on left side of receiver; serial number on top of receiver, inspector's marks on left side of barrel, left side of breech block, butt plate tang, left side of stock, and top of butt stock comb.
The Ballard Carbine, .44 Caliber, Type II, featured a "split" breech block patented by Joseph Merwin and Edward P. Bray on January 5, 1864. This design incorporated a percussion cap nipple in the front of the breech block, enabling firing either a rimfire cartridge or combustible cartridge.

GOOD—$2,750   **FINE—$4,750**

BILHARZ, HALL & CO. CARBINE, .54 CALIBER, PAPER CARTRIDGE, PERCUSSION

James D. Julia Auctioneers, Fairfield, Maine

James D. Julia Auctioneers, Fairfield, Maine

Made by Bilharz, Hall & Co., Pittsylvania Court House, Virginia, ca. 1863. Total production: Fewer than 100.
Overall length: 40".
Breechloader (rising breech), single shot.
Type I: Top left side of the barrel stamped with a large "P". Below it and at a right angle is a similarly large "CS". The front sight is an iron blade rising from a broad base. The extreme rear end of the lever has an open loop (about three-fourths of a complete circle)
Type II: Marked with only a large "P" stamped on the barrel. Front sight is a brass blade rising from a brass base. The Type II carbine is recognizable from the full, circular loop on the loading lever.

On September 16, 1862, Captain Edward B. Smith, assistant ordnance officer to the Confederate Chief of Ordnance paid Bilharz, Hall & Co. $4,500 for "100 breech-loading carbines" utilizing a "rising breech"—a unique lever-action, breech loading design.

ALL TYPES:
GOOD—$15,000   FINE—$45,000

James D. Julia Auctioneers, Fairfield, Maine

BURNSIDE CARBINE, SECOND MODEL, .54 CALIBER, COPPER CARTRIDGE, PERCUSSION

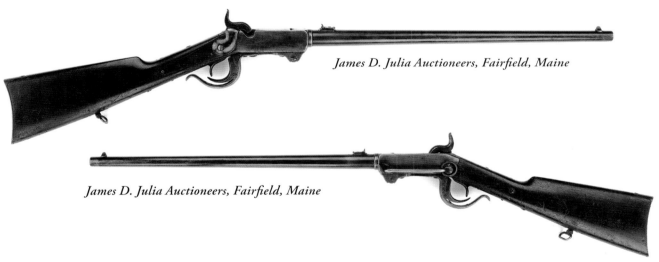

James D. Julia Auctioneers, Fairfield, Maine

James D. Julia Auctioneers, Fairfield, Maine

Manufactured by Bristol Firearms Company, Bristol, Rhode Island (early examples) and Burnside Rifle Company, Providence, Rhode Island (later examples), 1861. Total production: approximately 1,640–2,000.

Overall length: 39-1/2". Weight: 6 lbs. 12 oz.

Breechloader, falling breech block, single shot.

"BRISTOL FIREARM CO." or "BURNSIDE RIFLE CO. / PROVIDENCE=R.I." on lock plate to rear of hammer; "CAST STEEL 1861" on barrel; "BURNSIDE'S PATENT / MARCH 25TH, 1856" on receiver, over the serial number; inspector's mark on left side of butt stock; "G. P. FOSTER PAT / APRIL 10TH 1860" on the right side of some lever locks.

The Second Model of Burnside Carbine was distinguished by a curved locking device for the operating lever / trigger guard, mounted on the inner side of the bow, instead of the ungainly locking lever that wrapped under the hammer on the First Model carbines. The Second Model lacked a fore stock. Furniture was iron, and the receiver was described as casehardened, but usually seen as blued. The round, blued, 21" barrel had a 1/4"-wide reinforcing band where it joined the receiver. The front sight was 3/4" from the muzzle and a folding, single-leaf rear sight was 5/8" from the front of the receiver.

GOOD—$1,900   FINE—$4,500

Amoskeag Auction Company, Inc.

BURNSIDE CARBINE, THIRD MODEL, .54 CALIBER, COPPER CARTRIDGE, PERCUSSION

Manufactured by Burnside Rifle Company, Providence, Rhode Island, 1862. Total production: Approximately 1,500–2,000.

Overall length: 39-1/2". Weight: 6 lbs. 14 oz.

Breechloader, falling breech block, single shot.

"BURNSIDE RIFLE CO. / PROVIDENCE=R.I." on lock plate to rear of hammer; "CAST STEEL" (sometimes followed by "1862") on barrel; "BURNSIDE'S PATENT / MARCH 25TH, 1856" on receiver, over the serial number; "G. P. FOSTER PAT / APRIL 10TH 1860" on the right side of some lever locks.

The Third Model of Burnside Carbine was distinguished from the Second Model principally by the addition of a black walnut fore stock attached to the barrel with a single iron band; the elimination of the reinforcing band on the barrel; and a slightly modified hammer. Production of this model was from March to October 1862.

GOOD—$1,250   FINE—$3,500

Burnside Carbine, Fourth Model (or, Transition Type), .54 Caliber, Copper Cartridge, Percussion

Manufactured by Burnside Rifle Company, Providence, Rhode Island, 1863–64. Total production: Approximately 7,000.

Overall length: 39-1/2". Weight: 6 lbs. 14 oz.

Breechloader, falling breech block, single shot.

"BURNSIDE RIFLE CO. / PROVIDENCE=R.I." on lock plate to rear of hammer; "CAST STEEL" (sometimes followed by year "1863" or "1864") on barrel; "BURNSIDE'S PATENT / MARCH 25TH, 1856" on receiver, over the serial number; "G. P. FOSTER PAT / APRIL 10TH 1860" on the right side of some lever locks; inspector's mark on left side of butt stock.

The Fourth Model of Burnside Carbine (formerly classified in some references as "Transition Type") was similar to the Third Model, except for a radically different breech mechanism, with a hinged center part of the breech block which facilitated loading of the cartridge.

GOOD—$950   FINE—$3,500

BURNSIDE CARBINE, FIFTH MODEL, .54 CALIBER, COPPER CARTRIDGE, PERCUSSION

Manufactured by Burnside Rifle Company, Providence, Rhode Island, ca. 1863–65. Total production: Approximately 43,000.

Overall length: 39-1/2". Weight: 7 lbs. 2 oz.

Breechloader, falling breech block, single shot.

"BURNSIDE RIFLE CO. / PROVIDENCE=R.I." on lock plate to rear of hammer; "CAST STEEL" followed by year on barrel; "BURNSIDE'S PATENT / MODEL OF 1864" on top of receiver, over the serial number; inspector's marks in cartouches on left side of butt stock.

By far the most numerous of the Burnside Carbines, the Fifth Model (formerly classified in some references as the Fourth, or Standard, Model) was distinguished from the Fourth Model mainly by the new "BURNSIDE'S PATENT / MODEL OF 1864" mark on top of the receiver; the inclusion of a hinged, double-pivoting breech block patented by Isaac Hartshorn on March 31, 1864; and the inclusion of a prominent screw in the center of the right side of the receiver, which improved the action of the breech. The carbine featured a round, blued barrel with single-leaf rear sight graduated to 500 yards 9/16" to the front of the receiver, and wide-base, iron-blade front sight 3/4" from the muzzle.

GOOD—$900   **FINE—$3,000**

Rock Island Auction Company

Amoskeag Auction Company, Inc.

MODEL 1855 COLT REVOLVING CARBINE, .44 OR .56 CALIBER PAPER CARTRIDGE, PERCUSSION

Made at Colt factory, Harford, Connecticut, ca. 1857-1864. Total production estimated at 4,435.

Overall length: 36-1/2" or 39-1/2".

Single action, 6 shot.

Top of frame marked, "COLT'S PT. /1856" and "ADDRESS COL. COLT / HARTFORD CT. U.S.A." Left side of frame stamped behind the recoil shield, "COLT'S PATENT / NOV. 24TH, 1857".

Though varying lengths will be found, there are three basic types of Model 1855 Colt carbines:

Type I: .44 Caliber, iron furniture, double-spurred trigger guard, double sling swivels and swivel ring.

Type II: .44 Caliber, iron furniture, no spurs on trigger guard, double sling swivels and swivel ring.

Type III: .56 Caliber, five-shot, iron furniture, brass trigger guard, just a swivel ring. Top of frame marked, "COL. COLT HARTFORD CT. USA". Carbines in the 10000-12000 may also have British proof marks on the barrel and brass butt plates.

Model 1855 Colt carbines can be quickly recognized by the lack of a forestock, the presence of swivels and/or sling rings, and military style rear sights.

The first government order for Model 1855 carbines was for two cavalry carbines placed in March 1859. In 1860, the Ordnance Department ordered four more. Though the Ordnance Department did not order any but these six, small numbers did find their way into Union soldiers' hands. Company B, 11th New York Cavalry received 63. The 2nd Missouri Cavalry receive 300. The 9th Missouri Cavalry is reported to also have received Colt carbines. Similarly, Colt carbines were used by Confederate troops. The 1st Virginia Cavalry and a portion of the 8th Virginia Infantry received Colt carbines. Total numbers issued—to either Union or Southern troops—unfortunately, is not known.

TYPE I: GOOD—$3,250   FINE—$10,500
TYPE II: GOOD—$3,250   FINE—$10,500
TYPE III: GOOD—$3,250   FINE—$12,000

Amoskeag Auction Company, Inc.

MODEL 1855 COLT REVOLVING ARTILLERY CARBINE, .56 CALIBER PAPER CARTRIDGE, PERCUSSION

Made at Colt factory, Harford, Connecticut, ca. 1857-1864. Total production estimated at 4,435.

Overall length: 39-1/2".

Single action, five shot.

Top of frame marked, Top of frame marked, "COL. COLT HARTFORD CT. USA". Left side of frame stamped behind the recoil shield, "COLT'S PATENT / NOV. 24TH, 1857".

The Artillery Carbine was the only member of the Model 1855 Colt carbine family to have a fore stock and a ramrod (actually, a cleaning rod). Held in place with two barrel bands, the barrel was fitted with a bayonet lug to accept a saber bayonet.

The first government order for Model 1855 carbines included 62 artillery carbines and bayonets placed in March 1859. These were sent to the State of North Carolina for the use of its militia. In 1860, the Ordnance Department ordered two more. Total numbers issued—to either Union or Southern troops—unfortunately, is not known.

GOOD—$3,750   FINE—$17,000

*Rock Island
Auction Company*

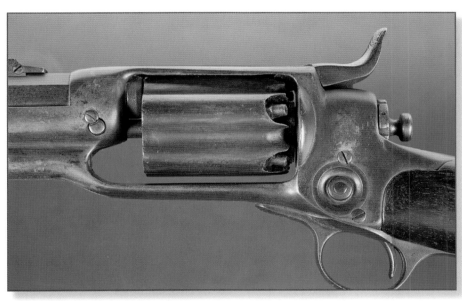

Rock Island Auction Company

*James D. Julia
Auctioneers,
Fairfield, Maine*

CONFEDERATE SHARPS TYPE CARBINE, .52 CALIBER, PAPER OR LINEN CARTRIDGE, PERCUSSION

Made by S.C. Robinson and Confederate Government, Richmond, Virginia, ca. 1862-1864. Total production: Approximately 5,000 of both types.

Overall length: 38-1/2".

Breechloader, falling breech block, single shot.

Type I: Made by S.C. Robinson during 1862 and 1863, the first 1,900 carbines were marked on the lock plate, "S.C. ROBINSON. / ARMS MAUFACTORY. / RICHMOND, VA. / 1862" with a serial number at the rear of the lock. The top of the barrel was usually marked in front of the rear sight, "S.C. ROBINSON / ARMS MANUFACTORY". In addition, most were marked behind the rear sight, "RICHMOND, VA. / [year]".

Type II: Production was not interrupted when the C.S. Government purchased Robinson's factory in March 1863. Serial numbers picked up where Robinson left them (at about 1,900). Type II carbines are identical to Type I with the exception of the markings. The only markings on the Type II carbines is "RICHMOND, VA." Stamped at the top of the barrel breech along with the serial number at the rear of the lock. The C.S. Government-run factory produced approximately 3,100 of the Type II carbines.

TYPE I: GOOD—$7,000   FINE—$20,000
TYPE II: GOOD—$6,500   FINE—$17,500

COSMOPOLITAN CARBINE, .52 CALIBER, PAPER CARTRIDGE, PERCUSSION

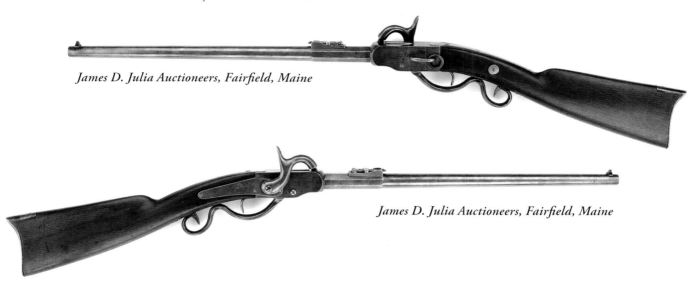

James D. Julia Auctioneers, Fairfield, Maine

James D. Julia Auctioneers, Fairfield, Maine

Manufactured by Cosmopolitan Arms Company, Hamilton, Ohio, ca. 1859–62. Total production: Approximately 1,140.
Overall length: 39". Weight: 6 lbs. 9 oz.

Breechloader, falling breech block, single shot.

"COSMOPOLITAN ARMS CO." in curve over "HAMILTON O. US. / GROSS' PATENT / 1859" on lock plate
to rear of hammer (a few examples substitute "UNION / RIFLE" for "GROSS' PATENT / 1859"); "UNION / RIFLE"
vertically on the front of the right side of the receiver; serial number on bottoms of receiver and barrel.

The Cosmopolitan carbine featured a lever-actuated breech mechanism patented by Henry Gross. The barrel, 19-1/8"
to the frame, was blued; the barrel was round, with a 3-1/2"-long octagonal section at the breech. Furniture was blued iron.
The lock plate was flat with beveled edge. Rear sight was a folding leaf; front sight was an iron block and blade. There was
no fore stock; the butt stock was of black walnut, with curved butt plate. It is known that the 5th and 6th Illinois Volunteer
Cavalry Regiments were armed with Cosmopolitan carbines.

There were two types of Cosmopolitan carbine:

Early Type: On early examples of the carbine, the operating lever incorporated two enclosed loops, the front one
comprising the trigger guard and the rear loop functioning as a guard for the locking latch.

Contract Type: The operating lever was of a complex curved shape, with the trigger and locking latch guards being open
instead of enclosed.

EARLY TYPE: GOOD—$2,750   **FINE—4,750**
CONTRACT TYPE: GOOD—$2,500   **FINE—$4,500**

GALLAGHER CARBINE, EARLY PRODUCTION, .50 CALIBER, PAPER AND FOIL CARTRIDGE, PERCUSSION

Manufactured by Richardson & Overman, Philadelphia, Pennsylvania, ca. 1861. Total production: over 17,700 of early
and standard production models.

Overall length: 39-1/8". Weight: 7 lbs. 8 oz.

Breechloader, pivoting barrel, single shot.

"GALLAGHER / PATENTED JULY 17TH 1860 / [serial number, from 1 up] on lock plate to rear of hammer;
inspector's initials on left side of stock, opposite lock plate.

The Gallagher carbine featured a unique breechloading mechanism whereby operating the lever caused the barrel to
slide forward and tilt down for loading. Early-production examples were rifled with five grooves. The Gallagher had iron
furniture, blued barrel and butt plate, casehardened receiver, and black walnut butt stock (there was no fore stock). There
also was a patch box, usually casehardened, and a sling ring bar on left side of the stock opposite the lock plate.

GOOD—$1,250   **FINE—$3,000**

*Rock Island
Auction Company*

GALLAGHER CARBINE, STANDARD PRODUCTION, .50 CALIBER, PAPER AND FOIL OR COPPER CARTRIDGE, PERCUSSION

Manufactured by Richardson & Overman, Philadelphia, Pennsylvania, ca. 1861–64. Total production: over 17,000 of early and standard-production models.

Overall length: 39-1/8". Weight: 7 lbs. 8 oz.

Breechloader, pivoting barrel, single shot.

"MANUFACTD BY / RICHARDSON & OVERMAN / PHILADA / [serial number] and "GALLAGHER'S PATENT / JULY 17TH 1860" on lock plate to rear of hammer; inspector's initials on left side of stock, opposite the lock.

The standard-production model of the Gallagher Carbine was similar to the early model, with different lock plate markings. Early cartridges were made of paper and foil, while latter on a cartridge with a copper case with a flash hole in the base was introduced. The carbine was used by a number of Union volunteer cavalry units, including the 2nd, 3rd, 4th, and 6th Ohio; 13th Tennessee; and 3rd West Virginia. After the Civil War, some Gallagher carbines were converted to other calibers or to smoothbore shotguns.

GOOD—$1,100   FINE—$2,500

GALLAGHER CARBINE, FINAL MODEL, .56-52 CALIBER, RIMFIRE CARTRIDGE

Manufactured by Richardson & Overman, Philadelphia, Pennsylvania, 1865. Total production: Approximately 5,000.

Overall length: 39-1/8". Weight: 7 lbs. 8 oz.

Breechloader, pivoting barrel, single shot.

"MANUFACTD BY / RICHARDSON & OVERMAN / PHILADA / [serial number] and "GALLAGHER'S PATENT / JULY 17TH 1860" on lock plate to rear of hammer; inspector's initials on left side of stock, opposite the lock.

In 1865, about 5,000 standard production Gallagher carbines were rechambered for the Spencer .56-52 rimfire cartridge. This alteration included installing a firing pin unit in place of the percussion nipple, and a cartridge case extractor. The units were delivered in May 1865, too late for service in the Civil War. In 1870 France purchased 2,500 or more of this model.

GOOD—$950   FINE—$2,300

GIBBS CARBINE, .52 CALIBER, PAPER OR LINEN CARTRIDGE, PERCUSSION

Manufactured by Phoenix Armory, New York City, 1863. Total production: 1,052.
Overall length: 39". Weight: 7 lbs. 6 oz.
Breechloader, pivoting barrel, single shot.
"L. H. GIBBS / PAT'D / JANY 8, 1856" on top of breech; "B" on left side of barrel near breech; "US" on butt plate tang; number stamped on hidden side of barrel band tang; "WM F. BROOKS / MANFR NEW YORK" on lock plate to front of bolster on early examples; on later examples, "WM F. BROOKS / MANFR NEW YORK / 1863" in same location, and eagle on lock plate to rear of hammer.

From May to July 1863 the Phoenix Armory (William F. Brooks and William W. Marston, props.) delivered 1,052 Gibbs carbines to the government. Volunteer cavalry units equipped with the Gibbs carbine included the 10th Missouri and 13th and 16th New York. By actuating the operating lever of the carbine, the barrel slid forward and down, exposing the casehardened breech for loading. The carbine had a round, blued, 22" barrel with folding, two-leaf rear sight and brass blade front sight. Other features included a black walnut fore stock and butt stock, blued side plate on left side with 2-1/2" sling ring rod, and curved, blued butt plate.

GOOD—$2,500   FINE—$5,000

GREENE CARBINE, .54 CALIBER, COMBUSTIBLE CARTRIDGE, PERCUSSION

Manufactured by Massachusetts Arms Company, Chicopee Falls, Massachusetts, 1855–57. Total production: 300.
Overall length: 38-1/2". Weight: 7 lbs. 12 oz.
Breechloader, rotating barrel, single shot.
"MASS. ARMS CO / CHICOPEE FALLS" stamped on lock plate to rear of hammer; "MAYNARD'S PATENT / SEP. 22, 1845" in circular shape on tape-primer door; "GREENE'S PATENT. / JUNE 27. 1854" on breech tang.

Operating the Greene carbine's breech mechanism was accomplished by unlocking it by squeezing the forward trigger and manually twisting the barrel sleeve, and then pushing the barrel forward and manually rotating it to the right, exposing the breech for loading. The carbine had a round, blued barrel, blade front sight and long-range rear sight, blued receiver, and brass patch box on side of butt stock.

A variant made for export to England had an overall length of 34-3/8", 18" barrel, weight of 7 lbs. 8 oz., and, in addition to the aforementioned markings, a crown over "VxR" on the lock plate to rear of the hammer, as well as British proof marks and numbers on the butt stock. There is no evidence that the British Type Greene carbines were used in the Civil War.

GOOD—$5,000   FINE—$15,500

*Rock Island
Auction Company*

GWYN & CAMPBELL CARBINE, TYPE I, .52 CALIBER, PAPER AND LINEN CARTRIDGE, PERCUSSION

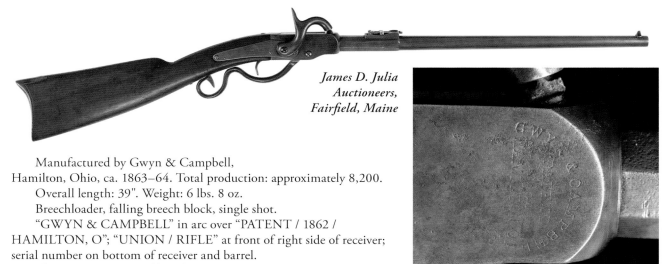

James D. Julia Auctioneers, Fairfield, Maine

Manufactured by Gwyn & Campbell,
Hamilton, Ohio, ca. 1863–64. Total production: approximately 8,200.
  Overall length: 39". Weight: 6 lbs. 8 oz.
  Breechloader, falling breech block, single shot.
  "GWYN & CAMPBELL" in arc over "PATENT / 1862 /
HAMILTON, O"; "UNION / RIFLE" at front of right side of receiver;
serial number on bottom of receiver and barrel.
  The Gwyn & Campbell Carbine, Type I (also sometimes called the
Union Carbine or Grapevine Carbine had a patented falling breech mechanism actuated by an intricately curved operating
lever that also served as a trigger and locking latch guard. Other features that distinguished this type from the Type II were
rounded hammers, a pointed lever-locking latch, and a barrel that was 1/2" longer than the Type II. Features common
to both types were a browned, rounded barrel with octagonal section at the breech, long-range rear sight, 16"-long black
walnut butt stock, and flat lock plate with beveled edge.

GOOD—$1,250   FINE—$2,750

GWYN & CAMPBELL CARBINE, TYPE II, .52 CALIBER, PAPER AND LINEN CARTRIDGE, PERCUSSION

Manufactured by Gwyn & Campbell, Hamilton, Ohio, ca. 1863–64. Total production: approximately 8,200.
  Overall length: 38-1/2". Weight: approximately 6 lbs. 8 oz.
  Breechloader, falling breech block, single shot.
  "GWYN & CAMPBELL" in arc over "PATENT / 1862 / HAMILTON, O"; "UNION / RIFLE" at front of right side
of receiver; serial number on bottom of receiver and barrel.

GOOD—$1,200   FINE—$2,750

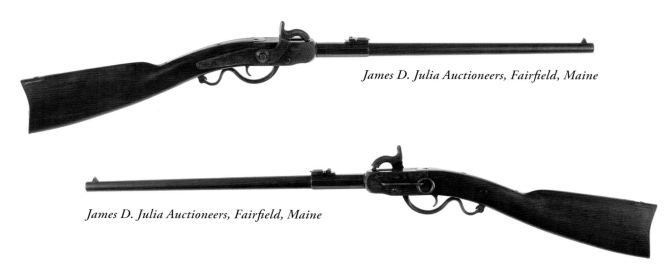

James D. Julia Auctioneers, Fairfield, Maine

James D. Julia Auctioneers, Fairfield, Maine

JENKS CARBINE (AMES), .54 CALIBER, LOOSE POWDER AND BALL OR PAPER CARTRIDGE AND BALL, PERCUSSION

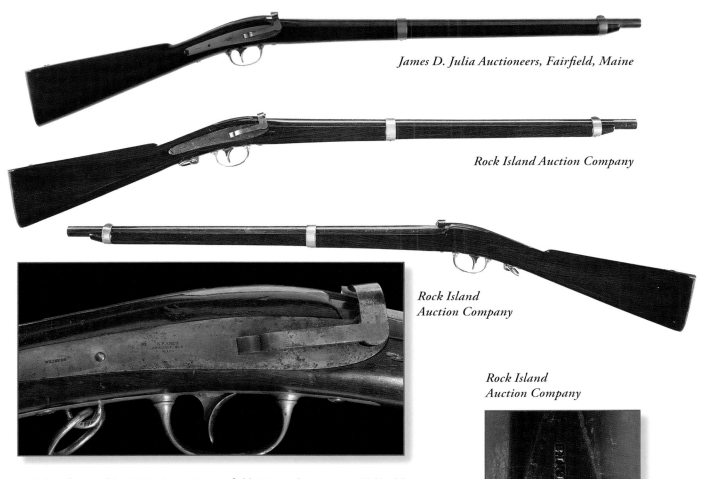

James D. Julia Auctioneers, Fairfield, Maine

Rock Island Auction Company

Rock Island Auction Company

Rock Island Auction Company

Manufactured by N. P. Ames, Springfield, Massachusetts, ca. 1841–46. Total production: Approximately 4,250.

Overall length: 41". Weight: 6 lbs.

Breechloader, sliding breech bolt, single shot.

"N. P. AMES / SPRINGFIELD / MASS" at center of lock plate; "WM JENKS / USN (or "USR") / [inspector's initials, JCB, JL, RC, or RP] / P / [year]" on top of breech; inspector's initials within cartouche on left side of stock near breech; serial numbers on major parts.

The Jenks Carbine featured a sliding breech block actuated by a top lever, patented by William Jenks in 1838. Ignition was by a percussion cap struck by a "mule ear" side hammer. The 24-1/2" round barrel was rifled with six grooves and browned with lacquer; some late-production units had a small, fixed rear sight screwed to the top of the breech. All furniture bright brass, including two barrel bands, each screwed to the bottom of the stock. To the rear of the trigger guard bow was a sling ring.

EASTMAN ALTERATION:

Arthur M. Eastman bought a large consignment of Jenks-Ames carbines from the U. S. Navy in 1861 and had alterations made to them, to include altering the round loading aperture to oval, rifling the bores with six narrow grooves, milling a v-groove into the breech cover to serve as the rear sight, and mounting a sling ring on the trigger guard.

STANDARD MODEL: GOOD—$1,250   FINE—$3,500

EASTMAN ALTERATION: GOOD—$1,000   FINE—$2,750

*James D. Julia
Auctioneers,
Fairfield, Maine*

JENKS-REMINGTON CARBINE, .54 CALIBER, PAPER CARTRIDGE AND BALL, PERCUSSION

Manufactured by E. Remington & Son, Herkimer, New York, 1847–48. Total production: approximately 1,000.

Overall length: 41". Weight: 6 lbs.

Breechloader, sliding breech bolt, single shot.

"REMINGTON'S / HERKIMER / N.Y." on lock plate; "WM JENKS / USN / RC / P / [year]" on top of breech ("CAST STEEL" between "P" and year on some specimens); inspector's initials on left side of stock near breech.

The Jenks-Remington Carbine was manufactured by E. Remington & Son using the same machinery that N. P. Ames had used to make the Jenks Carbine. The Remington version was similar to the Ames, with the exceptions of different markings and the inclusion of a Maynard tape priming device as the ignition system. Although the U.S. Navy used many of these carbines in the Mexican War, it is unclear how many saw service in the Civil War.

EASTMAN ALTERATION:

In 1861, Arthur M. Eastman bought a substantial quantity of the U. S. Navy's Jenks-Remington carbines and had alterations made to them, including rifling the bores with six narrow grooves, converting the round loading aperture to oval, milling a V-groove in the breech cover to serve as a rear sight, and attaching a sling ring to the trigger guard.

STANDARD MODEL: GOOD—$1,450   **FINE—$4,000**
EASTMAN ALTERATION: GOOD—$1,250   **FINE—$3,750**

JENKS-MERRILL CARBINE, .54 CALIBER, LINEN CARTRIDGE, PERCUSSION

Altered by James H. Merrill, Baltimore, Maryland, ca. 1858–60. Total production: Approximately 300.

Overall length: 41". Weight: 6 lbs. 2 oz.

Breechloader, sliding breech bolt, single shot.

"J. H. MERRIL BALTO. / PAT. JULY 1858" or "JAS. H. MERRILL / BALTO. PATENTED / JULY 1858" on top of breech lever; "WM JENKS / USN (or "USR") / RC / P / [year]" on top of breech.

The Jenks-Merrill carbine was similar to the Ames-manufactured Jenks carbines, with several modifications. Most conspicuously, there was a new back-action hammer and vertical percussion cap nipple, instead of the mule-ear hammer and horizontal nipple of the Ames version. The Merrill alteration was made to specimens with round loading apertures, and the alteration included plugging the aperture, with loading now to be done through the rear of the breech. The alteration also included a new, casehardened breech lever patented by Merrill. It had at the front an oval catch that latched to the rear of the long-range rear sight.

GOOD—$3,000   **FINE—$7,000**

JOSLYN CARBINE MODEL 1855, .54 CALIBER, PAPER CARTRIDGE, PERCUSSION

James D. Julia Auctioneers, Fairfield, Maine

Manufactured by A. H. Waters & Company, Milbury, Massachusetts, ca. 1855–56. Total production: Approximately 1,200.

Overall length: 38-1/4". Weight: 7 lbs. 4 oz.

Breechloader, hinged breech bolt, single shot.

"A. H. WATERS & CO. / MILBURY MASS" on lock plate to front of hammer; "PATD BY / B. F. JOSLYN. / AUG. 23, 1855" on operating lever; serial number on left side of breech lever; inspector's initials on stock opposite lock.

The Joslyn Carbine Model 1855 included a patented breech mechanism operated by half-cocking the hammer and sliding forward a ring at the rear of the lever, allowing the shooter to lift the operating lever/breech block. The carbines had a round, 21" blued barrel with three rifling grooves; bright brass furniture except for a blued iron swivel ring and bar on the left side; single barrel band; and casehardened breech, breech lever, and lock.

GOOD—$2,500   FINE—$5,000

JOSLYN CARBINE MODEL 1862, .52 CALIBER, RIMFIRE CARTRIDGE

Rock Island Auction Company

Manufactured by Joslyn Fire Arms Company, Stonington, Connecticut, ca. 1862. Total production: approximately 3,500.

Overall length: 38-7/8". Weight: 6 lbs. 10 oz.

Breechloader, pivoting breech block, single shot.

"JOSLYN FIRE ARMS CO / STONINGTON, CONN." on lock plate to front of hammer; "B.F. JOSLYN'S PATENT / OCTOBER 8TH 1861 / JUNE 24TH 1862" over serial number on top of breech block; serial number on breech tang; inspector's initials on left side of stock opposite lock.

The Joslyn Carbine Model 1862 featured a pivoting breech block with a hook-style friction latch and an exposed firing pin extension on its rear face. The round, blued, 22" barrel was rifled with three broad grooves and mounted with a front blade sight and two-leaf long-range rear sight. All furniture was bright brass, including a single oval barrel band; the lock plate was casehardened. A few early-production examples were percussion, with cap nipple in the rear face of the breech block. Some later, transitional units had Model 1864-type breech blocks.

GOOD—$1,250   FINE—$3,000

JOSLYN CARBINE MODEL 1864, .52 CALIBER, RIMFIRE CARTRIDGE

Manufactured by Joslyn Fire Arms Company, Stonington, Connecticut, ca. 1864–65. Total production: Approximately 12,500.

Overall length: 38-7/8". Weight: 6 lbs. 10 oz.

Breechloader, pivoting breech block, single shot.

"JOSLYN FIRE ARMS CO / STONINGTON CONN. / 1864" on lock plate to front of hammer; "B.F. JOSLYN'S PATENT / OCTOBER 8TH 1861 / JUNE 24TH 1862" on rear face of breech block; serial number on breech tang; inspector's initials on left stock opposite lock.

In addition to different markings, the 1864 Model of the Joslyn Carbine varied from the 1862 Model in that all furniture was casehardened iron (as opposed to all brass on the Model 1862 version), and the pivoting breech block had a knurled, spring operated catch and a protective circular guard around the firing pin extension. There are also variations within the Model 1864 carbines, including different Calibers (including .44 and .58 rimfire) and barrel lengths.

GOOD—$1,200   **FINE—$2,750**

Rock Island Auction Company

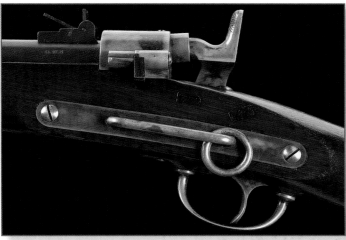

KEEN, WALKER & CO. CARBINE, .54 CALIBER, PAPER CARTRIDGE, PERCUSSION

Made by Keen, Walker & Co., Danville, Virginia, ca. 1862. Total production: Fewer than 300.

Overall length: 40".

Breechloader, tilting breech, single shot.

The only marking is a "P" on the breech barrel.

Produced on contract with the C.S. Government with either a blued or browned barrel, the brass or bronze frame carbine is externally quite similar to the U.S. Maynard carbine. As the lever is lowered, the breech block tilts upwards allowing the operator to slip in a paper cartridge. A percussion cap placed on a cone ignites the charge. A ring on a bar on the left side of the stock permits the carbine to be carried on a wide, over-the-shoulder cavalry sling.

GOOD—$15,000   **FINE—$30,000**

James D. Julia Auctioneers, Fairfield, Maine

Collection of Frank Reile, photo by Alya Alberico

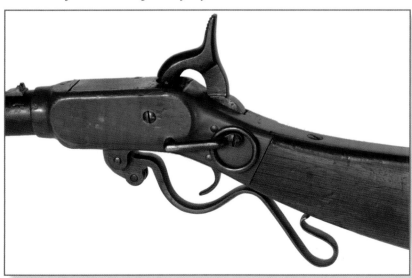

Collection of Frank Reile, photo by Alya Alberico

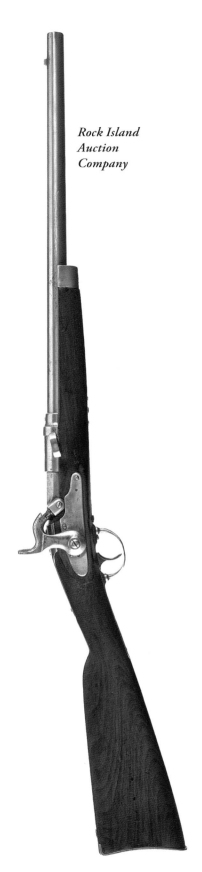

*Rock Island
Auction
Company*

LINDNER CARBINE, TYPE I, .58 CALIBER, PAPER CARTRIDGE, PERCUSSION

Manufactured by Edward Lindner / Amoskeag Manufacturing Company, Manchester, New Hampshire, ca. 1861–62. Total production: 501.

Overall length: 38-3/4". Weight: 6 lbs.

Breechloader, hinged breech block, single shot.

"EDWARD LINDNER'S / PATENT / MARCH 29, 1859" on top of breech block (some examples had no markings).

The Lindner Carbine, Type I, incorporated a patented breech mechanism whereby a locking collar was rotated, allowing the spring-actuated, hinged breech block to swing up for forward loading. The carbine had a round barrel rifled with three grooves, bright iron furniture, sling ring on the left side of the stock opposite the lock, and two-leaf rear sight on the breech tang. Lindner delivered 501 Type I carbines to the U.S. government in November 1862.

GOOD—$2,500   FINE—$5,000

LINDNER CARBINE, TYPE II, .58 CALIBER, PAPER CARTRIDGE, PERCUSSION

Manufactured by Edward Lindner / Amoskeag Manufacturing Company, Manchester, New Hampshire ca. 1863–64. Total production: Approximately 6,000.

Overall length: 38-3/4". Weight: 6 lbs.

Breechloader, hinged breech block, single shot.

"U [spread eagle] S / AMOSKEAG MFG CO / MANCHESTER, N.H." to front of lock plate; year to rear of lock plate; "EDWARD LINDNER'S / PATENT / MARCH 29, 1859" on top of breech block.

The Lindner Carbine, Type II, was similar to the Type I carbine of the same manufacturer, with exceptions including: markings stamped on the lock plate; differently shaped lock plate and stock; rear sight positioned to front of breech block; and sling ring mounted to the rear of the trigger guard bow. The U.S. Ordnance Department ordered 6,000 of these carbines in April 1863 but refused to accept delivery; ten years later, the carbines were sold to France.

GOOD—$2,250   FINE—$3,000

MAYNARD CARBINE, TYPE I, .35 AND .50 CALIBER, COPPER CARTRIDGE, PERCUSSION

Manufactured by the Massachusetts Arms Company, Chicopee Falls, Massachusetts, ca. 1858–59. Total production: approximately 5,000.

Overall length: 36-1/2". Weight: 6 lbs.

Breechloader, hinged barrel, single shot.

"MANUFACTURED BY / MASS. ARMS CO. / CHICOPEE FALLS" on left side of receiver; "MAYNARD ARMS CO. / WASHINGTON" on right side of receiver; "MAYNARD PATENTEE / MAY 27, 1851 / JUNE 17, 1856" on patch box cover; inspector's initials on top of stock to rear of breech tang; inspector's and subinspector's initials inside patch box of some examples.

The Maynard Carbine, Type I, was produced with .35- and .50-caliber barrels that were 20" in length, with a 5" octagonal section at the breech. Loading was accomplished by lowering the trigger guard/operating lever, which caused the hinged barrel to tilt downward, exposing the breech for loading. The carbine incorporated a Maynard tape priming device. Furniture was iron. A tang sight was mounted on the stock to the rear of the breech, and some late examples had a sling ring on the underside of the stock. The manufacturer sold many units of this carbine to several Southern states immediately before the start of the Civil War, and it was considered an official CSA firearm.

GOOD—$2,250   FINE—$5,500

MAYNARD CARBINE, TYPE II, .50 CALIBER, COPPER CARTRIDGE, PERCUSSION

Manufactured by the Massachusetts Arms Company, Chicopee Falls, Massachusetts, ca. 1863–65. Total production: approximately 20,200.

Overall length: 36-7/8". Weight: approximately 6 lbs.

Breechloader, hinged barrel, single shot.

"MANUFACTURED BY / MASS. ARMS CO. / CHICOPEE FALLS" on right side of receiver; "EDWARD MAYNARD / PATENTEE / MAY 27, 1851 / DEC. 6, 1859" on left side of receiver; serial number on underside of barrel; inspector markings on left side of stock.

The Maynard Carbine, Type II, varied from the Type I in the following respects: The Type II had a percussion nipple instead of the Maynard tape priming device. The rear tang sight and patch box were omitted. The Type II was offered in .50 caliber only. And, a sling ring and rod were mounted on the left side of the receiver.

GOOD—$1,150   FINE—$2,750

*James D. Julia
Auctioneers,
Fairfield, Maine*

*James D. Julia
Auctioneers,
Fairfield, Maine*

MERRILL CARBINE, TYPE I, .54 CALIBER, PERCUSSION, COMBUSTIBLE CARTRIDGE

Made by J. H. Merrill, Merrill Patent Firearms Company, Baltimore, Maryland, ca. 1861–63. Total production: Unknown, but several thousand at least.

Overall Length: 37-3/8". Weight: 6 lbs. 8 oz.

Breechloading, sliding breech block, single shot.

"J.H. MERRILL BALTO. / PAT. JULY 1858 / APL. 9 MAY 21–28–61" on lock plate to front of hammer; "J.H. MERRILL BALTO. / PAT. JULY 1858" on top of breech lever; serial number on lock plate to rear of hammer; inspector's initials on stock opposite lock.

The Merrill Carbine, Type I, had a 22-1/8" round, blued (or bright) barrel, rifled with three grooves. Loading was accomplished by unlatching and lifting the breech lever, which caused the copper-faced breech block to slide back, exposing the breech. The carbine took a paper, foil, or rubber cartridge. All furniture was bright brass, including a single, oval barrel band and patch box. A few specimens have tinned metal, probably for naval use, and some browned barrels have been noted.

GOOD—$1,250   **FINE—$3,750**

James D. Julia Auctioneers, Fairfield, Maine

James D. Julia Auctioneers, Fairfield, Maine

James D. Julia Auctioneers, Fairfield, Maine

MERRILL CARBINE, TYPE II, .54 CALIBER, PERCUSSION, COMBUSTIBLE CARTRIDGE

Made by J. H. Merrill, Merrill Patent Firearms Company, Baltimore, Maryland, ca. 1861–63. Total production: Approximately 14,500.

Overall Length: 37-3/8". Weight: 6 lbs. 8 oz.

Breechloading, sliding breech block, single shot.

"J.H. MERRILL BALTO. / PAT. JULY 1858 / APL. 9 MAY 21–28–61" on lock plate to front of hammer; eagle to center of lock plate; year on lock plate to rear of hammer; "J.H. MERRILL BALTO. / PAT. JULY 1858" on breech lever; inspector's initials on stock opposite lock.

The Merrill Carbine, Type II, was similar to the Type I, except for the markings, as noted above. In addition, the Type II lacked the patch box (except in a few very early examples) and had a different rear sight, different shaped stock (the fore-end being fuller and rounder), and different latch on the breech-operating lever.

GOOD—$1,400   **FINE—$4,000**

Rock Island Auction Company

Inspector's cartouche on Type II Merrill carbine. Rock Island Auction Company

MERRILL, LATROBE & THOMAS CARBINE, .58 CALIBER, PERCUSSION, PAPER CARTRIDGE

Made by S. Remington, Ilion, New York, ca. 1855. Total production: Approximately 170.

Overall Length: 38". Weight: 7 lbs.

Breechloading, single shot.

"S. REMINGTON / ILION, NY" to rear of lock plate; "MERRILL, LATROBE & THOMAS / BALTIMORE, MD. / PATENT APPLIED FOR" on top of receiver; serial number on underside of breech lever.

The Merrill, Latrobe & Thomas Carbine featured a patented breech mechanism with an operating lever pivoted to the left side of the receiver and a sliding rammer housed in the wrist of the stock. All furniture was bright brass, including the single barrel band and patch box. The 21" barrel, rifled with three grooves, was round and blued. The stock was black walnut, 25" long. The carbine had a Maynard tape primer box to the front of the hammer.

GOOD—$12,500   **FINE—$35,00**

*James D. Julia
Auctioneers,
Fairfield, Maine*

U.S. MODEL 1833 HALL-NORTH CARBINE, .52 AND .58 CALIBER, COMBUSTIBLE CARTRIDGE, PERCUSSION

Manufactured by Simeon North, Middletown, Connecticut, 1834–39. Total production: 7,163.

Overall length: 45". Weight: 8 lbs. 3 oz.

Breechloader, hinged receiver, single shot.

"U.S. / S. NORTH / MIDLTN / CONN. / [year]" on top of receiver (examples marked "S. NORTH" on receiver are rare, while examples with gold medallion with "S. NORTH / MIDDLETOWN" are exceedingly rare); inspector's initials on right frame.

The U.S. Model 1833 Hall-North carbine was the first percussion firearm to be officially adopted by any military service in the world. Manufactured under contract by Simeon North and based on Hall's patented design, the carbines featured a rear-hinged receiver that pivoted upward for front loading once a spur latch (which included a sliding safety catch) to the front of the trigger was released. The smoothbore, round, 26-3/16" barrel was fastened to the walnut stock by two bands. An implement box was fitted into the lower side of the butt stock. The barrel and furniture were finished with brown lacquer, except for the casehardened receiver. The nipple was mounted directly on the receiver, without a bolster. A sling ring was mounted toward the rear of the trigger plate; the plate had two ridges to the rear of the guard. Also included was a 25-1/4" combination ramrod and bayonet enclosed in the forward part of the stock.

Two basic types existed:

.58 Caliber: In 1834, 1,028 were produced, most of which went to the 1st U.S. Dragoons at Fort Gibson, Arkansas Territory.

.52 Caliber: From about 1836 to 1839, 6,135 of this Caliber were manufactured, with most going to the 2nd U.S. Dragoons in Florida, and a special run of 100 units sent to a Mobile, Alabama, militia unit (these are numbered from 1 to 100 at the top rear of the breech block and lack U.S. inspector's marks.

.58 CALIBER: GOOD—$2,750   FINE—$7,000
.52 CALIBER: GOOD—$2,000   FINE—$4,500

U.S. MODEL 1836 HALL CARBINE, TYPES I AND II, .64 CALIBER, COMBUSTIBLE CARTRIDGE, PERCUSSION

Manufactured by Harper's Ferry Armory, 1837–40. Total production: 2,020.
Overall length: 43". Weight: 7 lbs. 12 oz.
Breechloader, hinged receiver, single shot.
"J. H. Hall / U.S. / [year]" on top of receiver.

The U.S. Model 1836 Hall Carbine was produced for the 2nd U.S. Dragoons and was similar to the U.S. Model 1833 Hall-North Carbine, with some exceptions, including but not limited to: The smoothbore barrel was .64 caliber. The shank of the hammer featured a prominent round hole. The sling ring, actually an eye bolt, was on the left side of the wrist of the stock. The bands were secured to the stock by pins. The receiver's spur latch lacked the sliding safety. The nipple was mounted on a bolster. And, the barrel was 23" long.

Two basic types existed, with minor variations in the stocks and barrel diameters, and:

Type I: Manufactured before 1836; lacked the implement box in butt stock.

Type II: Made from 1839 to 1840; included the implement box.

BOTH TYPES: GOOD—$1,750 FINE—$4,000

James D. Julia Auctioneers, Fairfield, Maine

James D. Julia Auctioneers, Fairfield, Maine

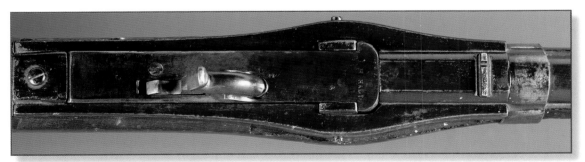

James D. Julia Auctioneers,
Fairfield, Maine

U.S. MODEL 1840 HALL-NORTH CARBINE, TYPES I AND II, .52 CALIBER, COMBUSTIBLE CARTRIDGE, PERCUSSION

Amoskeag Auction Company, Inc.

Manufactured by Simeon North, Middletown, Connecticut, 1840–43. Total production: 6,501.

Overall length: 40". Weight: 7 lbs. 12 oz.

Breechloader, hinged receiver, single shot.

"U.S. / S. NORTH / MIDLTN / CONN. / [year]" on top of receiver.

This carbine was similar to the U.S. Model 1833 Hall-North carbine, .52 Caliber, except the 1840 model had a shorter, 21" barrel and a buttonhead ramrod. The implement box was eliminated in all but a few examples. In addition, the spur-type latch of the 1833 model was eliminated in favor of two styles of operating levers, according to the two types of the 1840 model carbine:

Type I: An L, or elbow-shaped operating lever was mounted on the front of the trigger plate. In 1840, 500 units of this type were delivered, making it the rarest of Hall breechloaders.

Type II: From 1840 to 1843, 6,001 units were manufactured, featuring a fishtail-shaped breech lever. Some late-

James D. Julia Auctioneers, Fairfield, Maine

production examples had an 8-1/2" sling bar and ring on the left side, attached to the lower band and rear of the frame, with the resulting elimination of the lower barrel-band spring.

TYPE I: GOOD—$3,750   FINE—$7,000

TYPE II: GOOD—$1,750   FINE—$3,750

U.S. MODEL 1842 HALL CARBINE, .52 CALIBER, COMBUSTIBLE CARTRIDGE, PERCUSSION

Manufactured by Harpers Ferry Armory, ca. 1842–43. Total production: 1,001.

Overall length: 40". Weight: 8 lbs. 3 oz.

Breechloader, hinged receiver, single shot.

"H. FERRY / US / 1842" on top of receiver.

This, the last carbine to be produced by Harpers Ferry Arsenal, was similar to the U.S. Model 1840 Hall Carbine, Type II, except that it had bright-finished brass furniture. The entire production run was issued to the 1st U.S. Dragoons.

GOOD—$4,750   FINE—$8,750

U.S. MODEL 1843 HALL-NORTH CARBINE, .52 CALIBER SMOOTHBORE, COMBUSTIBLE CARTRIDGE, PERCUSSION

Manufactured by Simeon North, Middletown, Connecticut, 1844–53. Total production: 10,500.

Overall length: 40". Weight: 8 lbs. 4 oz.

Breechloader, hinged receiver, single shot.

"U.S. / S. NORTH / MIDLTN / CONN. / [year]" on top of receiver; "STEEL" stamped on the barrel to rear of rear sight on post-1848 examples; sub-inspector markings on barrel near breech; inspector mark "WAT" on right cheek piece of some stocks.

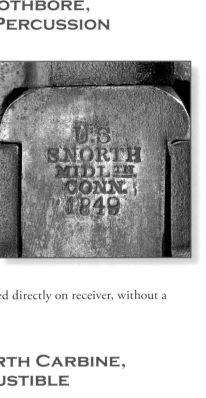

This model of Hall-North carbine featured a thumb lever for operating the breech block apparatus on the right side of the frame. The carbine had a 21" round barrel, two barrel bands, lacquer-browned finish on barrel and furniture, casehardened breech, and nipple mounted directly on receiver, without a bolster.

GOOD—$1,500   FINE—$3,250

U.S. MODEL 1843 HALL-NORTH CARBINE, .58 CALIBER RIFLED, COMBUSTIBLE CARTRIDGE, PERCUSSION

Originally manufactured by Simeon North, Middletown, Connecticut, 1844–53; converted to .58-Caliber rifled by W. W. Marston, New York City, 1861. Total conversions: 5,000.

Overall length: 40". Weight: 8 lbs. 4 oz.

Breechloader, hinged receiver, single shot.

Markings presumably the same as the U.S. Model 1843 Hall-North Carbine, .52 Caliber smoothbore.

In August 1861, Gen. John C. Frémont purchased from a private contractor 5,000 unused U.S. Model 1843 Hall-North carbines, which W. W. Marston of New York had recently converted from .52-caliber smoothbore to .58-Caliber rifled. It later developed that the carbines had been purchased from the New York arsenal for $3.50 apiece and resold, after being rifled, to Frémont for a $19 markup. A government corruption investigation followed, and was in part the reason for Frémont's removal from command.

GOOD—$1,500   FINE—$3,250

Rock Island Auction Company

MORSE CARBINE, .50 CALIBER, METALLIC CENTERFIRE CARTRIDGE

Made by State Military Works, Greenville, South Carolina, 1864. Total production: Approximately 1,000 of all types. Overall length: 40".

Breechloader, tilting breech, single shot.

Serial number stamped on bottom of frame. Very late production examples marked "MORSE" on the right frame plate.

James D. Julia Auctioneers, Fairfield, Maine

James D. Julia Auctioneers, Fairfield, Maine

Type I: The latching mechanism depends on a moveable iron rod inside the brass operating lever. This rod also functions as the firing pin. Barrels on Type I carbines may be part octagon or all round. The sides of the breech lever have three, deep-cut indentations. Probably less than 200 produced.

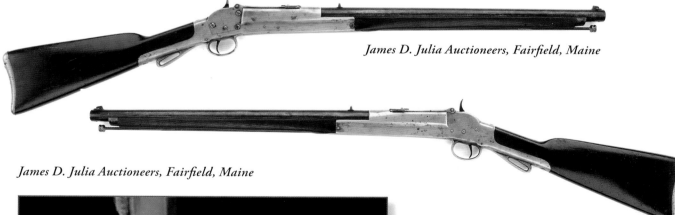

James D. Julia Auctioneers, Fairfield, Maine

James D. Julia Auctioneers, Fairfield, Maine

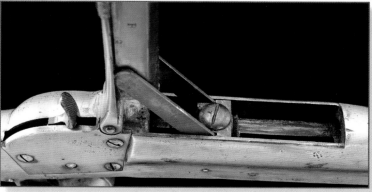

Type II: The latching mechanism incorporates a flanged, iron rod in a channel in the operating lever above the moveable iron rod found on Type I carbines. This flanged rod is attached to an iron plate with knurled front edge that cover the top portion of the operating lever. The action is locked by the latch when it engages the bolt head on the breechblock. Serial number range is from about 200 to 350.

Type III: The same latching mechanism as the Type II except that the forward end of the flanged rod has a broad, flat projecting flange that extends beneath the knurled iron plate. The sliding breechblock is made of iron instead of brass or bronze.

Morse carbines were issued primarily to South Carolina militia troops, perhaps accounting for the relatively high survival rate. Nevertheless, the Morse carbine is a fixture of Confederate small arms history.

TYPE I: GOOD—$10,250   FINE—$29,000
TYPE II: GOOD—$9,000   FINE—$26,000
TYPE III: GOOD—$8,500   FINE—$20,000

James D. Julia Auctioneers, Fairfield, Maine

James D. Julia Auctioneers, Fairfield, Maine

Collection of William C. Weber

Collection of William C. Weber

PERRY MILITARY CARBINE .54 CALIBER, PAPER OR LINEN CARTRIDGE, PERCUSSION

Manufactured by the Perry Patent Arms Company, Newark, New Jersey, ca. 1855–57. Total production: Approximately 200.

Overall length: 39". Weight: approximately 7 lbs.

Breechloader, pivoting breech block, single shot.

Numerous variations of maker's marks on breech blocks and receivers, such as "PERRY PATENT ARMS CO.", "PERRY'S PATENTED ARM", "A.D. PERRY / PATENTED", "PERRY PATENTED ARMS / NEWARK, N.J.", etc.; serial number on top of barrel near receiver and on top of receiver.

The Perry Carbine featured a pivoting breech block, operated by an integral trigger assembly/lever which, when pushed down and forward, tilted the breech block up, exposing the chamber for loading. The carbine also included a patented percussion cap magazine in the butt stock, which fed caps onto the nipple. The furniture was blued iron, with casehardened receiver. Earliest specimens included a brass patch box in the butt stock and/or a sling ring on the left side of the receiver (production carbines lacked a sling ring); in addition, the receiver was shorter than that of the production carbine. Perry also manufactured a sporting version of this carbine.

GOOD—$3,000   FINE—$7,000

REMINGTON CARBINE .46 CALIBER, RIMFIRE CARTRIDGE, PERCUSSION

Rock Island Auction Company

Rock Island Auction Company

Manufactured by E. Remington & Sons, Ilion, New York, ca. 1864-65. Total production: approximately 5,000.

Overall length: 34-1/8". Weight: approximately 7 lbs.

Breechloader, split breech block, single shot.

"REMINGTON'S ILION, N.Y. / PAT. DEC. 23, 1863 MAY 3 & NOV. 16, 1864" on breech tang; serial number on underside of barrel near receiver; inspector's initials on left side of butt stock.

The Remington Carbine .46 caliber, also known as the "Split Breech Remington," featured a split-block breech mechanism, an early version of the rolling block. It had a blued, 20" round barrel, rifled with three grooves. Other features included a two-piece black walnut stock; iron furniture, including a single oval barrel band secured by a spring on the underside of the fore stock; and iron-blade front sight and single-leaf folding rear sight. A .56-50 rimfire version of the carbine was manufactured, but was delivered too late to for service in the Civil War.

GOOD—$1,250   FINE—$5,000

SHARPS MODEL 1851 CARBINE, TYPE I, .52 CALIBER, PAPER OR LINEN CARTRIDGE

Manufactured by Robbins & Lawrence, Windsor, Vermont, for Sharps Rifle Manufacturing Co., Hartford, Connecticut, ca. 1852–55. Total production: approximately 1,457.

Overall length: 37-3/8". Weight: 7 lbs.

Breechloader, falling breech block, single shot.

"ROBBINS / & / LAWRENCE" on barrel; "C. SHARPS / PATENT / 1848" and serial number on breech tang; "EDWARD MAYNARD / PATENTEE / 1845" on tape primer door; serial number on breech block; martial specimens with "U.S. / S.P.K." and "U.S. / 1852" on heel of butt plate (U.S. Dragoons), or "USN" with small, 5-pointed star between each letter, on heel of butt plate (U.S. Navy).

The Sharps Model 1851 Carbine, Type I, featured a 21-5/8" round, bright-finished barrel with a .52-caliber bore and rifled with six grooves. It incorporated the patented Maynard tape primer system. The base of the hammer was enclosed within the lock, and a spring set in the fore stock retained the operating lever pin. Some examples had a 9" sling ring bar attached to the left side of the barrel band and the left side of the frame. All furniture was brass, including the patch box found on some specimens. Some 175 stands were issued to the 1st and 2nd U.S. Dragoons in Texas and New Mexico in the mid-1850s, while 60 were delivered to the U.S. Navy in 1853. The dragoon- and navy-issued carbines had extra markings, as noted above.

GOOD—$7,000   **FINE—$20,000**

Amoskeag Auction Company, Inc.

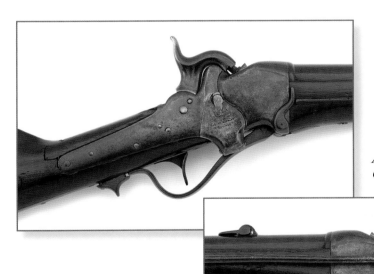

Amoskeag Auction Company, Inc.

Rock Island Auction Company

SHARPS MODEL 1851 CARBINE, TYPE II (SPORTING), .36, .44, AND .52 CALIBER, PAPER OR LINEN CARTRIDGE

James D. Julia Auctioneers, Fairfield, Maine

Manufactured by Robbins & Lawrence, Windsor, Vermont, for Sharps Rifle Manufacturing Co., Hartford, Connecticut, ca. 1852–55. Total production: approximately 400.

Overall length: 37-3/8", or other, according to barrel length. Weight: approximately 7 lbs.

Breechloader, falling breech block, single shot.

"SHARPS' RIFLE / MANUFG CO. / HARTFORD, CONN" on top of barrel; "C. SHARPS / PATENT / 1848" and serial number on breech tang; "EDWARD MAYNARD / PATENTEE / 1845" on tape primer door; serial number on breech block.

Sharps manufactured a sporting version of its Model 1851 carbine, with browned or blued barrel, round or octagonal, in .36, .44, and .52 caliber. Lacking the sling ring bar of the Model 1851 Type I carbine to hold the barrel band in place, the Type II's band was screwed to the fore stock. Some examples had blued and engraved frames.

GOOD—$4,000 **FINE—$10,000**

SHARPS MODEL 1852 CARBINE, TYPE I, .52 CALIBER, PAPER OR LINEN CARTRIDGE

James D. Julia Auctioneers, Fairfield, Maine

Manufactured by Robbins & Lawrence, Windsor, Vermont, for Sharps Rifle Manufacturing Co., Hartford, Connecticut, ca. 1853–55. Total production: 4,400.

Overall length: 37-5/8". Weight: approximately 7 lbs. 10 oz.

Breechloader, falling breech block, single shot.

"C. SHARPS / PATENT / 1848" and serial number on breech tang; "C. SHARPS / PATENT / 1848" on lock plate to rear of hammer; U.S. Army-purchased specimens stamped with "U.S. / J.H." or "U.S. / S.K.P." on top of barrel; U.S. Navy specimens with "USN" with small, 5-pointed star between each letter, on heel of butt plate.

The Sharps Model 1852 Carbine, Type I, was similar to the Sharps 1851 Carbine, Type I, with the primary new distinguishing feature being the elimination of the Maynard tape primer device in favor of the "slanted-breech" pellet primer system of Sharps' own design. Type I carbines had bright-finished barrels and brass furniture. In the mid-1850s, 225 units were delivered to the U.S. Army and 150 to the U.S. Navy.

GOOD—$3,750 **FINE—$12,500**

SHARPS MODEL 1852 CARBINE, TYPE II, .36, .44, OR .52 CALIBER, PAPER OR LINEN CARTRIDGE

Rock Island Auction Company

Manufactured by Robbins & Lawrence, Windsor, Vermont, for Sharps Rifle Manufacturing Co., Hartford, Connecticut, ca. 1853–55. Total production: Approximately 600.

Overall length: approximately 37-5/8", varying with barrel length. Weight: approximately 7 lbs. 10 oz.

Breechloader, falling breech block, single shot.

"ROBBINS / & / LAWRENCE" or "SHARPS' RIFLE / MANUFG CO / HARTFORD CONN." on top of barrel; "C. SHARPS / PATENT / 1848" and serial number on breech tang; "C. SHARPS / PATENT / 1852" on lock plate to rear of hammer.

The Sharps Model 1852 Carbine, Type II, was a sporting model with browned octagonal or round barrels of different lengths. Like the Sharps Model 1852 Carbine, Type I, it eliminated the Maynard tape primer system in favor of Sharps' own pellet primer mechanism.

GOOD—$3,000   FINE—$5,500

SHARPS MODEL 1853 CARBINE, .52 CALIBER, PAPER OR LINEN CARTRIDGE

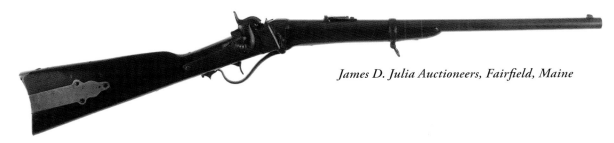

James D. Julia Auctioneers, Fairfield, Maine

Manufactured by Robbins & Lawrence, Windsor, Vermont, for Sharps Rifle Manufacturing Co., 1854–56; Sharps Rifle Manufacturing Co., Hartford, Connecticut, 1856–57. Total production: 10,500.

Overall length: 37-5/8". Weight: approximately 7 lbs. 10 oz.

Breechloader, falling breech block, single shot.

"SHARPS / PATENT / 1852" on lock plate to rear of hammer on early-production specimens, with "SHARPS" substituted by "SHARP'S" on later-production carbines; "C. SHARPS / PATENT / 1848" and serial number on breech tang; "SHARPS RIFLE / MANUFG. CO. / HARTFORD, CONN." on barrel.

The Sharps Model 1853 Carbine was similar to the Sharps Model 1852 Carbine, with the main identification point being the sprung stud on the right side of the frame to retain the operating lever pin, instead of the fore-stock-mounted spring of the Model 1852. The brass patch box gave way on later-production examples to iron, and several variations in the sling-ring rod have been observed. An estimated 250 bore U.S. inspector's stampings. Abolitionist groups shipped approximately 900 stands of the Model 1853 to "Bloody Kansas" for the use of Free Staters in the 1850s, and some of those in the 10,000–11,000 and 12,000–18,000 serial number ranges were shipped back east for the use of John Brown's raiders in their 1859 attack on Harper's Ferry.

GOOD—$2,000   FINE—$5,500

Sharps Model 1855 Carbine, Type I, .52 Caliber, Paper or Linen Cartridge

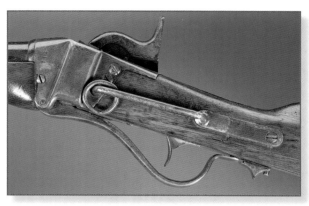

Rock Island Auction Company

Manufactured by the Sharps Rifle Manufacturing Co., Hartford, Connecticut, ca. 1856–57. Total production: approximately 701.

Overall length: 37-5/8". Weight: approximately 7 lbs. 10 oz.

Breechloader, falling breech block, single shot. "EDWARD MAYNARD / PATENTEE 1845" on tape primer door; "SHARPS / PATENT / 1848" and serial number on breech tang; "SHARPS RIFLE / MANUFG. CO. / HARTFORD, CONN." U.S. Army purchases: "US / J.H." on barrel. U.S. Navy purchases: "USN" with five-pointed star between the letters; "SCR / 1857" on finial of patch box.

The last Sharps slanting-breech carbine, the Model 1855 Carbine reverted to the Maynard tape primer system, but in most respects it was similar in design and operation to Sharps Model 1853 carbine. The Type I, or military version, had a 21-3/4" round barrel (bright or blued), brass furniture (including a patchbox), a short sling-ring bar attached to the left side of the wrist of butt stock and the frame, and, on most examples, a long rear sight with a sliding V-notch bar. The U.S. Ordnance Department obtained 600 stands of the Type I, while the U.S. Navy bought 101 (known as Type Ia). According to weapons expert Norm Flayderman, the Navy-purchased carbines had shortened, 18" barrels and .577-caliber bores.

Type Ia: Of the Navy order, 50 were equipped with the Rollin White patented cocking device. The Navy found these to be wholly ineffective and removed all but 12 from service. These 50 have the additional lock marking "R. WHITES / PATENT / 1855" behind the hammer.

Type I: Good—$7,500   Fine—$25,000
Type Ia: Good—N/A   Fine—N/A

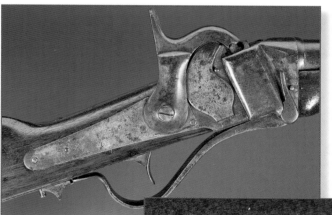

Rock Island Auction Company

SHARPS MODEL 1855 CARBINE, TYPE II, .52 CALIBER, PAPER OR LINEN CARTRIDGE

Manufactured by the Sharps Rifle Manufacturing Co., Hartford, Connecticut, ca. 1856–57. Total production: Approximately 95.

Overall length: 37-5/8". Weight: approximately 7 lbs. 10 oz.

Breechloader, falling breech block, single shot.

"EDWARD MAYNARD / PATENTEE 1845" on tape primer door; "SHARPS RIFLE / MANUFG. CO. / HARTFORD, CONN." on barrel; "SHARPS / PATENT / 1848" and serial number on breech tang.

The Sharps Model 1855 Carbine, Type II, was the civilian version, with only approximately 95 having been made. It was similar to the Type I, except without martial stampings.

GOOD—$4,750   **FINE—$14,000**

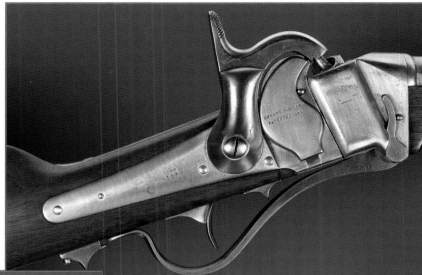

Rock Island Auction Company

SHARPS MODEL 1855 CARBINE, TYPE III, .577 CALIBER, PAPER OR LINEN CARTRIDGE

Manufactured by the Sharps Rifle Manufacturing Co., Hartford, Connecticut, ca. 1855–57. Total production: Approximately 3,000.

Overall length: approximately 37". Weight: approximately 7 lbs. 10 oz.

Breechloader, falling breech block, single shot.

"EDWARD MAYNARD / PATENTEE 1845" on tape primer door; "SHARPS RIFLE / MANUFG. CO. / HARTFORD, CONN." on barrel; "SHARPS / PATENT / 1848" and serial number on breech tang; British proof marks on the barrel and breech tang.

In 1857, 3,000 stands of the Sharps Model 1855 Carbine, Type III, were delivered to the British government. This type was similar to the Sharps Model 1855 Carbine, Type I, but with a 21" barrel, a short, four-leaf rear sight about half-way between the breech and the barrel band; brass furniture except for the iron barrel band, and British proof and inspectors' marks.

GOOD—$4,000   **FINE—$8,000**

SHARPS MODEL 1855 CARBINE, TYPE IV, .577 CALIBER, PAPER OR LINEN CARTRIDGE

Rock Island Auction Company

Manufactured by the Sharps Rifle Manufacturing Co., Hartford, Connecticut, ca. 1855–57. Total production: Approximately 3,000.

Overall length: approximately 35". Weight: approximately 7 lbs. 10 oz.

Breechloader, falling breech block, single shot.

"EDWARD MAYNARD / PATENTEE 1845" on tape primer door; "SHARPS RIFLE / MANUFG. CO. / HARTFORD, CONN." on barrel; "SHARPS / PATENT / 1848" and serial number on breech tang; British proof marks on the barrel and breech tang.

In addition to the 3,000 stands of Sharps Model 1855 Carbines, Type III, delivered to the British government in 1857, another 3,000 of the Sharps Model 1855 Carbine, Type IV, were delivered to that government the same year. It was similar to the Type III, but with a shortened barrel (18" or 19", according to different authorities). An indeterminate quantity of Type III and Type IV carbines were returned to the United States and used in the Civil War.

GOOD—$4,000   FINE—$8,000

Rock Island Auction Company

SHARPS MODEL 1859 CARBINE, .52 CALIBER, PAPER OR LINEN CARTRIDGE

Manufactured by the Sharps Rifle Manufacturing Co., Hartford, Connecticut, ca. 1859. Total production: Probably fewer than 10,000.

Overall length: 39-1/8". Weight: 7 lbs. 12 oz.

Breechloader, falling breech block, single shot.

"SHARPS RIFLE / MANUFG. CO. / HARTFORD, CONN." on barrel to front of rear sight; "C. SHARPS' PAT. / OCT. 5th 1852" on lock to rear of hammer; "R.S. LAWRENCE' PAT. / APRIL 12TH 1859" on lock above hammer; "C. SHARPS' PAT. / SEPT. 12TH 1848" on left side of frame; "R.S. LAWRENCE / PATENTED / FEB 15TH 1859" on base of rear sight; serial number on tang of breech frame.

The most prominent design change of the Sharps Model 1859 carbine over preceding models was the change from the slant breech to a "vertical" or "straight" breech and the revival of the Sharps pellet priming system last seen in the Sharps Model 1853 carbine. However, the Model 1859 had a new, patented Lawrence pellet-cutoff mechanism, permitting the use of standard percussion caps in addition to percussion pellets. Other features of the carbine included a 22" blued barrel rifled with six grooves, casehardened frame, brass furniture, and a 2-9/16" sling ring rod attached to the rear of the left side of the frame and to the butt stock.

GOOD—$2,500   FINE—$7,000

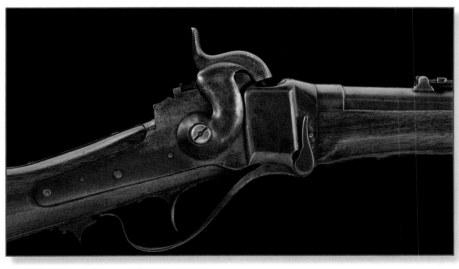

*Rock Island
Auction Company*

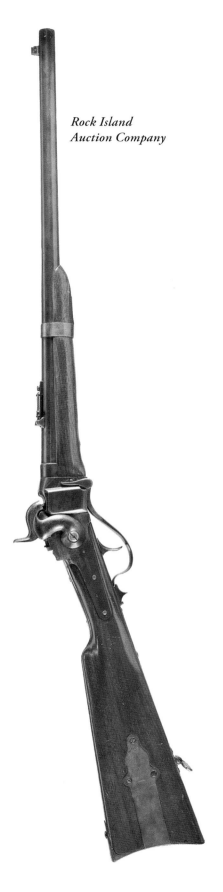

*Rock Island
Auction Company*

SHARPS NEW MODEL 1859 CARBINE, .52 CALIBER, PAPER OR LINEN CARTRIDGE

Manufactured by the Sharps Rifle Manufacturing Co., Hartford, Connecticut, ca. 1859–63. Total production: approximately 33,000.

Overall length: 39-1/8". Weight: 7 lbs. 12 oz.

Breechloader, falling breech block, single shot.

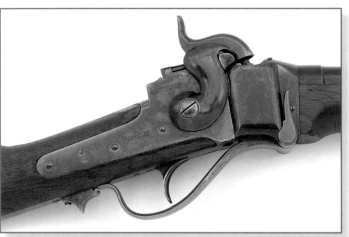

Amoskeag Auction Company, Inc.

"NEW MODEL 1859" on barrel between breech and rear sight; "SHARPS RIFLE / MANUFG. CO. / HARTFORD, CONN." on barrel to front of rear sight; "C. SHARPS' PAT. / OCT. 5th 1852" on lock to rear of hammer; "R.S. LAWRENCE' PAT. / APRIL 12TH 1859" on lock above hammer; "C. SHARPS' PAT. / SEPT. 12TH 1848" on left side of frame; "R.S. LAWRENCE / PATENTED / FEB 15TH 1859" on base of rear sight; "R.S. LAWRENCE / PATENT / DEC. 20. 1850" AND "H. CONANT / PATENT / APR. 1ST 1856" on rear face of breech block; serial number on tang of breech frame.

Amoskeag Auction Company, Inc.

Rock Island Auction Company

The Sharps New Model 1859 carbine improved the Sharps Model 1859 carbine by introducing a patented gas-check design with two ridged, friction-fitting seals on the rear face of the breech block. The improved breech block on the New Model carbine was stamped with the two Lawrence and Conant patent markings listed above. Serial numbered approximately in the 30000–75000 range.

There were two basic versions of the New Model 1859 carbine:

Early Type: About the first 3,000 stands had all brass furniture, including the patchbox. The State of Georgia purchased over half of these before the Civil War.

Late Type: Most of the production run of the New Model 1859 carbine, some 30,000 stands, had all iron furniture, including patch box. The U.S. Navy bought a few examples without the sling ring and bar in the serial number range of 40,000–44,000.

EARLY TYPE: GOOD—$2,500   FINE—$7,000
LATE TYPE: GOOD—$1,750   FINE—$3,750

Rock Island Auction Company

Rock Island Auction Company

Rock Island Auction Company

SHARPS NEW MODEL 1863 CARBINE, .52 CALIBER, PAPER OR LINEN CARTRIDGE

*Rock Island
Auction
Company*

Manufactured by the Sharps Rifle Manufacturing Co., Hartford, Connecticut, ca. 1859–63. Total production: approximately 60,000. Overall length: 39-1/8". Weight: 7 lbs. 12 oz. Breechloader, falling breech block, single shot. "NEW MODEL 1863" on barrel between breech and rear sight; "SHARPS RIFLE / MANUFG. CO. / HARTFORD, CONN." on barrel to front of rear sight; "C. SHARPS' PAT. / OCT. 5th 1852" on lock to rear of hammer; "R.S. LAWRENCE' PAT. / APRIL 12TH 1859" on lock above hammer; "C. SHARPS' PAT. / SEPT. 12TH 1848" on left side of frame; "R.S. LAWRENCE / PATENTED / FEB 15TH 1859" on base of rear sight; "R.S. LAWRENCE / PATENT / DEC. 20. 1850" AND "H. CONANT / PATENT / APR. 1ST 1856" on rear face of breech block; serial number on tang of breech frame.

The Sharps New Model 1863 carbine differed from the Sharps Model 1859 carbine by having an enlarged cleanout screw in the breech block, as well as the "NEW MODEL 1863" stamping on the barrel. Serial numbers ranged from approximately 75000 to 140000.

There were two basic versions of the Sharps New Model 1863 carbine:

Early Type: Around the first 20,000 stands had all iron furniture, including the patchbox.

*Rock Island
Auction
Company*

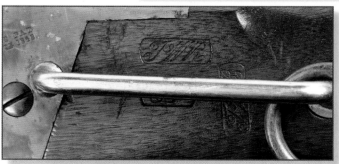

www.AdvanceGuardMilitaria.com

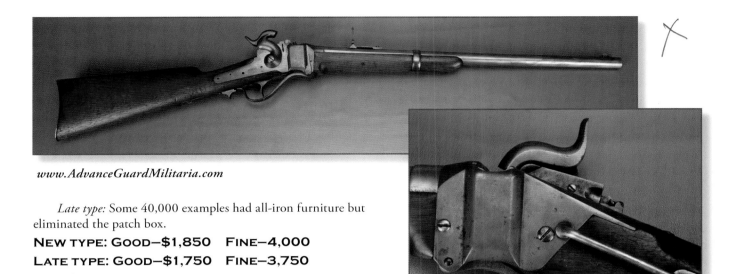

www.AdvanceGuardMilitaria.com

Late type: Some 40,000 examples had all-iron furniture but eliminated the patch box.

NEW TYPE: GOOD—$1,850   FINE—4,000
LATE TYPE: GOOD—$1,750   FINE—3,750

www.AdvanceGuardMilitaria.com

SHARPS NEW MODEL 1865 CARBINE, .52 CALIBER, PAPER OR LINEN CARTRIDGE

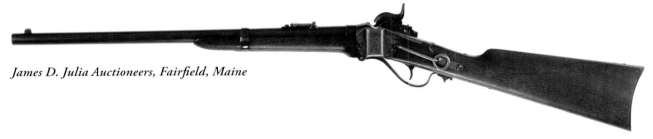

James D. Julia Auctioneers, Fairfield, Maine

Manufactured by the Sharps Rifle Manufacturing Co., Hartford, Connecticut, ca. 1865. Total production: approximately 5,000

Overall length: 39-1/8". Weight: 7 lbs. 12 oz.
Breechloader, falling breech block, single shot.
"NEW MODEL 1865" on barrel between rear sight and breech; "SHARPS RIFLE / MANUFG. CO. / HARTFORD, CONN." on barrel to front of rear sight; "C. SHARPS' PAT. / OCT. 5th 1852" on lock to rear of hammer; "R.S. LAWRENCE' PAT. / APRIL 12TH 1859" on lock above hammer; "C. SHARPS' PAT. / SEPT. 12TH 1848" on left side of frame; "R.S. LAWRENCE / PATENTED / FEB 15TH 1859" on base of rear sight; "R.S. LAWRENCE / PATENT / DEC. 20. 1850" AND "H. CONANT / PATENT / APR. 1ST 1856" on rear face of breech block; serial number on tang of breech frame.

The Sharps New Model 1865 carbine was similar to the late-production Sharps New Model 1865 carbine (i.e., no patchbox), but with the substitution of the "NEW MODEL 1865" stamping on the barrel. Serial numbered in the 140000–145000 range.

GOOD—$1,750   FINE—$4,500

James D. Julia Auctioneers, Fairfield, Maine

SHARPS & HANKINS MODEL 1862 ARMY CARBINE, .52 CALIBER, RIMFIRE CARTRIDGE

Rock Island Auction Company

Manufactured by Sharps & Hankins, Philadelphia, Pennsylvania, ca. 1862–65. Total production: 500 or more. Overall length: 38-5/8". Weight: 7 lbs. 10 oz.

Breechloader, single shot.

"SHARPS / & / HANKINS / PHILADA" on right side of frame; "SHARPS / PATENT / 1859" on left side of frame; serial number on all major parts; "P/ HKH" or an anchor stamped on leather barrel sleeve on some examples.

The Sharps & Hankins Model 1862 army carbine featured a patented breechloading mechanism involving a lever-actuated forward-sliding barrel. The 23-5/8" round, blued barrel had a breech chambered for the .52-56 Sharps & Hankins rimfire cartridge. Early-production carbines had the firing pin on the hammer; more frequently seen is the floating firing pin at the rear of the frame of later-production examples. The frame, operating lever, and hammer were casehardened; furniture was steel, except for the brass butt plate. Variations included a sling swivel under the butt stock, or no sling swivel; and a 4-1/2" fore stock secured with a single band, or, more often, no fore stock.

GOOD—$1,150   **FINE—$4,000**

SHARPS & HANKINS MODEL 1862 CAVALRY, .52 CALIBER, RIMFIRE CARTRIDGE

Manufactured by Sharps & Hankins, Philadelphia, Pennsylvania, ca. 1862–65. Total production: approximately 1,000. Overall length: 33-5/8".

Breechloader, single shot.

"SHARPS / & / HANKINS / PHILADA" on right side of frame; "SHARPS / PATENT / 1859" on left side of frame; serial number on all major parts.

212Amoskeag Auction Company, Inc.

Some 1,000 Sharps & Hankins carbines were delivered to New York Stat4e for use by the 9th and 11th New York Volunteer Cavalry Regiments. They were similar to Sharps & Hankins Model 1862 army carbine, except with a shortened, 19" blued barrel and a sling ring on the left side of the frame in lieu of a sling swivel on the butt stock. The metal parts of some specimens have tinned finishes and naval inspector's mark "P / HJH".

GOOD—$1,250   **FINE—$4,500**

Rock Island Auction Company

Amoskeag Auction Company, Inc.

SHARPS & HANKINS MODEL 1862 NAVY CARBINE, .52 CALIBER, RIMFIRE CARTRIDGE

Manufactured by Sharps & Hankins, Philadelphia, Pennsylvania, ca. 1862–65. Total production: approximately 11,000.

Overall length: 38-5/8". Weight: 7 lbs. 10 oz.

Breechloader, single shot.

"SHARPS / & / HANKINS / PHILADA" on right side of frame; "SHARPS / PATENT / 1859" on left side of frame; serial number on all major parts; "P/ HKH" or an anchor stamped on leather barrel sleeve on some examples.

The Navy version of the Sharps & Hankins Model 1862 carbine was similar to the army version of this carbine, with the principal difference being the leather cover fitted over the entire barrel, to help prevent rusting. This leather sleeve was secured by a steel band at the muzzle and two screws at the breech. The U.S. Navy reportedly procured 6,686 of these carbines, out of an estimated total production of 11,000.

GOOD—$1,100   FINE—$3,250

James D. Julia Auctioneers, Fairfield, Maine

Rock Island Auction Company

SMITH BREECHLOADING CARBINE, .50 CALIBER, COMBUSTIBLE CARTRIDGE, PERCUSSION

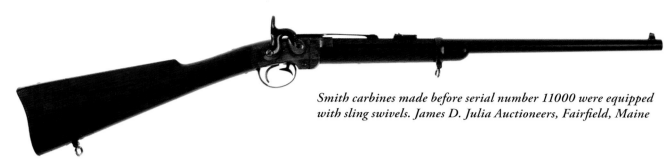

Smith carbines made before serial number 11000 were equipped with sling swivels. James D. Julia Auctioneers, Fairfield, Maine

Manufactured by American Machine Works, Springfield, Massachusetts; American Arms Company and Massachusetts Arms Company, Chicopee Falls, Massachusetts, ca. 1860–65. Total production: 30,062.

Overall length: 39-1/2". Weight: 7 lbs. 8 oz.

Breechloader, hinged barrel, single shot.

"ADDRESS / POULTENEY & TRIMBLE / BALTIMORE, U.S.A." over "SMITH'S PATENT / JUNE 23 1857" on left side of frame, along with one of three markings to the front of this: "AMERICAN ARMS CO. / CHICOPEE FALLS", "MANUFACTURED MY / AM'N M'CH'N WKS /. SPRINGFIELD, MASS", or "MANUFACTURED BY / MASS. ARMS CO / CHICOPEE FALLS"; serial number on rear face of breech

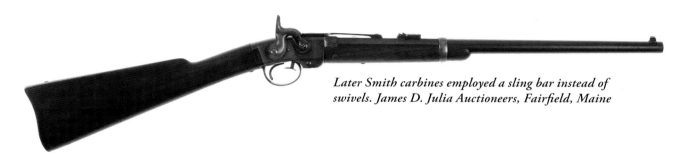

Later Smith carbines employed a sling bar instead of swivels. James D. Julia Auctioneers, Fairfield, Maine

This carbine patented by Gilbert Smith featured a breechloading mechanism whereby pressing a T-shaped latch lifter to the front of the trigger allowed the barrel to swing downward, permitting the shooter to insert a .50-Caliber cartridge of India rubber or brass foil covered with paper. The frame and hammer were casehardened, while the 21-5/8" blued barrel was rifled with three grooves. All furniture was blued iron. The two-piece stock was black walnut. Specimens under serial number 11000 had sling swivels on the butt stock and barrel band; later units had a sling ring to the left of the breech. Poulteney & Trimble of Baltimore, agents for the Smith Carbine, arranged for the American Arms Company, American Machine Works, and Massachusetts Arms Company to manufacture the carbines, with the U.S. government purchasing 30,062 stands. Volunteer cavalry regiments known to have used these carbines included the 1st Massachusetts, 7th Pennsylvania, and 9th Ohio.

GOOD—$1,450   FINE—$3,000

SPENCER MODEL 1860 CARBINE, .52 CALIBER, RIMFIRE CARTRIDGE

Manufactured by Spencer Repeating Rifle Company, Boston, Massachusetts, ca. 1863–65. Total production: Approximately 50,000.

Overall length: 39". Weight: approximately 8 lbs., 4 oz.

Breechloader, seven shot.

"SPENCER REPEATING / RIFLE CO. BOSTON, MASS. / PAT'D MARCH 6, 1860" on top of frame to front of breech; serial number on top of frame to rear of breech.

Initial deliveries of the Spencer Model 1860 Carbine began in October 1863, though reports that many of carbines were already in the field by that time. Serial umbers range of the Model 1860 is 11000 to 61000.

GOOD—$1,850   FINE—$4,000

James D. Julia Auctioneers, Fairfield, Maine

SPENCER MODEL 1865 CARBINE, .50 CALIBER, RIMFIRE CARTRIDGE

 Manufactured by Spencer Repeating Rifle Company, Boston, Massachusetts, ca. 1865–66. Total production: 21,511.

Overall length: 37". Weight: approximately 8 lbs.

Breechloader, seven shot.

"SPENCER REPEATING / RIFLE CO. BOSTON, MASS. / PAT'D MARCH 6, 1860" on top of frame to front of breech; serial number on top of frame to rear of breech. Barrel breech also marked "M 1865".

The Spencer Model 1865 Carbine was similar to the standard Spencer repeating carbine, except with a 20" instead of 22" barrel, and a .50-caliber bore instead of .52-caliber. Serial numbers were in the 1–23000 range, and roughly half of the carbines had the Stabler cut-off switch, which allowed the shooter to select between manually loading single cartridges at the breech or loading by means of the seven-shot tubular magazine.

GOOD—$1,600   FINE—$2,7500

SPENCER MODEL 1865 CARBINE, BURNSIDE CONTRACT, .50 CALIBER, RIMFIRE CARTRIDGE

James D. Julia Auctioneers, Fairfield, Maine

Manufactured by Burnside Rifle Company, Providence, Rhode Island, ca. 1865. Total production: 34,000.
Overall length: 37". Weight: approximately 8 lbs.
Breechloader, seven shot.
"SPENCER REPEATING RIFLE / PAT'D MARCH 6, 1860 / MANUF'D AT PROV. R.I. / BY BURNSIDE RIFLE CO. / MODEL 1865" on top of frame to front of breech; serial number on top of frame to rear of breech.
Burnside Rifle Company's contract version of the Spencer Model 1865 Carbine was similar to Spencer-made version, except with three-groove rifling instead of six-groove. Serial numbers were in the 1–34000 range, with the U.S. government taking delivery of 30,502 stands. Over half of the carbines were equipped with the Stabler cut-off switch.

GOOD—$1,600   **FINE—$2,750**

STARR PERCUSSION CARBINE, .54 CALIBER, PAPER/LINEN CARTRIDGE

James D. Julia Auctioneers, Fairfield, Maine

Manufactured by Starr Arms Company, Yonkers, New York, ca. 1858–65. Total production: 20,601.
Overall length: 37-5/8". Weight: 7 lbs. 6 oz.
Breechloader, falling breech block, single shot.
"STARR ARMS CO / YONKERS, N.Y." on lock plate to rear of hammer and on barrel to front of rear sight; "STARR'S PATENT / SEPT. 14TH 1858" on breech tang; serial number on right side of breech reinforcing band and inspector's initials on left side of reinforcing band and left side of butt stock (in a cartouche).
First tested in January 1858, the Starr Percussion Carbine saw extensive service in the western campaigns in the Civil War. Its 21" round, blued barrel was rifled with five grooves. The lock and breech frame were casehardened, while the oval barrel band and butt plate were brass. A sling ring was stapled to the left side of the frame. Unlatching and lowering the lever/trigger guard caused the breech block to drop down, opening the breech for loading a cartridge. Ignition was by means of a percussion nipple. A number of low-serial number specimens have 18" barrels. The 1st Arkansas Volunteer Cavalry Regiment (U.S.A.) stamped its Starr Percussion Carbines with "1 / ARK / [company letter]" on top of the breech frame, but the buyer should ascertain the authenticity of such markings, as it is easy to duplicate the crudely stamped characters.

GOOD—$1,250   **FINE—$3,000**

STARR CARTRIDGE CARBINE, .52 CALIBER, RIMFIRE CARTRIDGE

Manufactured by Starr Arms Company, Yonkers, New York, ca. 1864–65. Total production: 5,002.
Overall length: 37-5/8". Weight: 7 lbs. 6 oz.
Breechloader, falling breech block, single shot.
"STARR ARMS CO / YONKERS, N.Y." on lock plate to rear of hammer and on barrel in front of rear sight; "STARR'S PATENT / SEPT. 14TH 1858" on breech tang; serial number on right side of breech reinforcing band and inspector's initials on left side of band and, on some specimens, on left side of butt stock (in a cartouche).

The Starr Cartridge Carbine was similar in appearance to the Starr Percussion Carbine, except with a smaller hammer with a straight shank, brass or iron barrel band and butt plate, and a .52-caliber bore, to accept a Spencer .56-52 rimfire cartridge. Starr tested the carbine in January 1865 and delivered 5,002 stands to the U.S. government from late March to early April 1865.

GOOD—$1,100   **FINE—$2,750**

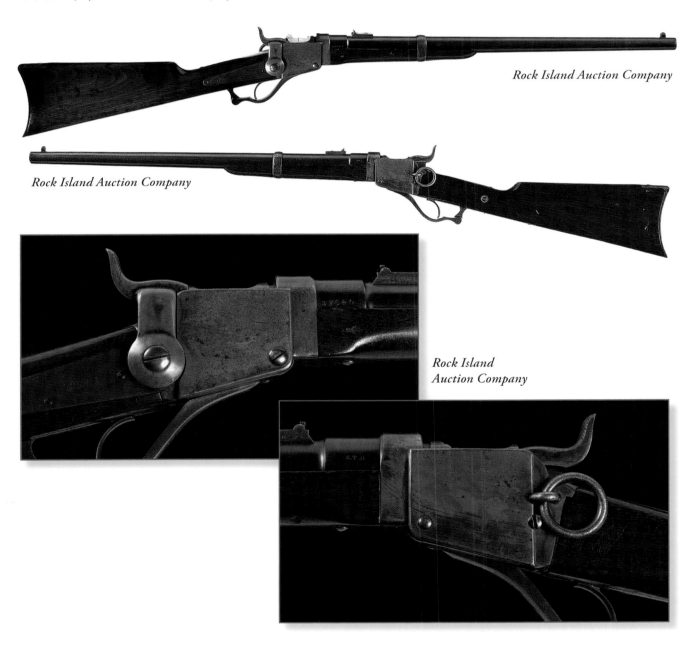

Rock Island Auction Company

Rock Island Auction Company

*Rock Island
Auction Company*

TARPLEY CARBINE, .52 CALIBER, PAPER CARTRIDGE, PERCUSSION

Made by Tarpley, Garrett & Company, Greensboro, North Carolina, ca. 1863-1864. Total production: Approximately 300.

Overall length: 39-1/4".

Breechloader, falling breech block, single shot.

Upper tang of frame stamped, "JH TARPLEY'S. / PAT FEB 14. / 1863." Serial numbers stamped on all primary pieces. Some carbines have stocks stamped "MANUFACTURED BY / J.&F. GARRETT & CO / GREENSBORO N.C. CSA."

The iron furniture was case-hardened in mottled colors, and the round barrels were blued. Each carbine was fitted with a brass front sight and an iron, two-leaf rear sight. A saddle ring and bar mounted on the left side allowed a horse rider to carry the carbine from a sling. The State of North Carolina received 200 Tarpley carbines in 1863. In addition to military contracts, the Tarpley carbine is the only Confederate arm known to also have been sold commercially.

GOOD—$55,000   FINE—$100,000

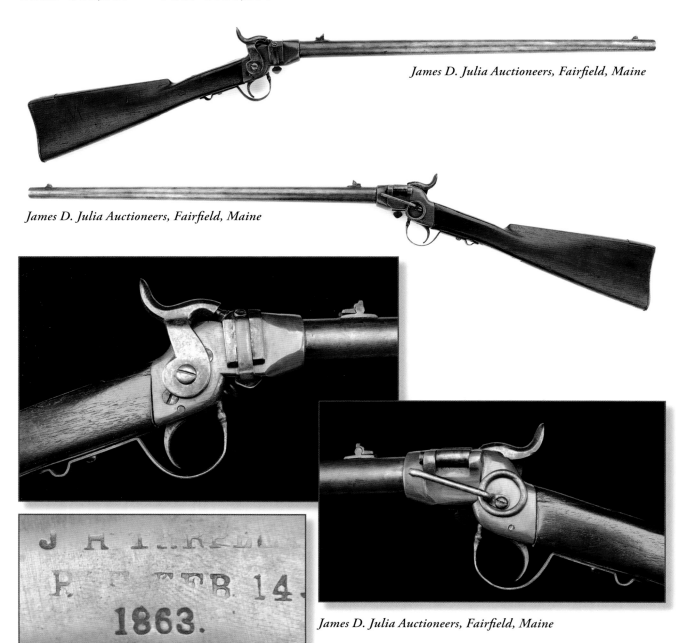

James D. Julia Auctioneers, Fairfield, Maine

James D. Julia Auctioneers, Fairfield, Maine

James D. Julia Auctioneers, Fairfield, Maine

TRIPLETT & SCOTT REPEATING CARBINE, .50 CALIBER, RIMFIRE CARTRIDGE

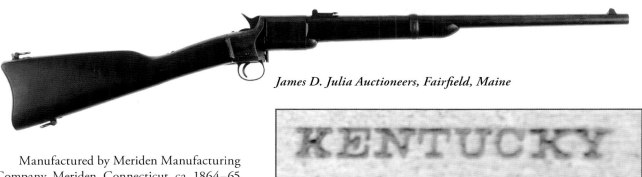

James D. Julia Auctioneers, Fairfield, Maine

Manufactured by Meriden Manufacturing Company, Meriden, Connecticut, ca. 1864–65. Total production: 5,000.

Breechloader, rotating barrel, seven shot.

"TRIPLETT & SCOTT / PATENT / DEC. 6, 1864" on left side of frame; "MERIDEN MAN'FG. CO. / MERIDEN, CONN." and serial number on right side of frame; "KENTUCKY" on left side of breech; "N / W.B." on left side of stock near butt plate on some examples..

The Triplett & Scott Repeating Carbine featured a breechloading mechanism whereby pressing a latch behind the hammer allowed the barrel to be rotated laterally, placing the opened breech in alignment with the mouth of the seven-shot tubular magazine in the butt stock. The carbine had iron furniture, including one barrel band and two sling swivels, on the top and bottom of the butt stock at the butt. Most barrels were 30", although 22" barrels have been reported. The State of Kentucky bought 5,000 of these carbines under a contract dated January 2, 1865.

GOOD–$1,500   FINE–$2,750

WARNER CARBINE, .50 CALIBER, RIMFIRE CARTRIDGE

James D. Julia Auctioneers, Fairfield, Maine

Manufactured by Massachusetts Arms Company, Springfield, Massachusetts, ca. 1864–65. Total production: 1,501. Overall length: 37-1/2". Weight: 6 lbs. 12 oz.

Breechloader, hinged breech block, single shot.

"JAMES WARNER, SPRINGFIELD, MASS. / WARNER'S PATENT" on left side of frame (this marking was absent on approximately the first 200 units); "CSL" stamped on left side of butt stock to rear of frame; serial number on underside of breech block.

The Warner Carbine featured a breech block hinged on the right side of the frame. Pressing a thumb lever to the left of the hammer unlocked the breech block, allowing it to be flipped up. A manual slide-type extractor was located beneath the fore stock. The carbine had a 20" round barrel, either blued or bright. Initially chambered for the Warner .50-caliber rimfire cartridge, large quantities of the carbine were later altered to accept the Spencer .56-50 rimfire cartridge. The butt stock and fore stock, which was secured to the barrel by a single iron band, were black walnut. The frame, trigger guard and tang, and butt stock were brass. A sling ring was secured to the left side of the frame by an eye bolt.

GOOD–$2,250   FINE–$4,750

WARNER CARBINE, GREENE SUBCONTRACT, .50 CALIBER, RIMFIRE CARTRIDGE

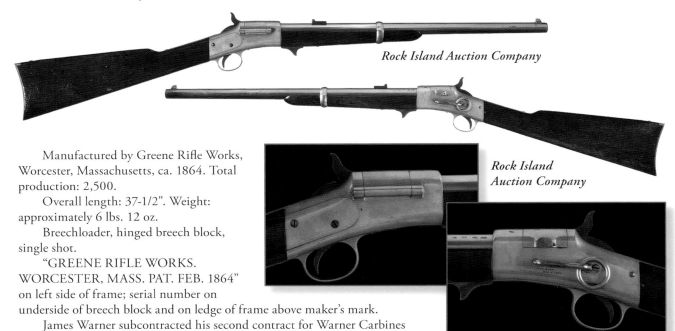

Rock Island Auction Company

Rock Island Auction Company

Manufactured by Greene Rifle Works, Worcester, Massachusetts, ca. 1864. Total production: 2,500.

Overall length: 37-1/2". Weight: approximately 6 lbs. 12 oz.

Breechloader, hinged breech block, single shot.

"GREENE RIFLE WORKS. WORCESTER, MASS. PAT. FEB. 1864" on left side of frame; serial number on underside of breech block and on ledge of frame above maker's mark.

James Warner subcontracted his second contract for Warner Carbines to Greene Rifle Works. Certain features of the Greene version differed from Warner's, the most prominent of which were: the extractor lever under the fore stock was noticeably larger; the separate breech-locking lever was omitted, with the hammer now acting as the breech-locking mechanism; a knurled-button breech block lifting handle replaced the plain projection of the Warner version; and the eye bolt that retained the sling ring was replaced by a rod.

GOOD—$2,000   FINE—$4,500

WESSON MILITARY CARBINE, TYPE I, .44 CALIBER, RIMFIRE CARTRIDGE

Amoskeag Auction Company, Inc.

Manufactured by Frank Wesson, Worcester, Massachusetts, ca. 1859–64. Total production: approximately 4,500.

Overall length: 39-1/2". Weight: 5 lbs. 12 oz.

Breechloader, hinged barrel, single shot.

"F. WESSON / WORCESTER, MASS." and "F. WESSON'S PATENT / OCT. 25, 1859 AND NOV. 11, 1862" on barrel; serial number on trigger guard.

The Wesson Military Carbine, Type I, had a breechloading mechanism comprising a hinged, downward-tilting barrel which was unlocked by pulling the forward of two triggers. Later examples with the 1862 patent mark had an "oscillating link" attached to the right side of the frame and barrel, which limited the downward travel of the barrel; earlier specimens lacked this feature. The carbine had an octagonal 24" blued barrel, rifled with five grooves. It also had an iron frame/fore arm, folding single-leaf rear sight, and black walnut butt stock (there was no fore stock). This model of the Wesson carbine lacked a cartridge extractor. Iron sling swivels were mounted on the rear of the trigger plate and on the underside of the barrel 7" from the muzzle.

GOOD—$750   FINE—$1,200

WESSON MILITARY CARBINE, TYPE I, KITTREDGE & CO. MARKED, .44 CALIBER, RIMFIRE CARTRIDGE

Manufactured by Frank Wesson, Worcester, Massachusetts, ca. 1859–64. Total production: Up to approximately 2,000.

Overall length: 39-1/2". Weight: 5 lbs. 12 oz.

Breechloader, hinged barrel, single shot.

Same markings as Wesson Military Carbine, Type I, with addition of "B. KITTREDGE & CO. / CINCINNATI, O." and, on some specimens, state militia markings.

Kittredge & Company, an Ohio arms agent and sporting arms dealer, furnished several states with Wesson Military Carbines, Type I, including but not limited to 1,366 to Kentucky and 760 to Indiana. Kittredge added its own marking to many of these carbines, as noted above, although it is not clear how many. Some examples also included state militia markings and command a large premium, but buyers should exercise extreme caution when considering these.

GOOD—$1,250   **FINE—$2,250**

Rock Island Auction Company

WESSON CARBINE, TYPE II, .44 CALIBER, RIMFIRE CARTRIDGE

Manufactured by Frank Wesson, Worcester, Massachusetts, ca. 1864–76. Total production: approximately 5,000.

Overall length: 39-1/2". Weight: Approximately 5 lbs. 12 oz.

Breechloader, hinged barrel, single shot.

"FRANK WESSON WORCESTER MASS / PATD.OCT. 25, 1859 & NOV. 11, 1862" on barrel; "B. KITTREDGE & CO. / CINCINNATI, O." on barrel of state-purchased examples; serial number on trigger guard.

The Type II Wesson Carbine differed from the Type I in that the oscillating link was moved to the left side of the breech and frame, and a manual cartridge extractor was added to the right side of the breech. According to firearms expert Norm Flayderman, the Type II was evidently issued in sporting configurations only.

GOOD—$375   **FINE—$800**

Rock Island Auction Company

CHAPTER 8
HANDGUNS - SINGLE-SHOT PISTOLS

Perhaps no other weapon represents the extent of the weapon shortage that existed in northern and southern armories at the beginning of the Civil War than the single-shot, muzzle-loading pistol. Never intended for much more than close-quarter combat, the single shot pistol had never fully achieved the status of a "front-line" weapon. The 19th century cavalry soldier's or naval crewman's weapon of first choice in close combat was their sword or cutlass. For combat on a wider scale, preference was given to their carbine or musketoon. The pistol was thought of as a last-resort weapon.

When thousands of men agreed to take up arms in 1861, it was left to the military to provide those arms. Arsenals and armories were ransacked and anything that could hold a charge, create a spark, or fill a holster was quickly dispersed.

Among the weapons found still in stock, but rarely used, were thousands of single-shot pistols. Rather than send cavalry soldiers to war with no weapons, officers issued the obsolete handguns.

Though the last single-shot pistol adopted by the U.S. Army was the Model 1855, the Confederacy did actually at least one model of single-shot pistol. Made with parts captured at Harpers Ferry, it was more a decision based on availability than one of demand. Like the musket, the single-shot pistol had become obsolete.

178

U.S. MODEL 1836 FLINTLOCK PISTOL (ASA WATERS CONTRACT), CONVERTED TO PERCUSSION, .54 CALIBER, COMBUSTIBLE CARTRIDGE

Manufactured by Asa Waters, Millbury, Massachusetts, ca. 1836–44; altered to percussion in the 1850s. Total original production: approximately 23,000; total number converted to percussion by Waters: Unknown.

Overall length: 14". Weight: 2 lbs. 10 oz. Muzzleloader, single shot.

"[Eagle head] / A. WATERS / MILBURY, MS / [year, between 1837 and 1843]" at center of lock plate on approximately the first 20,000 examples, made up to 1843; "[Eagle head] / A. H. WATERS & CO / MILBURY, MS / 1844" on approximately 3,000 specimens manufactured in 1844; some examples with state militia markings.

A large quantity of U.S. Flintlock Pistols, Model 1836, of the Asa Waters Contract were converted to percussion in the 1850s. These alterations incorporated all of the three principal percussion systems: French (or first U.S.) type, Belgian (or second U.S.) type, and a conversion whereby a section of breech was removed and a new breech section with integral nipple bolster was threaded into the barrel.

Rock Island Auction Company

GOOD–$450   FINE–$750

U.S. MODEL 1836 FLINTLOCK PISTOL (ROBERT JOHNSON CONTRACT), CONVERTED TO PERCUSSION, .54 CALIBER, COMBUSTIBLE CARTRIDGE

Manufactured by Robert Johnson, Middletown, Connecticut, ca. 1836–44; altered to percussion in the 1850s. Total original production: approximately 18,000; total number converted to percussion by Waters: Unknown.

Overall length: 14". Weight: 2 lbs. 10 oz. Muzzleloader, single shot.

"U.S. / R. JOHNSON / MIDDN CONN / [year]" at center of lock plate, militia markings on some examples.

In the 1850s, quantities of Robert Johnson-Contract U.S. Model 1836 flintlock pistols were converted to percussion.

Rock Island Auction Company

GOOD–$450   FINE–$750

U.S. MODEL 1836 FLINTLOCK PISTOL, M. A. BAKER BRAZED BOLSTER ALTERATION .54 CALIBER, COMBUSTIBLE CARTRIDGE, PERCUSSION

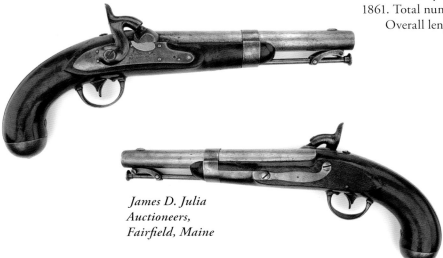

James D. Julia Auctioneers, Fairfield, Maine

Altered by M. A. Baker, Fayetteville, North Carolina, ca. 1861. Total number of alterations: Unknown.

Overall length: 14". Weight: approximately 2 lbs. 10 oz. Muzzleloader, single shot.

"N. CAROLINA" on top of barrel; other markings as on U.S. Flintlock Pistol, Model 1836, Asa H. Waters and Robert Johnson Contracts.

In 1861, the State of North Carolina contracted with M. A. Baker of Fayetteville, North Carolina, to convert a quantity of U.S. Model 1836 Flintlock Pistols to percussion. He effected this conversion by cutting out a quarter-section of the top right side of the breech, and brazing into the opening a bolster of the type used on the U.S. Model 1842 Percussion Musket. The hammer was of the Model 1842 type as well.

GOOD—$2,500   FINE—$6,000

A. H. WATERS SINGLE-SHOT PERCUSSION PISTOL, .54 CALIBER, COMBUSTIBLE CARTRIDGE

Manufactured by Asa Waters, Millbury, Massachusetts, ca. 1844–49. Total production: Unknown.

Overall length: 14". Weight: 2 lbs. 6 oz.

Muzzleloader, single shot.

Eagle head over "A. H. WATERS & CO / MILBURY, MASS" at center of lock plate of earliest examples; eagle head over "A.H. WATERS & CO / MILBURY, MASS / [year]" and government inspectors' marks on subsequent examples; no marks on stock.

The A. H. Waters single-shot percussion pistol was similar in shape and design to the U.S. Model 1836 flintlock pistol, but was manufactured as a percussion pistol and was not a conversion from flintlock. Further, it was privately developed and is considered a transitional pistol between the U.S. Model 1836 flintlock pistol and U.S. Model 1842 percussion pistol. Unlike the Model 1836 pistol, with its lock plate beveled to the front of the hammer, the Waters percussion pistol had a flat lock plate. There were several variations in percussion mechanisms (including cone nipple on barrel), with corresponding differences in hammers. Early-production specimens had bright iron furniture; later, some brass furniture parts were introduced.

GOOD—$750   FINE—$1,500

U.S. MODEL 1842 PERCUSSION PISTOL, H. ASTON CONTRACT, .54 CALIBER, COMBUSTIBLE CARTRIDGE

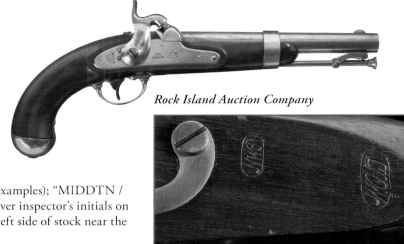

Rock Island Auction Company

Manufactured by H[enry]. Aston & Company, Middletown, Connecticut, ca. 1846–52. Total production: Approximately 30,000.

Overall length: 14". Weight: 2 lbs. 12 oz. Muzzleloader, single shot.

"US / H. ASTON" at center of lock plate (approximately first 24,000 examples); "US / H. ASTON & CO." at center of lock plate (approximately last 6,000 examples); "MIDDTN / CONN. / [year]" vertically to rear of lock plate; "US/P" over inspector's initials on breech; year stamped on barrel tang; inspector's mark on left side of stock near the side plate; naval contract specimens have anchor and naval inspector marks on top of breech.

This smoothbore pistol was similar to the U.S. Model 1836 flintlock pistol, with changes to include a percussion lock; a lock plate with all edges beveled and a rounded, rather than pointed, rear tip; trigger guard bow fastened to the trigger plate by two round spanner nuts instead of rivets; and brass furniture. It had an 8-1/2" round, bright-finished barrel with brass-blade front sight. The ramrod had a button-type head and was secured with a swivel. Of the total production, some 3,000 units were delivered to the U.S. Navy.

GOOD—$800 FINE—$3,000

WITH NAVY MARKINGS:
GOOD—$2,250   FINE—$5,500

U.S. MODEL 1842 PERCUSSION PISTOL, IRA N. JOHNSON CONTRACT, .54 CALIBER, COMBUSTIBLE CARTRIDGE

Manufactured by Ira N. Johnson, Middletown, Connecticut, ca. 1853–55. Total production: Approximately 10,000.

Overall length: 14". Weight: 2 lbs. 12 oz. Muzzleloader, single shot.

"US / I. N. JOHNSON" at center of lock plate; "MIDDTN / CONN. / [year: 1853, 1854, or 1855]" vertically to rear of lock plate; "US/P" over inspector's initials (including, among others, "JH" and "WAT") on breech; year stamped on barrel tang; inspector's mark on left side of stock near the side plate.

Rock Island Auction Company

When Ira N. Johnson, a partner in H. Aston & Company, secured a contract in March 1851 to supply the U.S. Ordnance Department with 10,000 Model 1842 percussion pistols, Johnson departed from the Aston firm and set up his own production company. His version of the Model 1842 percussion pistol was essentially the same as those manufactured by H. Alston & Company, except for the markings, as specified above.

GOOD—$800   FINE—$2,750

U.S. MODEL 1842 PERCUSSION PISTOL, PALMETTO ARMORY CONTRACT, .54 CALIBER, COMBUSTIBLE CARTRIDGE

James D. Julia Auctioneers, Fairfield, Maine

Manufactured by the Palmetto Armory, Columbia, South Carolina, 1852–53. Total production: 2,000.

Overall length: 14". Weight: 2 lbs. 12 oz. Muzzleloader, single shot.

"PALMETTO ARMORY" over S [5-pointed star or asterisk] C." in a circle, surrounding a palmetto tree, at center of lock plate; "COLUMBIA / S.C. 1852" vertically toward rear of lock plate; "1853" on barrel tang; "V / P / [palmetto tree]" on breech; "WM. GLAZE & CO." on left flat of barrel;

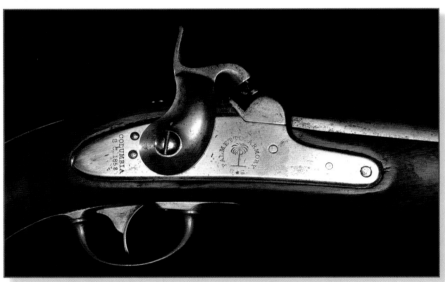

James D. Julia Auctioneers, Fairfield, Maine

The Palmetto Armory of William Glaze and Company (William Glaze and Benjamin Flagg) produced 2,000 U.S. Model 1842 percussion pistols in 1852 and 1853 for the use of the South Carolina militia. There is some evidence that the Palmetto Armory assembled these pistols from surplus and condemned parts from the two other contractors for the Model 1842 percussion pistols, H. Aston and I. N. Johnson. Considerable care should be exercised when considering a Model 1842 percussion pistol with Palmetto Armory marks, since numerous counterfeit examples were introduced into the market in the late 1950s with the original Waters or Johnson marks obliterated and fake Palmetto Armory marks added.

GOOD—$3,000   FINE—$8,000

U.S. NAVY PERCUSSION PISTOL, MODEL 1842 "BOX LOCK," N. P. AMES CONTRACT, .54 CALIBER, COMBUSTIBLE CARTRIDGE

Manufactured by N. P. Ames, Springfield, Massachusetts, ca. 1842–45; Total production: Approximately 2,000.

Overall length: 11-5/8". Weight: 2 lbs.

Muzzleloader, single shot.

"N.P. AMES / SPRINGFIELD, MASS" at center of lock plate; "USN / [year]" or "USR / 1843" vertically at rear of lock plate; proof marks and year on upper left side of barrel near breech; inspector's initials on left flat of stock.

James D. Julia Auctioneers, Fairfield, Maine

The U.S. Navy Percussion Pistol, Model 1842, was the first martial percussion pistol contracted by and delivered to the U.S. government. These smoothbore pistols were issued to the U.S. Navy and U.S. Revenue Cutter Service. The model was distinguished by its flat butt cap and box lock, which enclosed the lower part of the hammer. The 6" barrel was browned; all furniture was bright brass. The first 300 units had a raised lock plate with a beveled edge from the hammer forward, were dated 1842, and had proof mark "US / P" on the barrel. Subsequent units had a flat, flush lock plate stamped with the years 1843, 1844, and 1845.

EARLY PRODUCTION: GOOD–$3,250   FINE–$8,000
STANDARD MODEL: GOOD–$750   FINE–$2,000

U.S. NAVY PERCUSSION PISTOL, MODEL 1842 "BOXLOCK," DERINGER CONTRACT, .54 CALIBER, COMBUSTIBLE CARTRIDGE

Manufactured by Henry Deringer, Philadelphia, Pennsylvania, ca. 1845–47. Total production: Unknown; between 300–1,200.

Overall length: 11-5/8". Weight: 2 lbs.

Muzzleloader, single shot.

Three basic variations of marking schemes existed: 1) "DERINGER / PHILADELA" at center of lock plate. 2) "US / DERINGER / PHILADELA" at center of lock plate, and "DERINGER / PHILADEL'A" and "RP" on barrel near breech. 3) "US / DERINGER / PHILADELA" at center of lock plate, "U.S.N. / [year]" vertically at rear of lock plate, and "P" on barrel near breech.

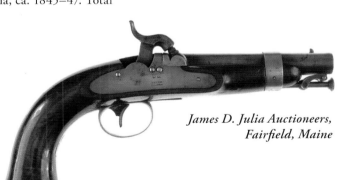

James D. Julia Auctioneers, Fairfield, Maine

Henry Deringer produced a version of the U.S. Navy Model 1842 percussion pistol under a contract of July 1, 1845, using the same tooling with which N. P. Ames had manufactured his slightly earlier version of the pistol. Less than half of the production run is thought to have been fitted with a brass front sight and fixed, V-notch sight on the barrel tang. Some specimens with the "US" lock plate marking had deep, seven-groove rifling instead of the standard smooth bore; these were the first rifled pistols made for the U.S. government.

GOOD–$550 FINE–$3,500 (DEPENDING ON MARKINGS)

U.S. MODEL 1855 PISTOL-CARBINE, .58 CALIBER, COMBUSTIBLE CARTRIDGE, PERCUSSION

Rock Island Auction Company

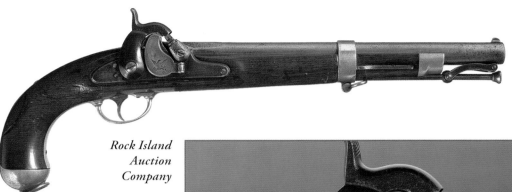

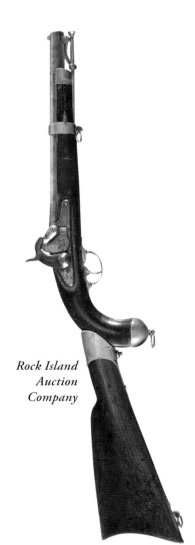

Rock Island Auction Company

Manufactured by Springfield Armory, Springfield, Massachusetts, ca. 1855–57. Total production: 4,021.

Overall length: 17-3/4" without shoulder stock affixed; 28-1/4" with shoulder stock. Weight: 3 lbs. 13 oz. pistol only; 5 lbs. 7 oz. pistol and stock.

Muzzleloader, single shot.

"U. S. / SPRINGFIELD" to front of lock plate; year to rear of lock plate; large spread eagle on tape-primer door; "V / P / [eagle head]" on left breech flat; batch number between 1 and 20 on back strap of pistol and yoke of shoulder stock; "US" on tang of butt plate of shoulder stock.

The U.S. Model 1855 pistol-carbine had a 12" barrel rifled with three wide lands and grooves. It came equipped with a detachable shoulder stock that attached to the back strap. All furniture was bright-finished brass, and the lock and barrel were finished bright. A two-leaf rear sight was mortised into the tang of the barrel. Other features included a ramrod swivel, a pommel ring fastened to the butt cap of the pistol, and sling swivels on the barrel band and the bottom of the butt stock.

Specimens will be found with and without the detachable shoulder stock.

WITHOUT SHOULDER STOCK: GOOD—$1,750   FINE—$6,500

"Fayetteville Armory" Model 1855 Pistol-Carbine, .58 Caliber, Combustible Cartridge, Percussion

Assembled by Fayetteville Armory, Fayetteville, North Carolina, ca. 1861. Total production: unknown.

Overall length: 17-3/4" without shoulder stock affixed; 28-1/4" with shoulder stock. Weight: 3 lbs. 13 oz. pistol only; 5 lbs. 7 oz. pistol and stock.

Muzzleloader, single shot.

"U. S. / SPRINGFIELD" to front of lock plate; year to rear of lock plate; large spread eagle on tape-primer door; "V / P / [eagle head]" on left breech flat; batch number between 1 and 20 on back strap of pistol and yoke of shoulder stock; "US" on tang of butt plate of shoulder stock.

Reportedly, the Fayetteville Armory in Fayetteville, North Carolina, assembled a quantity of Model 1855 pistol-carbines from parts captured at the Harper's Ferry Arsenal by Confederate forces in 1861. These arms were supposedly nearly identical to Springfield Armory's version, except the lock plate was not milled to accommodate the Maynard tape-priming magazine. Arms expert Norm Flayderman cautions that he has never seen an authentic example of this firearm or found independent verification that such a weapon actually existed.

If authenticated specimens are found, they presumably will be found with and without the detachable shoulder stock.

Good—N/A   Fine—N/A

J. and F. Garrett Single Shot Pistol, .54 Caliber, Paper Cartridge, Percussion

Made by J. and F. Garrett and Company, Greensboro, North Carolina, ca. 1862-1863. Total production: Approximately 500.

Overall length: 13-1/4".

Muzzleloader, Single-shot.

"G.W." or "S.R." over P stamped on breech end of barrel. Because it is likely that these pistols were made from parts captured at Harpers Ferry, it is unlikely these markings were not applied at the Garrett factory.

J. and F. Garrett also produced the Tarpley breechloading carbine. They assembled these pistols from captured parts and brass frame they cast themselves. The barrels and ramrods were intended, most likely, for the U.S. Model 1842 pistol. The 8-1/2" round barrels were left bright when assembled with to the cast brass frames.

Good—$1,750   Fine—$4,500

James D. Julia Auctioneers, Fairfield, Maine

CHAPTER 9

REVOLVERS

Though not the source of a great number of wounds or deaths during the Civil War, the revolver or pistol held a mystique for soldiers on both sides. Issued only to mounted troops, thousands of foot soldiers purchased handguns to carry in addition to their government-supplied weapons. In most cases, the only time they withdrew their handgun, though, was for a cleaning or posing in a warlike stance for the photographer.

The Union purchased 373,077 handguns during the Civil War, more than a fourth of which came from the Colt factory. Total Confederate purchases were probably near half of that number. Assuming there were 500,000 government purchases of handguns, this can only be considered a fraction of the weapons carried by soldiers, as period sales of handguns doubled the sales to government agencies.

ADAMS, .44 CALIBER, PERCUSSION REVOLVER

Made by London Armoury Company, London, England, 1859-1866. Total imported: Approximately 2,000.

Overall length: 12".

Double-action, five-shot.

Rock Island Auction Company

The top flat of the 6" barrel is stamped DEANE ADAMS DEANE, 30 KING ST, LONDON BRIDGE" and "LONDON ARMOURY" or "LONDON ARMOURY CO." The top left barrel flat is stamped "L.A.C." Revolvers intended for commercial resale usually are marked with the name and address of the retailer on either the barrel or top strap. The left side of the frame is stamped "ADAMS PATENT [serial number]". Serial numbers ending with an "R" denote that either Dean and Adams or the London Armoury Company produced the gun. A "P" represents Pryse and Redman, Birmingham. The suffix "C" was placed on Calisher & Terry-produced revolvers.

The U.S. Ordnance purchased only 1,075 Adams-type revolvers. Southern states and the Confederate government purchased at least 1,000 weapons.

GOOD—$850 FINE—$1,850

ALLEN & WHEELOCK NAVY, .36 CALIBER (AKA NO. 56) LIPFIRE REVOLVER

Made by Allen & Wheelock, Worcester, Massachusetts, ca. 1861-1862. Total production of about 500.

Overall length: 12-3/4". Weight: 2 lbs. 4 oz.

Single-action, six-shot.

Rock Island Auction Company

The left flat of the 4", 5", 6", 7-1/2" or 8" barrel is stamped in two lines, "ALLEN & WHEELOCK WORCESTER, MASS. U.S. / ALLEN'S PATENTS SEPT. 7, NOV. 9, 1858." Serial number is stamped on all major parts. The black walnut, two-piece grips are unmarked and varnished.

Produced for only about a year, the lipfire "Navy" and "Army" revolvers succeeded Allen & Wheelock's side-hammer percussion revolvers. Made to fire a .36-caliber cartridge (sometimes referred to as ".38 caliber"), the lipfire revolvers were the subject of a patent infringement suit from Smith & Wesson. Before the suit was resolved, however, Allen & Wheelock abandoned the design in favor of a new line of center-hammer percussion revolvers.

There are no known government contracts for either the lipfire Navy or Army models even though it was apparent that Allen & Wheelock designed these for military service.

GOOD—$750 FINE—$2,250

ALLEN & WHEELOCK ARMY, .44 CALIBER (AKA NO. 58) LIPFIRE REVOLVER

Made by Allen & Wheelock, Worcester, Massachusetts, ca. 1861-1863. Total production of about 250.

Overall length: 13-1/4". Weight: 2 lbs. 12 oz.

Single action, six-shot.

The left flat of the 7-1/2" half octagonal, half round barrel is stamped in two lines, "ALLEN & WHEELOCK WORCESTER, MASS. U.S. / ALLEN'S PATENTS SEPT. 7, NOV. 9, 1858." Serial number is stamped on all major parts. The black walnut, two-piece grips are unmarked and varnished. In addition to the serial number stamped on all major components, it also appears on the front face of the cylinder of type I and II revolvers and on the rear face of the cylinder of type III examples.

Production of the Allen & Wheelock Army lipfire revolver ceased in 1863, most likely due to pressure from the Smith & Wesson patent infringement suit. Prior to this, however, the Worcester, Mass., factory produced three versions of the .44 revolver.

Type I: Relatively narrow loading gate hinged near the top of the frame. This type most closely resembles Allen's September 24, 1861, patent drawing. Grips are evenly tapered.

Type II: The gate is wider and the gate lever larger than that of the first model. The hinge of the gate is located on the lower part of the frame behind the cylinder. Grips are flared, being about ¼" wider than first model grips.

Type III: Identical to type II revolver except that the grips are not flared. Serial number is on the rear face of the cylinder and on all major components.

There are no known government contracts for either the lipfire Navy or Army models. Nevertheless, collectors consider them secondary martial weapons.

TYPE I: GOOD—$1,100		**FINE—$5,000**
TYPE II: GOOD—$950		**FINE—$3,500**
TYPE III: GOOD—$875		**FINE—$3,000**

ALLEN & WHEELOCK NAVY, .36 CALIBER SIDE HAMMER REVOLVER, FIRST MODEL

Made by Allen & Wheelock, Worcester, Massachusetts, ca. 1857. Total production of about 100.

Overall length: 13-1/2". Weight: 2 lbs. 6 oz.

Single-action, six-shot.

Top barrel flat is stamped "ALLEN & WHEELOCK" and the upper left flat is stamped "ALLEN'S PATENT JAN. 13, 1857". The black walnut, two-piece grips are unmarked and varnished.

Allen & Wheelock's first martially-spirited revolver

James D. Julia Auctioneers, Fairfield, Maine

was the .36 caliber side hammer Navy models. The single action, six-shot revolver came in octagonal barrel lengths from 5-1/2" to 8", the latter being the most common.

A lateral friction style catch on the left side of the side plate held the trigger guard/loading lever in place on these first 100 side hammer Navy revolvers.

GOOD—$1,250   **FINE—$4,000**

ALLEN & WHEELOCK NAVY, .36 CALIBER SIDE HAMMER REVOLVER, STANDARD MODEL

Made by Allen & Wheelock, Worcester, Massachusetts, ca. 1858-1861. Total production of about 700.

Overall length: 13-1/2". Weight: 2 lbs. 6 oz.

Single action, six-shot

The single action, six-shot revolver came in octagonal barrel lengths from 5-1/2" to 8", the latter being the most common. The left barrel flat is stamped "ALLEN & WHEELOCK WORCESTER, MASS. U.S. / ALLEN'S PTS. JAN 13, DEC. 15, 1857, SEPT. 7, 1858." Serial (batch) number is stamped inside the loading lever/trigger guard. The black walnut, two-piece grips are unmarked and varnished.

The standard side hammer Navy revolver featured a spring-actuated catch at the forward section of the trigger guard that latched at the base of the rear guard arm. When it was released, it functioned as a loading arm. The rear contour of the cylinder arbor is narrower than on the first model. The hammer is also flatter and has sharper, beveled edges. Perhaps the most obvious difference, though, is that the distance between the cylinder face and the frame is slightly less than on the standard model as compared to the first model.

The Ordnance Department purchased 383 Allen & Wheelock revolvers in the early day of the war for a little more than $14 a revolver. This price would seem to indicate that the 383 weapons were, most likely, .36-caliber side hammer Navy revolvers. Artillerymen of the 1st Massachusetts Light Artillery carried Allen & Wheelock side hammer Navy revolvers, most likely the standard model.

GOOD—$1,150   **FINE—$3,500**

ALLEN & WHEELOCK NAVY, .36 CALIBER CENTER HAMMER PERCUSSION REVOLVER

Made by Allen & Wheelock, Worcester, Massachusetts, ca. 1861-1862. Total production fewer than 500.

Overall length: 12". Weight: 2 lbs. 6 oz.

Single-action, six-shot.

The left flat of the 7-1/2" full octagonal barrel is stamped "ALLEN & WHEELOCK WORCESTER, MASS. U.S. / ALLEN'S PT'S JAN. 13, DEC. 15, 1857, SEPT. 7, 1858" in two lines. Serial (batch) number is stamped on all major parts. The black walnut, two-piece grips are unmarked and varnished.

Rock Island Auction Company

Allen & Wheelock center hammers followed the side hammer series and is believed to precede the lipfire revolvers. No government contracts for this revolver are known, but collectors do consider it a secondary martial weapon.

GOOD—$750　　　**FINE—$3,000**

ALLEN & WHEELOCK NAVY, .44 CALIBER CENTER HAMMER PERCUSSION REVOLVER

Made by Allen & Wheelock, Worcester, Massachusetts, ca. 1861-1862. Total production of at least 700.

Overall length: 13-1/4". Weight: 2 lbs. 14 oz.

Single action, six-shot.

The left flat of the 7-1/2" half-octagonal, half-round barrel is stamped "ALLEN & WHEELOCK WORCESTER, MASS. U.S. / ALLEN'S PT'S JAN. 13, DEC. 15, 1857, SEPT. 7, 1858" in two lines. Serial (batch) number is stamped on all major parts. The black walnut, two-piece grips are unmarked and varnished.

Allen & Wheelock center hammers followed the side hammer series and is believed to precede the lipfire revolvers. Variations are known in the shape of the nipple wells and the method of attaching the nipples to the cylinder. The standard finish included a blued barrel, cylinder and frame. The hammer and trigger guard was usually case-hardened. Tinned or nickel finishes have also been observed.

James D. Julia Auctioneers, Fairfield, Maine

The U.S. government bought 536 "Allen's revolvers" on the open market in 1861. It is believed that these revolvers were all .44-caliber percussion models.

On December 31, 1861, the Ordnance Department purchased 198 Allen revolvers from William Read & Sons of Boston, Mass. Based on the $22 price, it is most likely that the 198 revolvers were the .44 caliber center hammer revolvers.

It is quite likely that Allen & Wheelock resumed the production of the .44 caliber Army models after discontinuing lipfire revolver production in 1863 due to the patent infringement suit brought on by Smith & Wesson.

Units known to have received small numbers of .44 Caliber Allen & Wheelock revolvers include the 2nd and 3rd Michigan Cavalry regiments and the 8th Pennsylvania Cavalry.

GOOD—$1,000　　　**FINE—$4,000**

ALSOP NAVY, .36 CALIBER PERCUSSION REVOLVER

Made by C.R. Alsop, Middleton Connecticut, ca. 1862-1863. Total production about 560.

Overall length: 9-5/8". Weight: 1 lbs. 4 oz.

Single-action, five-shot.

Produced in 3-1/2", 4-1/2", 5-1/2" and 6-1/2" barrel lengths. The top of the octagonal barrel stamped "C.R. ALSOP MIDDLETOWN CONN. / PATENTED JULY 17TH. AUGUST 7TH.1860 MAY 14TH. 1861" in two lines. The cylinder is stamped "C.H. ALSOP. PATENTED / NOV 26 TH. 1861" in two lines. On some revolvers, the upper left frame behind the cylinder is stamped "PATENTED JANY. 21ST 1862" in one line. Serial number found on the bottom grip strap. The grips are two-piece walnut and unmarked.

C.R. Alsop made two basic models of revolvers during 1862 and 1863, a pocket model and the Navy. Although no government contracts for either variety are known, collectors consider the Navy Model as a secondary martial weapons because a number seem to have been privately purchased and carried by soldiers.

First Model: The earliest version of the Navy revolver has a sliding safety bolt on the right side of the frame that blocks the spur trigger. Each of the first 100 had a fluted cylinder.

Rock Island Auction Company

GOOD—$1,150   **FINE—$3,750**

Rock Island Auction Company

Second Model: After the initial 100 revolvers, C.R. Alsop switched to a smooth, non-fluted cylinder and eliminated the safety device on the right side of the frame. Serial numbers of second model revolvers have been observed as high as 558.

GOOD—$850   **FINE—$3,000**

COLT MODEL 1849 POCKET, .31 CALIBER, PERCUSSION REVOLVER

James D. Julia Auctioneers, Fairfield, Maine

Made by Samuel Colt, Hartford, Conn., 1850-1873. Total production: Approximately 340,000.

Overall length: 11". Weight: 1 lb. 10 oz.

Single-action, five shot.

Markings: Three different barrel markings are known: "ADDRESS SAML COLT / NEW-YORK CITY" in two lines (used on 14400 through about 187000); "ADDRESS SAML COLT / HARTFORD CT." in two lines (164000 to about 206000) and "ADDRESS COL. SAML COLT NEW-YORK U.S. AMERICA" in one line (about 187000 to 340000). Very unusual, but "ADDRESS.COL: COLT. / LONDON" will be found in the very high serial range.

The case-hardened frame is marked on the left side, "COLT'S / PATENT" in two lines. The blued cylinder is roll-engraved on early examples with the Texas Ranger and Indian fight scene. Later revolvers (from about serial number 10,500) feature a stagecoach hold-up scene and "COLT'S PATENT" stamped in one line over the serial number. The oval, brass trigger guard on some, but not all, Model 1849 Pocket Revolvers is stamped "31 CAL" on the left side near the junction with the grips. Colt stamped the serial number on all major parts.

The Model 1849 Pocket Revolver was produced in 3", 4", 5" and 6" octagonal barrel lengths with or without an attached loading lever. A brass pin front sight was located ¼" from the muzzle while the rear sight was in the form of a "V" notch on the lip of the hammer.

Serial number range from about 12,000 to about 340000. Those produced before the end of the Civil War are numbered lower than 280000.

STANDARD MODEL: GOOD—$500   **FINE—$2,200**
MARTIALLY MARKED: GOOD—$6,000   **FINE—$20,000**

COLT MODEL 1851 NAVY, .36 CALIBER, PERCUSSION REVOLVER, FIRST MODEL

Made by Samuel Colt, Hartford, Conn., 1850-1851. Total production: Fewer than 1,250.

Overall length: 13". Weight: 2 lb. 10 oz.

Single-action, six shot.

Markings: The blued, octagonal 7-1/2" barrel is stamped "-ADDRESS SAML COLT NEW-YORK CITY-". The case-hardened frame is stamped on the left side, "COLT'S / PATENT" in two lines. A few First Model Navy revolvers include "U.S." under the frame marking and an inspector's cartouche on the one-piece black walnut grips. The blued cylinder is roll-engraved with scene depicting a naval battle between Texan and Mexican ships titled, "ENGAGED 16 MAY 1843". "COLT'S PATENT NO" with the serial number is stamped in one line.

The First Model Navy is recognizable from is square-back trigger guard and the wedge screw located under the wedge. Furthermore, the cylinder arbor on First Model Navy revolvers is grooved. Six safety pins are at the rear of he cylinder. Stop slots are rectangular with guide grooves.

Serial number range from about 1 to about 1250.

GOOD—$5,000   **FINE—$32,500**

Rock Island Auction Company

COLT MODEL 1851 NAVY, .36 CALIBER, PERCUSSION REVOLVER, SECOND MODEL

Made by Samuel Colt, Hartford, Conn., 1851. Total production: Approximately 3,000.

Overall length: 13". Weight: 2 lb. 10 oz.

Single-action, six shot.

Markings: The blued, octagonal 7-1/2" barrel is stamped "-ADDRESS SAML COLT NEW-YORK CITY-". The case-hardened frame is stamped on the left side, "COLT'S / PATENT" in two lines. A few Second Model Navy revolvers include "U.S." under the frame marking and an inspector's cartouche on the one-piece black walnut grips. The blued cylinder is roll-engraved with scene depicting a naval battle between Texan and Mexican ships titled, "ENGAGED 16 MAY 1843". "COLT'S PATENT NO" with the serial number is stamped in one line.

Rock Island Auction Company

The Second Model Navy is recognizable from is square-back trigger guard and the wedge screw located above the wedge. Furthermore, the cylinder arbor on Second Model Navy revolvers is slotted. Six safety pins are at the rear of the cylinder. Stop slots are rectangular with guide grooves.

Serial number range from about 1250 to about 4200.

GOOD—$3,250   FINE—$22,500

COLT MODEL 1851 NAVY, .36 CALIBER, PERCUSSION REVOLVER, THIRD MODEL

Made by Samuel Colt, Hartford, Conn., ca. 1851-ca. 1860. Total production: Approximately 86,000.

Overall length: 13". Weight: 2 lb. 10 oz.

Single-action, six shot.

Markings: The blued, octagonal 7-1/2" barrels of early Third Model revolvers are stamped "-ADDRESS SAML COLT NEW-YORK CITY-". Later examples are stamped, "ADDRESS SAML COLT HARTFORD CT." The case-hardened frame is stamped on the left side, "COLT'S / PATENT" in two lines. Those purchased by the U.S. Government include "U.S." under the frame marking and an inspector's cartouche on the one-piece black walnut grips. The blued cylinder is roll-engraved with scene depicting a naval battle between Texan and Mexican ships titled, "ENGAGED 16 MAY 1843". "COLT'S PATENT NO" with the serial number is stamped in one line.

James D. Julia Auctioneers, Fairfield, Maine

The Third Model Navy is recognizable from is small, oval brass trigger guard and brass backstrap. On early examples, the plunger screw enters from the right side. This changed at about serial number 30000, the plunger housing and loading groove were enlarged. The groove was heavily beveled. Six safety pins are at the rear of he cylinder. Stop slots are rectangular with guide grooves.

Considerable variation of Third Model Navy revolvers exist and include iron trigger guards and backstraps, revolvers designed to accept shoulder stocks and various barrel lengths.

Serial number range from about 4200 to about 92000.

GOOD—$900 FINE—$4,000

COLT MODEL 1851 NAVY, .36 CALIBER, PERCUSSION REVOLVER, FOURTH MODEL

Made by Samuel Colt, Hartford, Conn., ca. 1860.- 1873. Total production: Approximately 125,000.

Overall length: 13". Weight: 2 lb. 10 oz.

Single-action, six shot.

Markings: The blued, octagonal 7-1/2" barrels of early Fourth Model revolvers are stamped "ADDRESS SAML COLT HARTFORD CT." Later examples are stamped, "ADDRESS COL. SAML COLT NEW-YORK U.S. AMERICA". The case-hardened frame is stamped on the left side, "COLT'S / PATENT" in two lines. Those purchased by the U.S. Government include "U.S." under the frame marking and an inspector's cartouche on the one-piece black walnut grips. The blued cylinder is roll-engraved with scene depicting a naval battle between Texan and Mexican ships titled, "ENGAGED 16 MAY 1843". "COLT'S PATENT NO" with the serial number is stamped in one line.

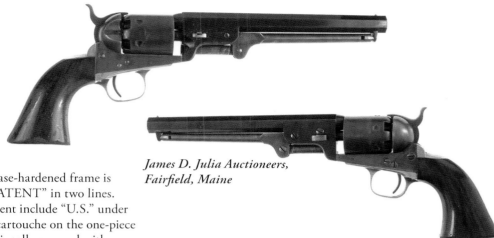

James D. Julia Auctioneers, Fairfield, Maine

Early fourth Model Colt 1851 Navy revolvers have a capping groove in the recoil shield. James D. Julia Auctioneers, Fairfield, Maine

The Fourth Model Navy is recognizable from is large, oval brass trigger guard and brass backstrap. Early examples will have a capping channel milled into the right hand recoil shield. The plunger screw enters from the left side. Six safety pins are at the rear of the cylinder. Stop slots are rectangular with guide grooves.

Considerable variation of Fourth Model Navy revolvers exist and include iron trigger guards and backstraps, revolvers designed to accept shoulder stocks, different sizes of loading lever catches and various barrel lengths.

Serial number range from about 85000 to about 215348.

GOOD—$900 FINE—$4,000

COLT MODEL 1855 SIDEHAMMER, .28 CALIBER, PERCUSSION REVOLVER

James D. Julia Auctioneers, Fairfield, Maine

Made by Samuel Colt, Hartford, Conn., 1857-ca. 1861. Total production: About 30,000.

Overall length: 8". Weight: 1 lb. 1 oz.

Single-action, five shot.

Markings: The 3-1/2" octagonal barrel stamped "COLT'S PAT. 1855—ADDRESS COL. COLT, HARTFORD, CT. U.S.A."

The .28 Caliber Sidehammer (a.k.a. "Root") Revolver went through an evolution:

1st Model: Barrel actually measures 3-7/1" and has the Hartford address without a pointing hand stamped with it. The cylinder is roll-engraved with a cabin and Indian scene. Collectors further break down the 1st Model into two types:

1st Model, Type A (serial number range 1-175): Capping groove on right recoil shield is ½".

1st Model, Type B (serial number ranger 176-475): Capping groove on right recoil shield is 5/8".

2nd Model (serial number range 476-25,000): The 3-1/2" barrel had the same stamping as the 1st Model, but with a pointing hand motif.

3rd Model, Type A (serial number range 25,001-30,000): Round, roll-engraved cylinder replaced by a fully fluted cylinder.

1ST MODEL (BOTH TYPES):
GOOD—$950 FINE—$6,500

2ND MODEL:
GOOD—$450 FINE—$1,500

3RD MODEL TYPE A:
GOOD—$450 FINE—$1,500

COLT MODEL 1855 SIDEHAMMER, .31 CALIBER, PERCUSSION REVOLVER

Made by Samuel Colt, Hartford, Conn., 1861-ca. 1872. Total production: About 1,350.

Overall length: 8". Weight: 1 lb. 1 oz.

Single-action, five shot.

Markings: The 3-1/2" octagonal barrel stamped "COLT'S PAT. 1855—ADDRESS COL. COLT, HARTFORD, CT. U.S.A."

The .31 Caliber Sidehammer (a.k.a. "Root") Revolver went through an evolution that continued where the .28 Caliber version left off:

3rd Model, Type B (serial number range 1-1,350): Fully fluted cylinder.

4th Model (serial number range 1,351-2,400): Hartford address without pointing hand. on barrel

5th Model, Type A (serial number range 2,401-8,000): Barrel marked "COL. COLT, NEW YORK".

5th Model, Type B (same number range as 5th Model, Type A): Has 4-1/2" barrel.

6th Model, Type A (serial number range, 8,001-11,074): 3-1/2" round barrel marked "COL. COLT, NEW YORK". Round cylinder roll-engraved with a stagecoach holdup scene.

6th Model, Type B (same serial number range as 6th Model, Type A): 4-1/2" round barrel.

7th Model, Type A (serial number range 11,075-14,000): 3-1/2" round barrel with New York address. Cylinder has stagecoach scene. Screw-in cylinder retains cylinder pin.

7th Model, Type B (same serial number range 7th Model, Type A): 4-1/2" round barrel with New York address. Cylinder has stagecoach scene. Screw-in cylinder retains cylinder pin.

3RD MODEL TYPE B:
GOOD—$475 FINE—$1,500

4TH MODEL:
GOOD—$475 FINE—$1,500

5TH MODEL TYPE A:
GOOD—$450 FINE—$1,100

5TH MODEL TYPE B:
GOOD—$600 FINE—$1,850

6TH MODEL (BOTH TYPES):
GOOD—$450 FINE—$1,100

7TH MODEL (BOTH TYPES):
GOOD—$650 FINE—$2,250

COLT MODEL 1860 ARMY, .44 CALIBER, PERCUSSION REVOLVER, FIRST MODEL

Made by Samuel Colt, Hartford, Conn., ca. 1860. Total production: Approximately 100.

Overall length: 13-1/2". Weight: 2 lb. 11 oz.

Single-action, six shot.

Markings: The blued, 7-1/2" or 8" barrels of First Model revolvers are stamped "ADDRESS SAML COLT HARTFORD CT." or "ADDRESS COL. SAML COLT NEW-YORK U.S. AMERICA". The case-hardened frame is stamped on the left side, "COLTS / PATENT" in two lines. The left shoulder of the trigger guard stamped "44 CAL". The full-fluted blued cylinder is stamped in one flute, "PATENTED SEPT. 10TH 1850" and the serial number may be found in another. No engraving was used on the fluted cylinder revolvers. Government purchased examples will have inspector cartouches on grips and stamps on various metal parts.

James D. Julia Auctioneers, Fairfield, Maine

The fluted cylinder, 7-1/2" barrel and short, Navy-style grips distinguish the First Model Army revolver. Virtually all of these Hartford-made revolvers have brass trigger guards and iron back straps, though a few brass back straps have been encountered in the very lowest serial numbers. Government purchased examples will have inspector cartouches on grips and stamps on various metal parts.

Fewer than 100 Colt Army revolvers were assembled with Navy size grips, 65 of which were shipped to fill a government contract. The earliest examples do not have a capping channel milled into the right side recoil plate. Those revolvers built to accommodate a shoulder stock have four-bolt frames.

Fluted cylinders are found on revolvers below serial number 8000. The shorter, 7-1/2" barrels were used on the First Model revolvers and are numbered below 400.

Serial number range from about 1-400.

GOOD—$3,500   FINE—$16,000

COLT MODEL 1860 ARMY, .44 CALIBER, PERCUSSION REVOLVER, SECOND MODEL

Made by Samuel Colt, Hartford, Conn., ca. 1860-1861. Total production: Approximately 7,000.

Overall length: 14". Weight: 2 lb. 11 oz.

Single-action, six shot.

Markings: The blued, 8" barrels of Second Model revolvers are stamped "ADDRESS SAML COLT HARTFORD CT." or "ADDRESS COL. SAML COLT NEW-YORK U.S. AMERICA". The case-hardened frame is stamped on the left side, "COLTS / PATENT" in two lines. The left shoulder of the trigger guard stamped "44 CAL". The full-fluted blued cylinder is stamped in one flute, "PATENTED SEPT. 10TH 1850" and the serial number may be found in another. No engraving was used on the fluted cylinder revolvers. Government purchased examples will have inspector cartouches on grips and stamps on various metal parts.

James D. Julia Auctioneers, Fairfield, Maine

Distinguishing characteristics of Second Model Army revolvers includes a fluted cylinder, 8" barrel and longer grips. Virtually all of these Hartford-made revolvers have brass trigger guards and iron back straps. Second Model 1860 revolvers were furnished with the longer Army, one-piece, black walnut grips. All of the Second Model revolvers had a capping channel milled on the right side of the recoil shield. Those revolvers built to accommodate a shoulder stock have four-bolt frames.

Serial number range from about 400 to about 8000.

GOOD—$2,500   FINE—$11,100

COLT MODEL 1860 ARMY, .44 CALIBER, PERCUSSION REVOLVER, THIRD MODEL

Made by Samuel Colt, Hartford, Conn., ca. 1861-1864.
Total production: about 42,000.
Overall length: 14". Weight: 2 lb. 11 oz.
Single-action, six shot.
Markings: The most common stamping on the blued, 8" barrels of Third Model revolvers read, "ADDRESS COL. SAML COLT NEW-YORK U.S. AMERICA"

James D. Julia Auctioneers, Fairfield, Maine

though some will be found with the earlier, "ADDRESS SAML COLT HARTFORD CT." The case-hardened frame is stamped on the left side, "COLTS / PATENT" in two lines. The left shoulder of the trigger guard stamped "44 CAL". The round, rebated cylinder is roll-engraved with the same scene as found on Colt Navy revolvers depicting action between the Texas and Mexican navies. Each cylinder is stamped "COLT'S PATENT NO" with the last four digits of the serial number. Government purchased examples will have inspector cartouches on grips and stamps on various metal parts.

Distinguishing characteristics of Third Model Army revolvers includes a round cylinder with roll engraving, 8" barrel, four-bolt frame and longer grips. Virtually all of these Hartford-made revolvers have brass trigger guards and iron back straps. All of the Third Model revolvers had a capping channel milled on the right side of the recoil shield.

Many Third and Fourth Model Army revolvers had the lower portion of the recoil shield milled away to accommodate the attachment of a shoulder stock. These revolvers will also have four-bolt frames. Collectors refer to these as "martial models" believing that this style was only used to fill government contracts. Collectors have labeled examples with full recoil shields and three-bolt frames as "civilian models" even though standardized three-bolt frames around serial number 25,000.

A few Third Model Army revolvers constructed to accept shoulder stocks will be found with a small, two-leaf folding rear sight mortised in the top of the barrel near the breech.

Serial number range from about 8000 to about 50000.

GOOD—$950   FINE—$7,500

Many Third and Fourth Model Army revolvers had the lower portion of the recoil shield milled away and four-bolt frames to accommodate a shoulder stock. James D. Julia Auctioneers, Fairfield, Maine

COLT MODEL 1860 ARMY, .44 CALIBER, PERCUSSION REVOLVER, FOURTH MODEL

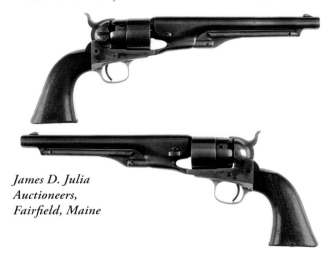

*James D. Julia
Auctioneers,
Fairfield, Maine*

COLT MODEL 1861 NAVY, .36 CALIBER, PERCUSSION REVOLVER

*James D. Julia
Auctioneers,
Fairfield, Maine*

Made by Samuel Colt, Hartford, Conn., ca. 1863-ca. 1872. Total production: about 150,000.

Overall length: 14". Weight: 2 lb. 11 oz.

Single-action, six shot.

Markings: The most common stamping on the blued, 8" barrels of Fourth Model revolvers read, "ADDRESS COL. SAML COLT NEW-YORK U.S. AMERICA" The case-hardened frame is stamped on the left side, "COLTS / PATENT" in two lines. The left shoulder of the trigger guard stamped "44 CAL". The round, rebated cylinder is roll-engraved with the same scene as found on Colt Navy revolvers depicting action between the Texas and Mexican navies. Each cylinder is stamped "COLT'S PATENT NO" with the last four digits of the serial number. Government purchased examples will have inspector cartouches on grips and stamps on various metal parts.

Distinguishing characteristics of Fourth Model Army revolvers includes a round cylinder with roll engraving, 8" barrel, three-bolt frame and longer grips. Virtually all of these Hartford-made revolvers have brass trigger guards and iron back straps. All of the Fourth Model revolvers had a capping channel milled on the right side of the recoil shield.

Many Third and Fourth Model Army revolvers had the lower portion of the recoil shield milled away to accommodate the attachment of a shoulder stock. These revolvers will also have four-bolt frames Collectors refer to these as "martial models" believing that this style was only used to fill government contracts. Collectors have labeled examples with full recoil shields and three-bolt frames as "civilian models" even though standardized three-bolt frames around serial number 25,000.

Serial number range from about 50,000 to about 200,500. Civil War production ended by 156,000.

GOOD—$900 FINE—$7,000

Made by Samuel Colt, Hartford, Conn., ca. 1861-ca. 1873. Total production: 38,843.

Overall length: 13". Weight: 2 lb. 10 oz.

Single-action, six shot.

Markings: Blued, round 7-1/2" barrel stamped "ADDRESS COL. SAML COLT NEW-YORK U.S. AMERICA". The case-hardened frame is stamped on the left side, "COLT'S / PATENT" in two lines. "36 CAL" stamped on left shoulder of brass trigger guard strap. Those purchased by the U.S. Government include "U.S." under the frame marking (though not confirmed as legitimate) and an inspector's cartouche on the one-piece black walnut grips.

Type I: The round, blued cylinder is roll-engraved with scene depicting a naval battle between Texan and Mexican ships titled, "ENGAGED 16 MAY 1843". "COLT'S PATENT NO" with the serial number is stamped in one line. About 100 between serial number 11,000 and 14,000 made to accept a shoulder stock.

Type II: Only about 100 in the serial range of 1 to 100 made with fluted cylinders. No engraved scene on the cylinder, but stamped on one of the flutes is "PAT. SEPT 10TH 1850".

Serial number range from 1 to about 38,843. Civil War production ended at about 28,000

TYPE I:
GOOD—$950   FINE—$8,000
TYPE II:
GOOD—$6,000   FINE—$40,000
MARTIALLY MARKED:
GOOD—$2,750   FINE—$17,500

COLT MODEL 1862 POCKET NAVY, .36 CALIBER, PERCUSSION REVOLVER

Made by Samuel Colt, Hartford, Conn., ca. 1863-ca. 1873. Total production: approximately 47,000.

Overall length: 11-1/2" (with 6-1/2" barrel). Weight: 1 lb. 12 oz.

Single-action, five shot.

Markings: Blued, octagonal barrel (in 4-1/2", 5-1/2" and 6-1/2") stamped on top flat "ADDRESS COL. SAML COLT NEW-YORK U.S. AMERICA". The case-hardened frame is stamped on the left side, "COLT'S / PATENT" in two lines. "36 CAL" stamped on left shoulder of brass trigger guard strap. The round cylinder (with 5/8" rebated section oat the rear) is roll-engraved with a stagecoach holdup scene and stamped "COLT'S PATENT" over "NO" and the serial number.

Serial number range from 1 to about 47,000.

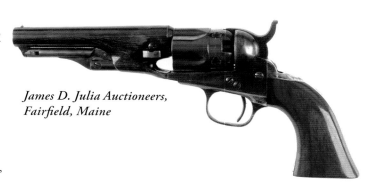

Rock Island Auction Company

GOOD—$625   **FINE—$2,750**

COLT MODEL 1862 POLICE, .36 CALIBER, PERCUSSION REVOLVER

Made by Samuel Colt, Hartford, Conn., ca. 1861-ca. 1873. Total production: Approximately 48,000.

Overall length: 11-1/2" (with 6-1/2" barrel). Weight: 1 lb. 10 oz.

Single-action, five shot.

Markings: Blued, round barrel (in 4-1/2", 5-1/2" and 6-1/2") stamped on the earliest examples, "ADDRESS SAML COLT HARTFORD CT." Later revolvers stamped, "ADDRESS COL. SAML COLT NEW-YORK U.S. AMERICA". The case-hardened frame is stamped on the left side in two lines, "COLT'S / PATENT". "36 CAL" stamped on left shoulder of the silver-plated brass trigger guard strap. The blued cylinder is rebated with a semi-fluted section forward of the rebate. "PAT SEPT. 10th 1850" stamped in one of the flutes.

James D. Julia Auctioneers, Fairfield, Maine

Grips are one-piece walnut. The frame, hammer and lever are case-hardened. Grip straps are silver-plated brass. Remaining parts are blued.

Serial number range from 1 to about 48,000.

EARLY: GOOD—$600   **FINE—$3,000**
LATE: GOOD—$650   **FINE—$4,750**

COLUMBUS FIRE ARMS NAVY, .36 CALIBER, PERCUSSION REVOLVER

Made by Columbus Fire Arms Manufacturing Company (L. Haiman and Bros.), Columbus, Georgia., 1863-1864. Total production: About 100.

Overall length: 13-1/2".

Single action, six-shot.

Serial number (beginning at "1") stamped in small size. Barrel marked in two lines, "COLUMBUS FIRE ARMS MANUF. CO / COLUMBUS, GA." Cylinder marked, "COLUMBUS FIRE ARMS/ MANUF. CO / COLUMBUS, GA." Trigger guard plate stamped "C.S." on some examples. Variations of these marking configuration exist.

In 1862, the Confederate government gave a contract to the Columbus Fire Arms company specifying an order for 10,000 Navy revolvers of he Colt type. By May 1863, production was underway. The following spring, the Confederate government purchased the business from L. Haiman and Bros. before they had assembled the first 100 revolvers.

The Columbus Fire Arms Navy has a round barrel that becomes octagonal near the cylinder. At least one example is known with a full octagonal barrel. The revolver is iron-framed with a brass trigger guard and grip straps.

FAIR—$75,000   **VERY GOOD—$150,000**

J. M. COOPER POCKET REVOLVER, 1ST MODEL, PHILADELPHIA-MADE, .31 CALIBER, COMBUSTIBLE CARTRIDGE, PERCUSSION

Rock Island Auction Company

Manufactured by Cooper Fire Arms Company, Philadelphia, Pennsylvania, ca. 1864. Total production: Unknown.

Double action, five shot.

"ADDRESS COOPER FIRE ARMS MFG. CO. FRANKFORD PHILA. PA. / PAT. JAN. 7, 1851 APR. 25, 1854 SEP. 4, 1860 / SEPT. 1, 1863 SEPT. 22, 1863"; serial numbered in approximately the 1–400 range.

J. M. Cooper & Company moved its armory from Pittsburgh to Philadelphia in 1864. The 1st Model of the firm's Philadelphia-made pocket revolvers featured new barrel markings, had the cylinder bolt on the right side of the frame, and lacked the nipple shield on the recoil shield. Grip straps were in most cases iron.

GOOD—$375   **FINE—$1,200**

J. M. COOPER POCKET REVOLVER, 1ST MODEL, PITTSBURGH-MADE, .31 CALIBER, COMBUSTIBLE CARTRIDGE, PERCUSSION

Rock Island Auction Company

Manufactured by J. M. Cooper & Co., Pittsburgh, Pennsylvania, 1850s–1864. Total production: Unknown.

Double action, five shot.

"MANFD BY J.M. COOPER & CO / PITTSBURGH PA / PATD APL 25, 1854 / PATD JAN. 7, 1851 / REISSD JULY 26, 1859" on barrel; serial number in the 1–100 range.

J. M. Cooper & Company manufactured the First Model of their Pocket Revolvers in Pittsburgh. Similar in appearance to the Colt Model 1849 Pocket Pistol, it had a .31-Caliber blued, octagonal barrel in lengths of 4", 5", or 6"; one-piece walnut grip; and brass grip straps. The round, five-shot cylinder lacked decorative engraving, and had ten oval or rectangular notches.

GOOD—$475   **FINE—$1,500**

J. M. COOPER POCKET REVOLVER, 2ND MODEL, PITTSBURGH-MADE, .31 CALIBER, COMBUSTIBLE CARTRIDGE, PERCUSSION

Manufactured by J. M. Cooper & Co., Pittsburgh, Pennsylvania, 1850s–1864. Total production: Unknown.

Double action, five shot.

Type I : "MANFD BY J.M. COOPER & CO / PITTSBURGH PA / PATD APL 25, 1854 / PATD JAN. 7, 1851 / REISSD JULY 26, 1859" on barrel; serial number in 1–100 range. Type II: "MANFD BY J.M. COOPER & CO PITTSH. PA PAT JAN. 7, 1851 / REIS'D JULY 26, 1859 PAT APR 25, 1854 PAT SEPT. 4, 1860" on barrel; serial number in the 1–900 range.

The 2nd Model of the J. M. Cooper Pocket Revolver was similar to the 1st Model, except with iron grip straps and a new serial-number range of 1–900. There were two basic variants:

Type I: About 100 examples had rectangular notches between each chamber on the cylinder.

Type II: Barrel markings were revised, as noted above; serial numbers in the 1–900 range.

TYPE I: GOOD—$475   **FINE—$1,400**
TYPE II: GOOD—$375   **FINE—$1,200**

J. M. COOPER POCKET REVOLVER, 2ND MODEL, PHILADELPHIA-MADE, .31 CALIBER, COMBUSTIBLE CARTRIDGE, PERCUSSION

Manufactured by Cooper Fire Arms Company, Philadelphia, Pennsylvania. Total production: Unknown.

Double action, five shot.

"COOPER FIRE ARMS MFG. CO. FRANKFORD PHILA. PA. / PAT. JAN. 7, 1851 APR. 25, 1854 SEP. 4, 1860 / SEPT. 1, 1863 SEPT. 22, 1863"; serial numbered in approximately the 400–11000 range.

On the 2nd Model of Cooper's Philadelphia-made pocket revolvers, the cylinder bolt was moved to the left side of the frame, the nipple shield was restored to the recoil shield, the word "ADDRESS" was deleted from the barrel marking, and the grip straps were usually brass.

GOOD—$350   **FINE—$1,100**

J. M. COOPER POCKET REVOLVER, 3RD MODEL, PHILADELPHIA-MADE, .31 CALIBER, COMBUSTIBLE CARTRIDGE, PERCUSSION

*Rock Island
Auction Company*

Manufactured by Cooper Fire Arms Company, Philadelphia, Pennsylvania. Total production: Unknown.

Double action, five shot.

"COOPER FIRE ARMS MFG. CO. FRANKFORD PHILA. PA. / PAT. JAN. 7, 1851 APR. 25, 1854 SEP. 4, 1860 / SEPT. 1, 1863 SEPT. 22, 1863"; serial numbered in approximately the 11000–15000 range.

The 3rd Model of the pocket revolver manufactured by J. M. Cooper in Philadelphia exchanged the five-shot cylinder for an enlarged, six-shot cylinder.

GOOD—$350   FINE—$1,100

J. M. COOPER NAVY REVOLVER, 1ST MODEL, .36 CALIBER, COMBUSTIBLE CARTRIDGE, PERCUSSION

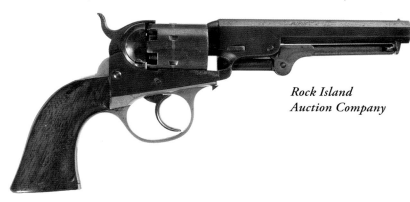

*Rock Island
Auction Company*

Manufactured by J. M. Cooper, Cooper Fire Arms Company, Philadelphia, Pennsylvania, ca. 1864. Total production: Approximately 400.

Overall length: 10-7/8".
Weight: 1 lb. 12 oz.

Double action, five shot.

"ADDRESS COOPER FIRE ARMS MFG. CO. FRANKFORD PHILA. PA. / PAT. JAN. 7, 1851 APR. 25, 1854 SEP. 4, 1860 / SEPT. 1, 1863 SEPT. 22, 1863"; serial number on cylinder and most major parts in approximately the 1–400 range.

J. M. Cooper's Navy Revolver, 1st Model, had a one-piece walnut grip; round, undecorated, five-shot cylinder; trapezoidal cylinder stops; casehardened frame and hammer; and, usually, an iron grip strap. Barrels were octagonal, blued, rifled with seven grooves, and were generally 5-7/8" long, but lengths of 4" and 5" are encountered. The barrel lug had a beveled loading groove on the right side.

GOOD—$600   FINE—$1,600

J. M. COOPER NAVY REVOLVER, 2ND MODEL, .36 CALIBER, COMBUSTIBLE CARTRIDGE, PERCUSSION

Manufactured by J. M. Cooper, Cooper Fire Arms Company, Philadelphia, Pennsylvania, ca. 1864–69. Total production: Approximately 14,600.

Overall length: 10-7/8". Weight: 1 lb. 12 oz.

Double action, five shot.

"COOPER FIRE ARMS MFG. CO. FRANKFORD PHILA. PA. / PAT. JAN. 7, 1851 APR. 25, 1854 SEP. 4, 1860 / SEPT. 1, 1863 SEPT. 22, 1863"; serial numbered in approximately the 400–15000 range on cylinder and most major parts.

The 2nd Model of J. M. Cooper's Navy Revolver varied from the 1st Model in several particulars: The barrel lug was slightly longer and had a loading groove that extended completely through the lug. The cylinder was 1/8" longer and was rebated, with the front half being of slightly larger diameter than on the 1st Model. (However, examples in the 500–1000 serial number range had cylinders that were 3/16" shorter than standard 2nd Model revolvers.) The grip straps were brass, and "ADDRESS" was eliminated from the marking on the barrel.

GOOD—$550   FINE—$1,500

J. Dance Revolver, .36 Caliber, Combustible Cartridge, Percussion

Rock Island Auction Company

Manufactured by J. H. Dance & Brothers, Columbia, Texas, 1862-1863. Total production: Approximately 50 to 150.

Overall length: 11-1/2".

Single action, six shot.

No maker's markings; serial numbers on some parts.

J. H. Dance & Brothers produced several hundred .36- and .44-caliber Colt-type revolvers at its Columbia, Texas, factory before moving from that location in 1863. The .36-caliber version has been described by some as a scaled-down Dragoon-type revolver, and by others as a Navy-type. Its primary distinguishing characteristic was a flat frame without a recoil shield. In addition to a round, blued, 7-3/8" barrel, it had bright brass grip straps and a one-piece walnut grip. Since counterfeit examples exist in the form of Colt 1851 Navy revolvers with the recoil shield ground off and other alterations, collectors are advised to exercise caution when considering Dance .36-caliber revolvers.

Fair—$40,000   **Very Good—$85,000**

The flat frame with no recoil shield is a distinctive hallmark of the J.H. Dance revolver. Rock Island Auction Company

J. DANCE REVOLVER, .44 CALIBER, COMBUSTIBLE CARTRIDGE, PERCUSSION

Manufactured by J. H. Dance & Brothers, Columbia, Texas, 1862-1863. Total production: approximately 275 to 350.

Overall length: 13-1/2".

Single action, six shot.

No maker's markings; serial numbers on some parts.

J. H. Dance & Brothers' .44-caliber revolver has been classified by some authorities as a Dragoon-type revolver, and by others as an Army-type. It was in effect a scaled-up version of Dance's .36-caliber revolver, with an 8" barrel. A few high-serial-number examples had octagonal instead of round barrels.

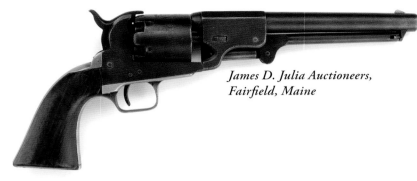

James D. Julia Auctioneers, Fairfield, Maine

FAIR—$25,000   VERY GOOD—$60,000

FREEMAN ARMY MODEL REVOLVER .44 CALIBER PERCUSSION REVOLVER, COMBUSTIBLE CARTRIDGE

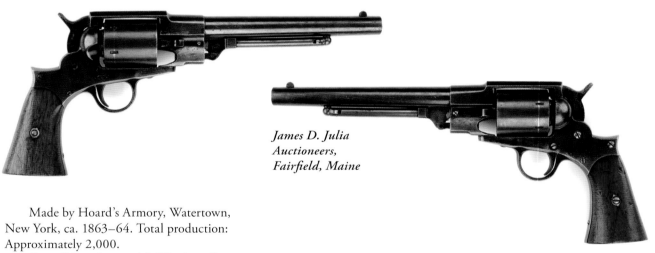

James D. Julia Auctioneers, Fairfield, Maine

Made by Hoard's Armory, Watertown, New York, ca. 1863–64. Total production: Approximately 2,000.

Overall length: 12-1/2". Weight: 2 lbs. 2 oz.

Single action, six shot.

"FREEMAN'S PAT. DECR 9, 1862 / HOARD'S ARMORY, WATERTOWN, N.Y." on top strap (Type II only); serial number (in sequence from 1) on cylinder.

The Freeman Army Revolver had a 7-1/2" round barrel, rifled with six grooves. It featured a blued finish, except for a casehardened hammer and lever.

Two basic types were produced:

Type I: Probably fewer of a dozen early-production examples had barrel threads visible through a cutout in the frame to the front of the cylinder, and a somewhat flattened recoil shield to the rear of the cylinder.

Type II: Barrel threads were not visible; recoil guard was fuller and round; and other minor details in the number of frame screws and the cylinder arbor release varied from the Type I revolver.

BOTH TYPES: GOOD—$1,400   FINE—$4,000

GRISWOLD & GUNNISON REVOLVER, .36 CALIBER, COMBUSTIBLE CARTRIDGE, PERCUSSION

Manufactured by Griswold & Gunnison, Griswoldville, Georgia, ca. 1862-64. Total production: Approximately 3,700.

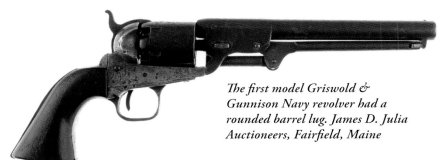

The first model Griswold & Gunnison Navy revolver had a rounded barrel lug. James D. Julia Auctioneers, Fairfield, Maine

The second model Griswold & Gunnison Navy revolver had an octagonal barrel lug. James D. Julia Auctioneers, Fairfield, Maine

Overall length: 13-1/4".

Single action, six shot.

No maker's markings; serial number starting at 1 on right side of frame and barrel and side of cylinder; secondary serial numbers on most parts (varies within one or two digits of the primary serial number); inspector's stamp on most major parts; Roman numeral benchmarks on frame and grip straps.

These revolvers, previously referred to in some works as the Griswold & Grier revolver, were produced under contract from the Confederate government by the factory of Samuel Griswold and A. W. Gunnison until Union cavalry burned the facility in November 1864. The chief identifying characteristics are the bright brass frame and grip straps; the safety pins between each nipple on the rear face of the cylinder; the twist marks on the cylinder; and the butt, which tilts upward to the rear. The revolver also features a 7-1/2" blued, dragoon-style barrel with six-groove rifling, right-twist, and one-piece walnut grip (many of which had the tendency to shrink).

There were two basic types of the Gunnison & Griswold revolver:

First Model: Rounded barrel lug.

Second Model: Octagonal barrel lug, serial numbers approximately 1500 and up..

FIRST MODEL: FAIR—$12,000   VERY GOOD—$25,000

SECOND MODEL: FAIR—$14,000   VERY GOOD—$30,000

HOPKINS & ALLEN DICTATOR MODEL REVOLVER, .36 CALIBER, COMBUSTIBLE CARTRIDGE, PERCUSSION

Manufactured by Hopkins & Allen, Norwich, Connecticut, ca. late 1860s–early 1870s. Total production:

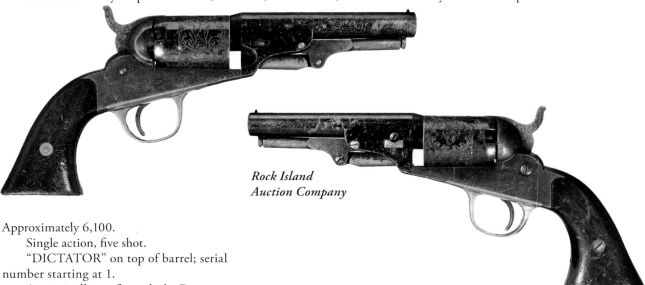

Rock Island Auction Company

Approximately 6,100.

Single action, five shot.

"DICTATOR" on top of barrel; serial number starting at 1.

As originally configured, the Dictator was a percussion revolver in .36 caliber. It included a blued finish, walnut grips, and a loading lever/plunger assembly. Around 1,000 of the Dictators were left in that configuration, but the remaining approximately 5,100 were altered to accept .38-caliber metallic rimfire cartridges. This conversion included elimination of the loading lever/plunger and altering the barrel lug to a smaller, more streamlined shape.

STANDARD MODEL: GOOD—$400   FINE—$1,250
FACTORY CONVERSION: GOOD—$250   FINE—$650

JOSLYN ARMY MODEL REVOLVER, EARLY MODEL, 44 CALIBER PERCUSSION REVOLVER, COMBUSTIBLE CARTRIDGE

Made by the Joslyn Firearms Company, Stonington, Connecticut, ca. 1861. Total production: Approximately 500.

Overall length: 14-3/8". Weight: 3 lbs.

Single action, 5 shot.

"B.F. JOSLYN / PATD MAY 4TH 1858" on top of barrel; serial number (in sequence, starting with 1) on rear face of cylinder and on barrel.

The Joslyn Army Model Revolver had an 8" rifled, octagonal barrel, with blued metal components, except for casehardened loading lever and side-mounted hammer. The two-piece black walnut grips had oil finish and partially checkered surface. The Early Model revolvers had a brass trigger guard and flat iron butt cap.

GOOD—1,500   FINE—5,000

JOSLYN ARMY MODEL REVOLVER, STANDARD PRODUCTION, 44 CALIBER PERCUSSION REVOLVER, COMBUSTIBLE CARTRIDGE

Made by the Joslyn Firearms Company, Stonington, Connecticut, ca. 1861–62. Total production: Approximately 2,500.

Overall length: 14-3/8". Weight: 3 lbs. Single action, 5 shot.

"B.F. JOSLYN / PATD MAY 4TH 1858" on top of barrel; serial number on rear face of cylinder and on barrel; anchor on bottom barrel flat or butt strap, or "USN" on butt, on U.S. Navy-procured examples.

The Standard Production model of the Joslyn Army Model Revolver differed from the Early Model in that all but the very-late-production specimens lacked butt caps, and they had iron trigger guards. Early in the Civil War, the Navy Department received a consignment of these pistols, and they have USN markings as described above.

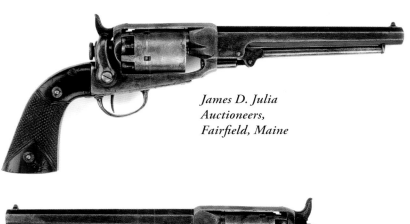

James D. Julia Auctioneers, Fairfield, Maine

GOOD—$1,400   FINE—$4,500

KERR PATENT, .44 CALIBER, PERCUSSION REVOLVER

James D. Julia Auctioneers, Fairfield, Maine

Made by London Armoury Company, London, England, 1858-1865. Total imported: Approximately 7,500.

Overall length: 10-3/4".

Single-action, five-shot.

The 5-1/2" barrel and cylinder have London proof marks. The lock plate is engraved, "LONDON ARMOURY." The right side of the frame is marked, "KERRS PATENT." The left side of the frame is stamped "LONDON ARMOURY" in an oval. The serial number is stamped on both the cylinder and the right side of the frame. Some are marked with "JS / [anchor]."

Type I: Loading lever has a hinge screw near the edge of the frame.

Type II: Loading lever is heavier than on the Type I and is recognizable from the centrally located hinge screw that is in line with the cylinder pin.

While the U.S. Government purchased only 16 Kerr revolvers in 1861, the Confederate government bought between 7,000 and 7,500 in the 3000-10000 serial number range. Though the revolver was made in both .36 and .44 calibers with a double-action version released in 1863, the Confederacy seemed to have only purchased single-action .44 caliber guns.

BOTH TYPES: GOOD—$2,000   FINE—$7,500

LEECH & RIGDON .36 CALIBER PERCUSSION REVOLVER, COMBUSTIBLE CARTRIDGE

Made by Leech & Rigdon, Columbus, Mississippi, and Rigdon & Ansley, Greensboro, Georgia, ca. 1863–64. Total production: approximately 1,500.

Overall Length: 13".

Single action, six shot.

"LEECH & RIGDON CSA" on top flat of barrel (some variations exist in this marking, such as "LEECH & RIGDON NOVELTY WORKS, CSA"; serial number in sequence from 1 on some parts; inspector or assembly marks on side of trigger guard; "W.H." inspector's mark on higher serial number examples.

The Leech & Rigdon revolver was a virtual copy of the Colt Model 1851 Navy Revolver. It had a 7-1/2" round barrel with an octagonal section near the frame. Other features included casehardened frame, blued barrel and cylinder, bright brass trigger guard and back strap, and one-piece walnut grips. Casting defects are common. Most of the production run was manufactured at Leech & Rigdon's Columbus, Mississippi, factory, with the last 500 or so being made at Rigdon & Ansley's Greensboro, Georgia, factory.

Collection Of Frank Reile,
Photo by Alya Alberico

FAIR—$12,500   **VERY GOOD—$30,000**

LEFAUCHEAUX MODEL 1854 REVOLVER, 12MM PINFIRE

James D. Julia
Auctioneers,
Fairfield, Maine

Most made by Lefaucheaux, Paris, France, but some made at the St. Etienne armory as well as by Belgian factories, ca. 1854-1866. Total imported: Unknown, but Union records indicate at least 12,639. Confederate purchases were between 2,000 and 5,000.

Barrel length: 6-1/2".

Single action, six shot.

Top of barrel engraved "IVon E. Lefaucheux Bvte S.G.D.G. a Paris". The same wording sometimes appears in an oval on the left side of the frame. "LF" and a small image of an opened revolver precede the serial number stamped on the right side of the frame.

The 12mm (roughly .47 caliber) revolver fired a metallic pinfire cartridge. Open framed, the revolvers featured round grips, round barrel and a lanyard ring. A hinged loading gate on the right side opens to insert the cartridge. A sliding rod under the barrel is available to assist in ejecting spent cartridges. Lefaucheaux produced two distinct versions of the Model 1854:

Cavalry Model: This is considered the "standard" model and can be identified by the finger spur on the trigger guard and a multi-contoured butt cap.

Navy Model: Has an oval trigger guard and a slightly rounded, oval-shaped butt cap.

The names of the two models were irrelevant when issuing the weapons. Variations of the Model 1854 exist, mostly in barrel length.

Despite never gaining wide acceptance among the troops, the U.S. Ordnance Department purchased at least 12,639. Confederate records are sketchy, but seem to point to between 2,000 and 5,000 Lefaucheaux pinfire revolvers purchased.

BOTH MODELS: GOOD—$450   FINE—$1,500

LeMat 1st Model Revolver, .42/.63 Percussion

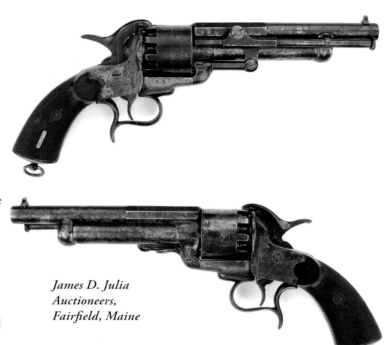

Made by Charles Girard & Co., Liege, Belgium, ca. 1861. Total production: Approximately 500.

Overall length: 13-5/8".

Single action, nine-shot (.42 caliber) and single shot (20 gauge—.63 caliber).

Top of barrel marked "Col. Le Mat's Patent" along with the LeMat trademark script "LM" within a circle.

The nine-shot revolver with a second 20-gauge barrel was an instant hit with Confederate troops. The barrel is part round and part octagonal. The loading lever is mounted on the right side. A lanyard swivel ring is affixed to the bottom of the grips. The trigger guard has a finger spur. Serial numbers range from 1 to about 450. It is believed that the virtually all of the 1st Model revolvers were shipped to the Confederacy to fulfill contracts.

James D. Julia Auctioneers, Fairfield, Maine

Good—$20,500   Fine—$50,000

LeMat Transition Model Revolver, .42/.63 Percussion

James D. Julia Auctioneers, Fairfield, Maine

Made by Charles Girard & Co., Paris, France, ca. 1861. Total production: Approximately 500.

Overall length: 13-5/8" - 14".

Single action, nine-shot (.42 caliber) and single shot (20 gauge—.63 caliber).

Markings vary and will be found in script or block letters. Identified Transition Model markings include: 1) "COL. LeMAT BTE.s.g.d.g. PARIS"; 2) SYST. LeMAT BTE s.g.d.g. PARIS"; "SYSTme LeMAT Bte S.G.D.G. PARIS"; 4) "LE MAT & GIRARD'S PATENT"; "LeMat's Patent"; and "Col. LeMat's Patent." In addition, some Transition Models will be marked will be marked on the cylinder with an "M" inside a recessed square. This was the inspector's mark of Confederate Navy Lieutenant William Murdaugh.

Transition Model revolvers incorporate characteristics of the 1st Model revolver into the 2nd Model. It appears this was done for no other reason than using up parts. Transition Model revolvers fall in the serial number range of approximately 450-950.

Good—$15,000   Fine—$25,000

LeMat 2nd Model Revolver, .42/.63 Percussion

Made by Charles Girard & Co., Paris, France, and Aston, Brothers, London, England, ca. 1861-1865. Total production: Approximately 2,000.

Overall length: 14".

Single action, nine-shot (.42 caliber) and single shot (20 gauge—.63 caliber).

Top of barrel marked in one of three ways: 1) "COL. LeMAT BTE.s.g.d.g. PARIS"; 2) SYST. LeMAT BTE s.g.d.g. PARIS"; or "SYSTme LeMAT Bte S.G.D.G. PARIS". Revolvers made in London were marked on the barrel, "LE MAT & GIRARD'S PATENT LONDON". In addition, the trademark "[star] / LM" will be found on the revolvers as well.

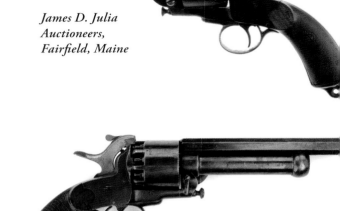

James D. Julia Auctioneers, Fairfield, Maine

The nine-shot revolver with a second 20-gauge barrel was an instant hit with Confederate troops. 2nd Model LeMats can be recognized by the completely octagonal barrel, trigger guard with no spur, and the loading lever mounted on the left side. In addition, the lanyard loop does not swivel as it did on the 1st Model. 2nd Model LeMats made in Paris are numbered from about 950 through 2500. The London-made revolvers are numbered from 1-128 and 5000 to about 5200. Made by the Aston Brothers of London, the barrels and cylinders of the English-made revolvers will also have London or Birmingham proof marks.

London-made 2nd Model LeMat revolver. James D. Julia Auctioneers, Fairfield, Maine

Good—$17,500   Fine—$30,000

W. W. Marston Pocket Model Revolver, .31 Caliber, Percussion, Combustible Cartridge

Made by W. W. Marston, New York City, c. 1858–early 1860s. Total production: approximately 13,000.

Overall length and weight: varies by type.

Single action, five or six shot.

For markings, see individual types below.

There were seven basic types of the W. W. Marston Pocket Model Revolver. The series featured a solid frame, walnut grips, Colt-type rammers on the first six types, and blued finish.

Type I: "Wm. W. Marston / Phenix Armory / New York City" on barrel; five-shot round cylinder; top surface of frame is flat (this feature remained up through the Fourth Type); serial number range ca. 1–1050.

Type II: "The Union / Arms Co." on barrel; five shot, round cylinder; serial number range ca. 1050–1500.

Type III: "The Union / Arms Co." on barrel; five-shot, round cylinder (with variations noted in shape of cylinder); serial number range ca. 1500–4000. This and subsequent types changed from a straight to a rounded edge of the grip where it meets the frame.

Type IV: "The Union / Arms Co." on barrel; five-shot, fluted cylinder; serial number range ca. 4000–6000.

Type V: "The Union / Arms Co." on barrel; top surface of frame is grooved rather than flat (this feature continued with the Sixth and Seventh Types); five-shot fluted cylinder; serial number range ca. 6000-8500

Type VI: Four possible markings on barrel: "The Union Arm / Arms Co.", "The Union Arms Co.", "Western Arms Co. New York", or "Western Arms Co. / Chicago, Ill."; six-shot round cylinder; serial number range ca. 8500–10000.

Type VII: "Union," "Western Arms Co. New York", or "Western Arms Co. / Chicago, Ill." on barrel; six-shot round cylinder; Whitney-type rammer; serial range ca. 10000–13000.

Type I: Good—$350   Fine—$1,100
Type II: Good—$375   Fine—$1,200
Type III: Good—$350   Fine—$1,100
Type IV: Good—$350   Fine—$1,100
Type V: Good—$350   Fine—$1,100
Type VI: Good—$375   Fine—$1,200
Type VII: Good—$350   Fine—$1,100

MARSTON NAVY MODEL .36 CALIBER PERCUSSION REVOLVER

Made by W. W. Marston, New York City, ca. late 1850s–early 1860s. Total production: 1,000.

Single action, six shot.

For markings, see individual types below.

Distinctive features of the Marston Navy Model Revolver included a six-shot round cylinder, plain or engraved with the same eagle, shield, and lion design as found on the Whitney Navy Revolver (suggesting that Whitney made the cylinders). The revolver had walnut grips and blued finish.

There were three variations:

Type I: Octagonal barrel; only markings were serial numbers, sequentially from 1.

Type II: "UNION ARMS CO." or "WESTERN ARMS CO." stamped on octagonal barrel; serial numbers ranged from 201 to 500.

Type III: "UNION ARMS CO." or "WESTERN ARMS CO." stamped on round barrel; serial numbers ranged from 501 to 1000.

Rock Island Auction Company

TYPE I: GOOD—$850   **FINE—$3,250**

TYPE II: GOOD—$900   **FINE—$3,500**

TYPE III: GOOD—$850   **FINE—$3,000**

MANHATTAN NAVY REVOLVER, SERIES I–IV, .36 CALIBER PERCUSSION REVOLVER

Series II Manhattan Navy Revolver. Rock Island Auction Company

Made by Manhattan Fire Arms Manufacturing Company, Newark, New Jersey, 1859–ca. 1864. Total production: Approximately 69,200.

Overall length and weight: varies by series.

Five shot, single action.

Markings vary by series, as detailed below.

The Manhattan .36-caliber revolvers were similar in design to the Colt Model 1851 Navy and Model 1849 Pocket revolvers. The Manhattan revolvers featured octagonal, rifled barrels (three grooves on earliest examples; subsequently, five grooves); blued finish; cylinders with five roll-engraved military scenes, and black walnut grips.

There were four series of Manhattan Navy Revolvers produced in the Civil War (Series V was produced in 1867 and 1868):

Series I: "MANHATTAN FIRE ARMS MFG. CO. NEW YORK" stamped on top flat of barrel (the company was incorporated in New York City, but the factory was in Newark, New Jersey); serial numbered 1–4200. Barrel lengths were 4", 5", 6", and 6-1/2". The first 800 units had 10 trapezoidal stop slots on the cylinder; subsequent units had rectangular slots.

Series II: Same barrel stampings as Series I, and "PATENTED DEC 27, 1859" vertically, toward the rear of the cylinder; serial numbers ca. 4200–14500. Barrel lengths of 4", 5", and 6-1/2".

Series III: Maker's mark changed to "MANHATTAN FIRE ARMS CO. NEWARK N.J."; "PATENTED DEC 27, 1859" toward rear of cylinder. Serial numbers ca. 14500–45200. Similar to Series II, but a semicircular spring plate was screwed to the front of the recoil shield on several thousand examples in the early part of the production run.

Series IV: Maker's mark changed to "MANHATTAN FIRE ARMS CO. NEWARK N.J. / PATENTED MARCH 8, 1864"; "PATENTED DEC 27, 1859" toward rear of cylinder; serial numbers ca. 45200–69200; some examples stamped "B. KITTREDGE & CO." on left barrel lug. The semicircular spring plate on the front of the recoil shield, patented March

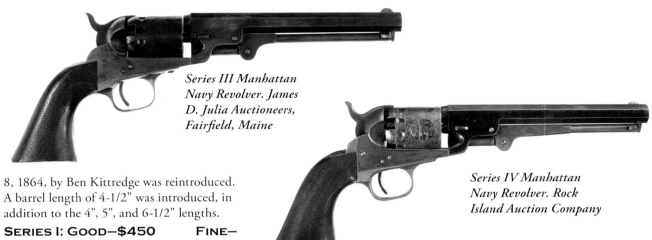

Series III Manhattan Navy Revolver. James D. Julia Auctioneers, Fairfield, Maine

Series IV Manhattan Navy Revolver. Rock Island Auction Company

8, 1864, by Ben Kittredge was reintroduced. A barrel length of 4-1/2" was introduced, in addition to the 4", 5", and 6-1/2" lengths.

SERIES I: GOOD—$450   FINE—1,500

SERIES II: GOOD—$450   FINE—$1,250

SERIES III: GOOD—$450   FINE—$1,250

SERIES IV: GOOD—$425   FINE—$1,250

MASSACHUSETTS ARMS CO. ADAMS PATENT POCKET REVOLVER .31 CALIBER COMBUSTIBLE CARTRIDGE, PERCUSSION

Made by Massachusetts Arms Company, Chicopee Falls, Massachusetts, ca. 1857–61. Total production: approximately 4,500.

Double action, five shot.

"MADE FOR ADAMS REVOLVING ARMS CO, N.Y. / BY MASS ARMS CO., CHICOPEE FALLS, / PATENT MAY 3, 1853, JUNE 3, 1856, APL. 7, 1857" stamped on top strap; serial number at bottom front of left side of frame.

Featuring a one-piece barrel and frame and based on British patents by Adams and Kerr, this five-shot pocket revolver was similar in design to the .36-Caliber Navy revolver by the same manufacturer.

GOOD—$450   FINE—$1,750

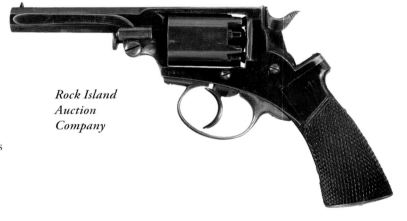

Rock Island Auction Company

Rock Island Auction Company

MASSACHUSETTS ARMS CO. ADAMS PATENT NAVY REVOLVER .36 CALIBER COMBUSTIBLE CARTRIDGE, PERCUSSION

Made by Massachusetts Arms Company, Chicopee Falls, Massachusetts, ca. 1857–61. Total production: approximately 1,000.

Overall Length: 11-1/2". Weight: 2 lbs. 9 oz.

Double action, five shot.

This revolver, based on a British design, featured a 6" octagonal barrel with three-groove rifling; a side-mounted loading lever; blued parts, except for casehardened butt cap and hammer; sliding cylinder safety catch, and checkered, two-piece black walnut grips.

Rock Island Auction Company

Top strap marked in three lines, "MANUFACTURED BY / MASS. ARMS CO. / CHICOPEE FALLS." The loading lever is stamped in two lines, "KERR'S PATENT ' APRIL 14, 1857." On some examples, the serial number also appears on the lever. On other samples, the serial number appears on the left front of the frame. The left side of the frame is stamped, in two lines, "ADAMS PATENT MAY 3D 1858" [this was, in fact, a stamping error—Adams patent was granted on May 3, 1853). Finally, the right side of the frame is stamped, "PATENT JUNE 3 1856."

Rock Island Auction Company

Between 1857 and 1858, the Massachusetts Arms Co. manufactured approximately 600 .36 Caliber double action revolvers, 500 of which fulfilled three separate 1858 Ordnance Department orders. The two-piece black walnut, checkered grips of government-accepted revolvers received an inspector's cartouche, most often, "LCA" (Lucius C. Allin), "WAT" (William A. Thornton) or "JT (Josiah Tatnal)".

GOOD—$850   **FINE—$2,250**

METROPOLITAN NAVY REVOLVER, .36 CALIBER COMBUSTIBLE CARTRIDGE, PERCUSSION

Made by the Metropolitan Arms Company, New York City, ca. 1864–66. Total production: approximately 6,063.

Overall length: 13". Weight: 2 lbs. 10 oz.

Single action, six shot.

Markings according to model, as described below.

Metropolitan Arms Company's copy of the Colt Model 1851 Third Model Navy Revolver had a 7-1/2" octagonal barrel rifled with seven grooves; blued cylinder and barrel; casehardened frame, loading lever, and hammer; and one-piece walnut grip.

Rock Island Auction Company

First Model: No markings except serial numbers from 1–63 and 1164–1799, cylinder not engraved.

H. E. Dimick order: Some 300 First Model revolvers were marked on top of barrel "MADE FOR H.E. DIMICK St LOUIS" or "H.E. DIMICK St LOUIS".

Standard Model: "METROPOLITAN ARMS CO. NEW-YORK" within pointed brackets on top of barrel; serial number on frame and on side of cylinder near rear, ranging from approximately 1800–7100; cylinders roll-engraved with scene of 1862 naval battle of New Orleans, inscribed "NEW ORLEANS APRIL 1862 W. L. ORMSBY Sc."

FIRST MODEL: GOOD—$1,000   **FINE—$3,500**

DIMICK ORDER: GOOD—$3,000   **FINE—$8,000**

STANDARD MODEL: GOOD—$1,250   **FINE—$3,750**

METROPOLITAN NAVY REVOLVER (COPY OF COLT MODEL 1861 NAVY REVOLVER), .36 CALIBER COMBUSTIBLE CARTRIDGE, PERCUSSION

Made by the Metropolitan Arms Company, New York City, ca. 1864–65. Total production: Probably fewer than 50.

Overall length: 13". Weight: 2 lbs. 10 oz.

Single action, six shot.

"METROPOLITAN ARMS CO. NEW-YORK" within angular brackets on top of barrel; no barrel markings on some specimens; serial number on frame and on side of cylinder near rear, ranging from 2300–2350; cylinders roll-engraved with scene of 1862 naval battle of New Orleans, inscribed "NEW ORLEANS APRIL 1862 W. L. ORMSBY Sc."

It is likely that the Metropolitan Arms Company produced fewer than fifty examples of its copy of the Colt Model 1861 Navy Revolver, making this an extremely rare revolver. It featured a 7-1/2" round barrel; blued finish; casehardened hammer, frame, and loading lever; brass blade front sight; silver-plated brass trigger guard; and brass back strap.

GOOD–$3,000   FINE–$7,000

METROPOLITAN POCKET/ POLICE REVOLVER, .36 CALIBER COMBUSTIBLE CARTRIDGE, PERCUSSION

Made by the Metropolitan Arms Company, New York City, ca. 1864–66. Total production: approximately 2,750.

Overall length: 10-5/8" (5-1/2" barrel version). Weight: 1 lb. 10 oz.

Single action, five shot.

"METROPOLITAN ARMS CO. NEW-YORK" on top of barrel in serial number range ca. 1800–1950 and ca. 2400–3850; no barrel markings on specimens in serial number range of ca. 1100–1800 and ca. 1950–2400; serial number from 1101 to ca. 3850 on frame and cylinder.

This weapon was a virtual copy of the Colt Model 1862 Pocket/Police Revolver. Unlike the Colt version, the Metropolitan had safety notches on the rear perimeter of the cylinder, and the loading lever was retained by a screw. The round, blued barrel was rifled with seven grooves, and came in 4-1/2", 5-1/2", and 6-1/2" lengths. The forward part of the blued cylinder was fluted.

GOOD–$450   FINE–$1,650
(DEPENDING ON SERIAL NUMBER)

MODEL 1860 PERRIN REVOLVER, 12MM, RIMFIRE BRASS CARTRIDGE

Rock Island Auction Company

Made by Perrin & Co., Paris, France, ca. 1861. Total imported : Unknown, but at least 550.

Barrel length: Available in 5-1/2" to 6".

Double-action, six shot.

Barrel stamped "PERRIN & Cie Bte". Serial number stamped on the left frame and/or the cylinder. On some examples, a small sunburst design with "PARIS" beneath it is stamped under the frame serial number. Low serial numbered examples also stamped on barrel, "INVon L. PERRIN Bte A PARIS" or "PERRIN BREVETTE A PARIS.

The Model 1860 Perrin revolver fired an internally primed cartridge. Identifying features of the revolver include an open frame, spurless hammer, a cylinder pin which could be used for ejecting spent casings, and a bright finish. At least three loading gate variations exist: the earliest hinged at the top that swung out and up. Second variation gates were also hinged at the top but swung back. Finally, the third style was hinged at the bottom and swung down. The U.S. Ordnance Department purchased first and second variation Perrin revolvers. Alexis Godillot sold 550 Perrin revolvers and cartridges to the Ordnance Department in 1861. Subsequent purchases by either Union or Confederate concerns are not known.

GOOD–$750 FINE–$2,000

PETTENGILL NAVY MODEL REVOLVER .34 CALIBER COMBUSTIBLE CARTRIDGE, PERCUSSION

C. S. Pettengill, New Haven, Connecticut, late 1850s. Total production: Approximately 900.

Overall Length: 10-3/8". Weight: 1 lb. 8 oz.

Double action, six shot.

"PETTENGILL'S / PATENT 1856" on top strap; "RAYMOND & ROBITAILLE / PATENTED 1858" on bottom strap to front of trigger guard; serial number on butt, cylinder, and bottom barrel flat.

The Pettengill Navy Model Revolver had a blued, octagonal, 4-5/8" barrel rifled with six grooves, and featured an internal hammer. The frame was iron, either blued or casehardened, and the loading lever casehardened. The two-piece grip was varnished rosewood. The first 250 or so examples had a split-type loading lever unit, while later specimens had a solid loading lever assembly.

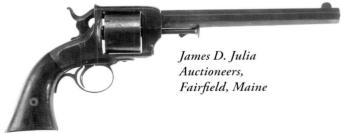

James D. Julia Auctioneers, Fairfield, Maine

GOOD—$700 FINE—$2,250

PETTENGILL ARMY MODEL REVOLVER .44 CALIBER COMBUSTIBLE CARTRIDGE, PERCUSSION

Made by C. S. Pettengill, New Haven, Connecticut, early 1860s. Total production: Approximately 3,400.

Overall Length: 14". Weight: 3 lbs.

Double action, six shot.

"PETTENGILL'S / PATENT 1856" and "RAYMOND & ROBITAILLE / PATENTED 1858" on top strap of early-production revolvers; "PETTENGILL'S / PATENT 1856" and "PAT'D JULY 22, 1856 AND JULY 27, 1858" on top strap of later revolvers; "PATENTED / NOV. 4, 1862" on bottom of frame; inspector's initials on left sides of frame and barrel on some specimens; serial number (about 1300 and up) on cylinder; "PETTENGILL'S PATENT" stamped on some barrels.

J.C. Devine, Inc

The Pettengill Army Model Revolver had a blued, octagonal, 7-1/8" barrel rifled with six grooves. The frame was casehardened and incorporated an internal hammer. The two-piece black walnut grip was stamped with inspector's initials on the left side. Military versions of the revolver had oil-finished grips, while civilian examples had varnished grips.

GOOD—$1,450   FINE—$4,500

MARTIALLY MARKED: GOOD—$1,750   FINE—$6,000

E. A. PRESCOTT SINGLE-ACTION NAVY REVOLVER, .38 CALIBER RIMFIRE

Made by E. A. Prescott, Worcester, Massachusetts, 1861–63. Total production: Several hundred.

Overall Length: 12-1/2". Weight: 1 lb. 12 oz.

Single action, six shot.

"E.A. PRESCOTT, WORCESTER, MASS. / PAT'D. OCT. 2, 1860" (or "PAT. OCT. 2, 1860") on barrel.

Probably no more than a few hundred of this rimfire revolver were manufactured before Prescott ceased production as a result of a successful patent-infringement suit by Smith & Wesson in late 1863. The revolver had

James D. Julia Auctioneers, Fairfield, Maine

a 7-5/16" blued barrel rifled with five grooves (although lengths of 6-1/2" and 8" also have been reported). Frames were generally silver-plated brass, although some were of iron. The trigger guard was brass, and the grips were polished rosewood.

GOOD—$775 FINE—$2,500

RAPHAEL 11MM CENTER-FIRE REVOLVER

French maker unknown, ca. 1854-61. 106 purchased by U.S. Ordnance Department.

Overall length: 10-1/2". Weight 1 lb. 4 oz.

Double action, six-shot.

Barrel is marked "Raphael / Paris" in one line. Some examples are unmarked. The serial number is located on below the barrel on the left side of the frame. "V" stamped on the inside of the cylinder rim.

On September 21, 1861, the Ordnance Department took delivery of 106 "breech-loading revolvers with appendages." The Department had paid George Raphael $26.33 per unit, ranking the revolvers among some of the most expensive of the war.

Raphael was neither a manufacturer nor designer. Some researchers have commented on the similarity of the Raphael's action to that of the 1854 Mangeot-Comblain design, suggesting that the revolvers were, indeed, made in France.

In 1900, purchased a lot of these revolvers from the New York Arsenal. In their 1927 catalog, Bannerman's offered 20 of the revolvers, without cartridges, for $15 each. Though Raphael is reported to have sold both 8mm- and 11mm-chambered revolvers of similar design; the engraving that accompanies Bannerman's description depicts the larger, 11mm double action revolver. Therefore, it is assumed that the original 1861 purchase was for the 11mm revolver. There is no evidence that the 8mm Raphael revolver was imported in any significant quantity during the Civil War.

GOOD—$375   FINE—$850

REMINGTON-BEALS NAVY, 36 CALIBER PERCUSSION REVOLVER

Made by E. Remington & Son, Ilion, New York, ca. 1861-1862. Total production: Approximately 14,500.

Overall length: 13-3/8". Weight: 2 lbs. 10 oz.

Single-action, six shot.

The 7-1/2" octagonal barrel is stamped "BEALS' PATENT. SEPT. 14. 1858. / MANUFACTURED BY REMINGTONS' ILION. N.Y." in two lines. The serial number is stamped under the barrel near the frame, on the trigger guard tab that fits into the frame, on the grip frame, and written on the inside of the grips. The 2" long, blued cylinder is unmarked, though the back of some are stamped with the serial number. The two-piece walnut grips are oil finished and when an inspector's cartouche is present, it will be found stamped only on the left grip.

Remington-Beals Navy, Type I. Rock Island Auction Company

The Remington-Beals Navy was the first martial-style revolver produced under Fordyce Beals' September 14, 1858, U.S. Patent. During the two years of production, the revolver underwent an evolution that can be broken down into four distinct variations:

Type I: The cylinder arbor has only one thumb piece or "ear," a design carried over from the Third Model Pocket Revolver. The arbor pin is 4-7/8" long. A much smaller in diameter, 9/10" long pin extends from the forward end of the arbor pin. This smaller pin was meant to keep the arbor from inadvertently being completely removed from the frame when it was withdrawn to release the cylinder. The loading lever has a slot milled in the top to accommodate the small extension.

The lever latch post, carried over from the Third Model Pocket Revolver, is dovetailed into the barrel. Later versions are threaded. The knurling on the high-spur hammer is a hand-cut diamond pattern. Screw escutcheons are made from German silver whereas escutcheons on later versions are of brass. The cylinder has no safety notches.

Remington & Sons produced approximately 175 revolvers that can be considered "Type I". Serial numbers range from 1-175

Type II: The cylinder arbor is approximately 1/5" in diameter being slightly thicker than on the Type I. The bottom of the arbor has a milled, flat surface runs for about two-thirds of its length. The rear of the arbor is round. Absent is the narrow pin extending from the forward part of the arbor found on the Type I. Furthermore, the arbor now sports two wings instead of just one.

The loading lever post is round with a convex bottom. The post screws into the bottom of the barrel and its diameter slightly overhangs the edges of the barrel flat.

Remington introduced a new serial number series with the introduction of the Type II revolver. The estimated range is 1-4000.

The extension on the cylinder pin is a unique feature of the Type I Navy. Rock Island Auction Company

Remington-Beals Navy, Type IV. Rock Island Auction Company

Type III: The lever latch post is smaller in diameter and does not extend beyond the barrel flat.

The knurling on the high-spur hammer is machine-cut in a crosshatch design. The estimated serial number range is 4,000-12,000.

Type IV: The lever latch post is very similar to that found on Type III revolvers, except that the bottom is half round and without shoulders. (that is, the surface between the barrel flat and the side of the latch post is a perfect 90-degree angle with no gap perceptible). The serial number range of Type IV revolvers is approximately 12,000-15,700 and overlaps with the Elliot Navy Model.

The Ordnance Department received about 50 Type IV revolvers in the 13,500-15,700 range although none were inspected. The Department also took delivery of 7,250 Beals Navy revolvers from Remington as open market purchases. Furthermore, it also purchased 3,949 from commercial dealers.

The Navy's Bureau of Ordnance received eight delivers for a total of 791 Remington Navy revolvers during 1862. The sloops *Ossipee* and *Sacramento* each received 60 of these revolvers.

TYPES I & II: GOOD—$950	**FINE—$4,000**
TYPES III & IV: GOOD—$750	**FINE—$2,250**
MARTIALLY MARKED: GOOD—$950	**FINE—$4,000**
NAVY MARKED: GOOD—$1,400	**FINE—$4,000**

REMINGTON-BEALS ARMY, 44 CALIBER PERCUSSION REVOLVER

Made by E. Remington & Son, Ilion, New York, 1862. Total production: Approximately 1,850.

Overall length: 13-3/4". Weight: 2 lbs. 14 oz.

Single-action, six shot.

The 8" octagonal barrel is stamped "BEALS' PATENT. SEPT. 14. 1858. / MANUFACTURED BY REMINGTONS' ILION. N.Y." in two lines. The serial number is stamped under the barrel near the frame, on the hooked trigger guard projection that fits into the frame, on the grip frame, and written on the inside of the grips. The 2" long, blued cylinder is unmarked, though the back of some are stamped with the serial number. The two-piece walnut grips are oil finished and when an inspector's cartouche is present, it will be found stamped only on the left grip.

Rock Island Auction Company

The Remington-Beals Army revolver has all of the features of the Remington-Beals Navy Type IV revolvers. Several parts of a Remington-Beals Army, such as the lever latch post, front German silver cone front sight, high spur hammer, trigger and screws, are interchangeable with those of a Type IV Navy.

The lever latch post is very similar to that found on Type IV Navy revolvers, except that the bottom is half round and without shoulders. (that is, the surface between the barrel flat and the side of the latch post is a perfect 90-degree angle with no gap perceptible). The frame, forward of the cylinder completely conceals the barrel threads. There are no safety notches between the cylinder's nipples.

Some authors have stated that the state of South Carolina bought 1,000 Remington-Beals Army revolvers in 1860. However, no documentation has emerged to confirm that Remington manufactured the Army model as early as 1860 or that South Carolina ordered and received any shipments from the company.

On July 29, 1861, the Ordnance Department placed an order Remington for 5,000 .44 caliber revolvers. Remington continued to deliver .36 caliber Navy revolvers to fulfill part of this contract, making the last delivery of the smaller revolver on May 31, 1862. On the same day, Remington delivered the first 850 .44 caliber Army revolvers. This first batch of 850 Beals Army revolvers were never inspected and, therefore, do not have any inspector cartouches.

In early July 1862, Major William A. Thornton personally inspected 750 Remington-Beals Army revolvers. These revolvers were marked with his "WAT" cartouche on the left grip. Other examples have been noted with the "CGC" cartouche of Charles G. Curtis. In all, the Ordnance Department received about 1,600 of the total production of about 1,850 revolvers.

GOOD—$1,150	**FINE—$3,750**
MARTIALLY MARKED: GOOD—$1,400	**FINE—$7,500**

REMINGTON ELLIOT NAVY, .36 CALIBER PERCUSSION REVOLVER

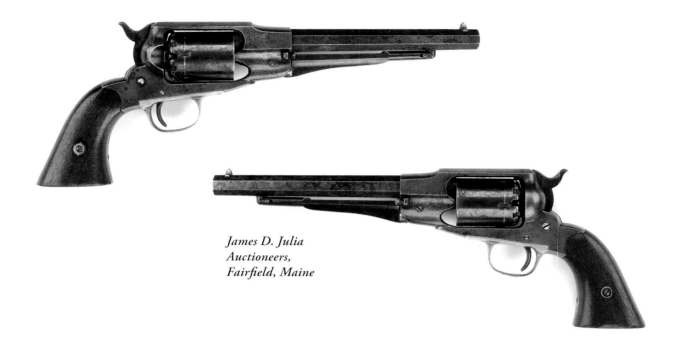

*James D. Julia
Auctioneers,
Fairfield, Maine*

Made by E. Remington & Son, Ilion, New York, ca. 1861-1862. Total production: Approximately 4,500.
Overall length: 13-3/8". Weight: 2 lbs. 10 oz.

Single-action, six shot.

The 7-3/8" octagonal barrel is stamped "PATENTED DEC.17 1861 / MANUFACTURED BY REMINGTONS'
ILION. N.Y." in two lines. On some examples, the rear of the loading lever is stamped "ELIOT'S PATENTS" (note that
the misspelling of "Elliot's" is a die maker's typographical error) The serial number is stamped under the barrel near the
frame, on the trigger guard projection that fits into the frame, on the grip frame, and written on the inside of the grips. The
2" long cylinder is unmarked, though the back of some are stamped with the serial number. The two-piece walnut grips are
oil finished and when an inspector's cartouche is present, it will be found stamped only on the left grip.

The arbor pin is about 3/8" longer than found on the Beals Navy revolver, Types II-IV. The head is not rebated into the
frame, enabling the arbor to be withdrawn from the cylinder and frame without having to first lower the loading lever. A
small friction spring mounted under the barrel holds the arbor pin in the frame.

The Elliot Navy abandoned the cylindrical latch post found on the Beals Navy. The new post is vertical on the forward
surface, but rear surface is cut at an angle and forms a catch at the bottom. Remington employed this fifth style of latch on
all subsequent production Army, Navy, Police, Belt and Pocket Model revolvers.

The Elliot loading lever features a new tapered lever release latch that provides a better grasp than on the earlier Beals.
The Elliot-style release latch was utilized on all subsequent Remington percussion revolvers.

The top of the frame nearest the hammer is beveled, previously having come to a sharp, nearly 90-degree angle on all
types of the Beals Navy model. Shortly after production began, around serial number 16,500, the frame directly in front
of the cylinder was slightly arched on both sides exposing the barrel threads. This was done in order to reduce incidents of
cylinder jamming due to powder fouling.

The serial number range is approximately 15,700- 20,200 and overlaps with that of Type IV Remington Beals Navy
revolvers.

Collectors often refer to this revolver as the "Model 1861 Navy" or the "Old Model Navy."

MARTIALLY MARKED: GOOD—$750 FINE—$2,500

NAVY MARKED: GOOD—$950   FINE—$3,250

REMINGTON ELLIOT ARMY, .44 CALIBER PERCUSSION REVOLVER

Made by E. Remington & Son, Ilion, New York, 1862. Total production: Approximately 8,500.

Overall length: 13-3/4". Weight: 2 lbs. 14 oz.

Single-action, six shot.

The 8" octagonal barrel is stamped "PATENTED DEC.17 1861 / MANUFACTURED BY REMINGTONS' ILION. N.Y." in two lines. The serial number is stamped on the bottom barrel flat near the frame and on the grip strap under the left grip on the trigger guard projection that fits into the frame, on the grip frame, and written on the inside of the grips. The 2" long cylinder is unmarked. The two-piece walnut grips are oil finished and when an inspector's cartouche is present, it will be found stamped only on the left grip.

The arbor pin is about 3/8" longer than found on the Beals Army revolver. The head is not rebated into the frame and a channel is cut into the top of the loading lever, enabling the arbor to be withdrawn from the cylinder and frame without having to first lower the loading lever. A small friction spring mounted under the barrel holds the arbor pin in the frame. The Elliot loading lever featured a new tapered lever release latch that provides a better grasp than on the earlier Beals.

The Elliot Army abandoned the cylindrical latch post found on the Beals Army. The new post is vertical on the forward surface, but rear surface is cut at an angle and forms a catch at the bottom. Remington employed this fifth style of latch on all subsequent production Army, Navy, Police, Belt and Pocket Model revolvers.

Shortly after production began, around serial number 6,500, the frame directly in front of the cylinder was slightly arched on both sides exposing the barrel threads. This was done in order to reduce incidents of cylinder jamming due to powder fouling.

The serial number range is approximately 2,000 to 10,500.

Collectors often refer to this revolver as the "Model 1861 Army" or the "Old Model Army."

STANDARD MODEL: GOOD—$700   FINE—$2,500

NEW JERSEY PURCHASE: GOOD—$700   FINE—$2,000

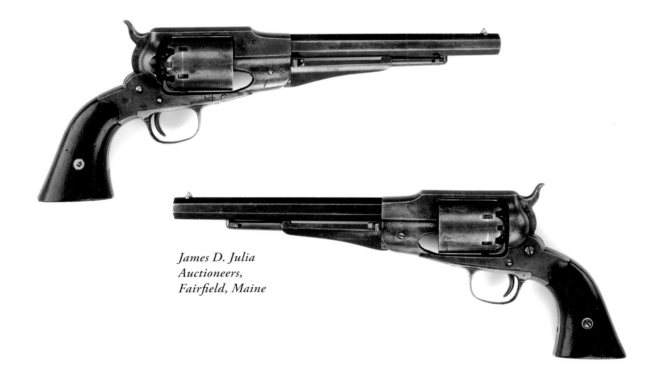

James D. Julia
Auctioneers,
Fairfield, Maine

REMINGTON MODEL 1863 NAVY, .36 CALIBER, PERCUSSION REVOLVER

Made by E. Remington & Sons, Ilion, New York, 1863-1878. Total production: Approximately 22,000.
Overall length: 13-3/8". Weight: 2 lbs. 10 oz.
Single-action, six shot.

The 7-3/8" barrel is stamped in three lines, "PATENTED SEPT. 14, 1858 / E. REMINGTON & SONS, ILION, NEW YORK U.S.A. / NEW MODEL". Revolvers in the 23,000 serial number range are marked on the barrel in two lines, "PATENTED SEPT. 14, 1858 / E. REMINGTON & SONS, ILION, NEW YORK U.S.A. / NEW MODEL".

Early examples of the Model 1863 Navy were fitted with brass or German silver cone front sights, but this was subsequently changed after about 27,000, to a pinched cylindrical sight style. A distinguishing characteristic of the New Model Navy is that the front of the steel frame is inlet to receive the finger lugs of the cylinder arbor. The rear of the frame and grip straps are shorter than earlier models. Also, the hammer spur is shorter and not at such a wide angle as the Model 1861 or Beals Navy.

The arbor pin of a Model 1863 is ¼" shorter than that of a Model 1861 Elliot Navy. The sides of the loading lever were contoured and not flat like those found on the Elliot. The 2" long, blued cylinder is milled with safety notches between the nipple wells.

Note: Post Civil War Model 1863 Navies are marked with two patent dates on the barrel: Sept. 14, 1858, and March 17, 1863.

The serial number range is from approximately 23,000 to 45,000.

James D. Julia Auctioneers, Fairfield, Maine

STANDARD MODEL: GOOD—$800   FINE—$2,250

MARTIALLY MARKED: GOOD—$950 FINE—$3,000

REMINGTON MODEL 1863 ARMY, .44 CALIBER, PERCUSSION REVOLVER

Made by E. Remington & Sons, Ilion, New York, 1863-1875. Total production: Approximately 126,000.
Overall length: 13-3/4". Weight: 2 lbs. 14 oz.
Single-action, six shot.

The 8" octagonal barrel is stamped in three lines, "PATENTED SEPT. 14, 1858 / E. REMINGTON & SONS, ILION, NEW YORK U.S.A. / NEW MODEL". Revolvers in the 20,000 serial number range are marked on the barrel in two lines, "PATENTED SEPT. 14, 1858 / E. REMINGTON & SONS, ILION, NEW YORK

James D. Julia Auctioneers, Fairfield, Maine

U.S.A. / NEW MODEL". The State of New Jersey bought 1,000 during the Civil War. These were stamped on the barrel, "N.J."

Early examples of the Model 1863 Army were fitted with brass or German silver cone front sights, but this was subsequently changed to a pinched cylindrical sight style after about serial number 50,000. A distinguishing characteristic of the New Model Army is that the front of the steel frame is inletted to receive the finger lugs of the cylinder arbor. The rear of the frame and grip straps are 3/16" shorter than earlier models. Also, the hammer spur is shorter and not at such a wide angle as the Model 1861 or Beals Army.

The arbor pin of a Model 1863 is ¼" shorter than that of a Model 1861 Elliot Army. The sides of the loading lever were contoured and not flat like those found on the Elliot. The 2" long, blued cylinder is milled with safety notches between the nipple wells.

Note: Post-Civil War Model 1863 Armies are marked with two patent dates on the barrel: Sept. 14, 1858, and March 17, 1863.

The serial number range is from approximately 10,000 to 150,000.

STANDARD MODEL: GOOD—$700   FINE—$2,500

NEW JERSEY PURCHASE: GOOD—$700   FINE—$2,500

REMINGTON NEW MODEL POLICE, .36 CALIBER, PERCUSSION REVOLVER

Made by E. Remington & Sons, Ilion, New York, 1865-1873. Total production: approximately 18,000.

Overall length: 11-1/2". Weight: 1 lbs. 8 oz.

Single-action, five shot.

Marked on the top strap in three lines: "PATENTED SEPT. 14, 1858 MARCH 17, 1863 / E. REMINGTON & SONS, ILION, NEW YORK U.S.A. / NEW MODEL".

Produced in 3-1/2", 4-1/2", 5-1/2" and 6-1/2" octagonal barrel lengths.

Blued, solid frame with integral walnut grips is cut away forward of the cylinder, exposing the barrel's threads. Front of frame is inlet to accept the finger lugs of the cylinder arbor. Like the belt model revolvers, the screws enter the frame from the right side.

The 1-/5/8" long blued cylinder is unmarked and has intermediate safety rest notches milled at the shoulder between the nipple wells.

Serial numbers are stamped on the bottom flat of the barrel near the frame and on the grip strap under the left, walnut grip.

The serial number range from 1 to about 18,000.

GOOD—$475   FINE—$1,200

REMINGTON NEW MODEL BELT, .36 CALIBER, PERCUSSION REVOLVER

Rock Island Auction Company

Made by E. Remington & Sons, Ilion, New York, 1865-1873. Total production: Approximately 3,000.

Overall length: 11-1/2". Weight: 2 lbs. 2 oz.

Single-action, six shot.

The 6-1/2" octagonal barrel is stamped in three lines, "PATENTED SEPT. 14, 1858 / E. REMINGTON & SONS, ILION, NEW YORK U.S.A. / NEW MODEL".

A distinguishing characteristic of the New Model Belt revolver are the frame screws that enter from the right side. The front of the frame is inlet to accommodate the finger lugs of the cylinder arbor. Barrel has a brass blade front sight.

The 1-7/8" long cylinder is blued and without markings. It does have intermediate safety rest notches

milled at the shoulder between the nipple wells.

The serial number range coincides with that of the Remington-Rider double-action revolver and is known nearing 8,000.

GOOD—$475   FINE—$1,400

REMINGTON-RIDER POCKET, .31 CALIBER, PERCUSSION REVOLVER

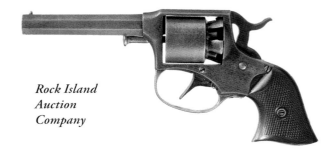

Rock Island Auction Company

Made by E. Remington & Sons, Ilion, New York, ca. 1860-1875. Total production: Approximately 1,200.

Overall length: 11-1/2". Weight: 2 lbs. 2 oz.

Single-action, six shot.

The 6-1/2" octagonal barrel is stamped in three lines, "PATENTED SEPT. 14, 1858 / E. REMINGTON & SONS, ILION, NEW YORK U.S.A. / NEW MODEL".

A distinguishing characteristic of the New Model Belt revolver are the frame screws that enter from the right side. The front of the frame is inlet to accommodate the finger lugs of the cylinder arbor. Barrel has a brass blade front sight.

The 1-7/8" long cylinder is blued and without markings. It does have intermediate safety rest notches milled at the shoulder between the nipple wells.

The serial number range coincides with the Remington-Rider double-action revolver and is known nearing 8,000.

GOOD—$350   FINE—$950

REMINGTON-RIDER NEW MODEL BELT, .36 CALIBER, PERCUSSION REVOLVER

Made by E. Remington & Sons, Ilion, New York, 1865-1873. Total production: Approximately 3,000.

Overall length: 11-1/2". Weight: 2 lbs. 4 oz.

Double-action, six shot.

The 6-1/2" octagonal barrel is stamped in two lines, "MANUFACTURED BY REMINGTON'S, ILION, N.Y. / RIDER'S PT. AUG. 17, 1858, MAY 3, 1859". Some marked, PATENTED SEPT. 14, 1858 / E. REMINGTON & SONS, ILION, NEW YORK U.S.A. / NEW MODEL" in three lines.

A distinguishing characteristic of the New Model belt revolvers is that the frame screws enter from the right side of the weapon. The 1-/7/8" long blued cylinder is unmarked. Round cylinders were the norm, but a number of New Model belt revolvers were produced with full-fluted cylinders as well. The round cylinders have intermediate safety rest notches milled at the shoulder between the nipple wells. On the fluted cylinders, the flutes function as safety rests.

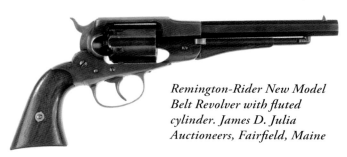

Remington-Rider New Model Belt Revolver with fluted cylinder. James D. Julia Auctioneers, Fairfield, Maine

The brass, oval trigger guard is much longer than on single-action revolvers. Remington-Rider New Model belt revolvers will be found with one of three front sight styles: iron cylindrical pinched style; German silver or brass cone; or a brass blade.

Serial numbers are stamped on the bottom flat of the barrel near the frame and on the grip strap under the left, walnut grip.

The serial number range coincides with the Remington New Model single-action belt revolver and is known to be as high as 8,000. Examples with fluted cylinders tend to be numbered lower than 650.

STANDARD MODEL: GOOD—$700   FINE—$2,250
FLUTED CYLINDER: GOOD—$850   FINE—$3,000

RIGDON, ANSLEY .36 CALIBER PERCUSSION REVOLVER, COMBUSTIBLE CARTRIDGE

Made by Rigdon, Ansley & Co., Augusta, Georgia ca. 1864–1864. Total production: Approximately 1,000.

Overall Length: 13".

Single action, six shot.

"AUGUSTA, GA. C.S.A." on top flat of barrel of serial number 1501-1700. "C.H. RIGDON" also stamped on examples. Above serial number 1700, "C.S.A." is frequently the only marking found on the barrel.

The 12 stop slots on the cylinder are the most recognizable features of the Rigdon, Ansley revolver. Beginning at 1501, the serial number range picks up where the Leech and Rigdon revolvers stopped.

Type I: Early production from 1501 to about 1700.

Type II: Serial number 1701. Barrel marked with "C.S.A." with no firm name nor an address.

James D. Julia Auctioneers, Fairfield, Maine

TYPE I: FAIR—$25,000   VERY GOOD—$60,000
TYPE II: FAIR—$17,500   VERY GOOD—$45,000

The Type II Rigdon, Ansley revolver was simply marked "C.S.A." on the top barrel flat. James D. Julia Auctioneers, Fairfield, Maine

ROGERS & SPENCER ARMY REVOLVER, .44 CALIBER, COMBUSTIBLE CARTRIDGE, PERCUSSION

Made by Rogers, Spencer & Co., Willowdale, New York, ca. 1864–1865. Total production: Approximately 5,800.

Overall length: 13-3/8". Weight: 3 lbs.

Single action, six shot.

"ROGERS & SPENCER / UTICA, N.Y." on top flat of barrel; "RPB" stamped in script on left grip; sub-inspector's initial on right side of frame; serial number on cylinder and on left side of frame below cylinder.

James D. Julia Auctioneers, Fairfield, Maine

The Rogers & Spencer Army Revolver was an improvement of the Austin T. Freeman revolver patented on December 9, 1862. It had a 7-1/2" blued, octagonal barrel rifled with five grooves; a solid, blued frame; and casehardened hammer and loading lever. The grips were two-piece, oil-finished walnut. Rogers, Spencer & Company delivered 5,000 of its Army Revolvers to the U.S. government from January to September 1865, but evidently none of them saw service in the Civil War. Francis Bannerman bought most of those revolvers in unused condition in 1901 and resold them to the public.

GOOD—$1,750   FINE—$4,250

SAVAGE & NORTH FIGURE 8 NAVY REVOLVER, 1ST MODEL, .36 CALIBER, COMBUSTIBLE CARTRIDGE, PERCUSSION

Made by Savage & North, Middletown, Connecticut, ca. 1856. Total production: Approximately 10 of 1st Model and 250 of variation of 1st Model.

Overall length: 14". Weight: 3 lbs. 6 oz.

Single action, six shot.

"E. SAVAGE. MIDDLETOWN. CT. / H.S. NORTH. PATENTED JUNE 17TH 1856" on top flat of barrel; serial number on most major parts.

Rock Island Auction Company

The 1st Model of the Savage & North Figure 8 Navy Revolver, of which only 10 examples are known to have been produced, had a brass frame that was round in cross section. The blued, octagonal barrel was rifled with three grooves. The nipples protruded nearly perpendicular to the outer surface of the blued cylinder. The hammer and loading lever were casehardened, and the two-piece grips were walnut. There was a prominent spur near the middle of the back strap. The unique "figure-8" trigger mechanism included a cocking lever (lower ring) and trigger (upper ring). Pulling the lever rearward cocked the hammer and drew the cylinder rearward, while returning the lever forward caused the cylinder to press forward against the barrel's breech, with a protrusion at the front of each chamber forming a gas seal at the breech.

After the initial production run of 10 revolvers, a variant of the 1st Model sometimes referred to as the "2nd Variation of the 1st Model" was produced that featured chamfers at the forward end of each chamber in the cylinder, instead of protrusions. This feature became standard in the series. Of the 250 units manufactured, 100 bore Ordnance Department inspectors' markings.

Rock Island Auction Company

FIRST VARIATION: GOOD—$6,000   FINE—$15,500

SECOND VARIATION: GOOD—$4,250   FINE—$11,000

SAVAGE & NORTH FIGURE 8 NAVY REVOLVER, 2ND MODEL, .36 CALIBER, COMBUSTIBLE CARTRIDGE, PERCUSSION

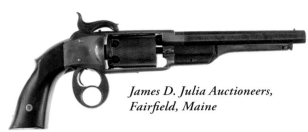

James D. Julia Auctioneers, Fairfield, Maine

Made by Savage & North, Middletown, Connecticut, ca. 1858. Total production: Approximately 100.

Overall length: 14". Weight: 3 lbs. 6 oz.

Single action, six shot.

"E. SAVAGE. MIDDLETOWN. CT. / H.S. NORTH. PATENTED JUNE 17TH 1856" on top flat of barrel; "H. S. NORTH, PATENTED APRIL 6, 1858" sometimes found on left side of plunger housing; serial number on most major parts.

This revolver was virtually identical to the 2nd variation of the 1st Model of the Savage & North Figure 8 Navy Revolver, except with a blued iron frame instead of brass, and a different loading rammer with a plunger housing. There were other subtle differences in the shapes of the grip, straps, and frame in front of the cylinder.

GOOD—$4,000   FINE—$10,000

SAVAGE & NORTH FIGURE 8 NAVY REVOLVER, 3RD MODEL, .36 CALIBER, COMBUSTIBLE CARTRIDGE, PERCUSSION

Made by Savage & North, Middletown, Connecticut, ca. 1858–60. Total production: between 100–400.

Overall length: 13-3/4". Weight: approximately 3 lbs. 6 oz.

Single action, six shot.

"E. SAVAGE. MIDDLETOWN. CT. / H.S. NORTH. PATENTED JUNE 17TH 1856" on top flat of barrel; "H. S. NORTH, PATENTED APRIL 6, 1858" sometimes found on rammer housing; serial number on most major parts.

Practically identical to the 2nd Model of the Savage & North Figure 8 Navy Revolver, the 3rd Model had a bronze (or, according to some sources, brass) frame with flattened sides and large, round recoil shield. The large spur on back strap of the first two models was replaced by a more subtle swell in the back strap and grip. The barrel length was 6-7/8", or 1/4" shorter than previous models.

GOOD—$4,000   FINE—$10,000

SAVAGE & NORTH FIGURE 8 NAVY REVOLVER, 4TH MODEL, .36 CALIBER, COMBUSTIBLE CARTRIDGE, PERCUSSION

Made by Savage & North, Middletown, Connecticut, ca. 1858–60. Total production: Approximately 50.

Overall length: 13-3/4". Weight: approximately 3 lbs. 6 oz.

Single action, six shot.

"E. SAVAGE. MIDDLETOWN. CT. / H.S. NORTH. PATENTED JUNE 17TH 1856" on top flat of barrel; "H. S. NORTH, PATENTED APRIL 6, 1858" sometimes found on rammer housing; serial number on most major parts.

The Fourth Model of the Savage & North Figure 8 Navy Revolver was basically the same design as the 3rd Model, except it had an iron frame. This model also had its own serial number range.

GOOD—$4,500   FINE—$12,000

James D. Julia Auctioneers, Fairfield, Maine

SAVAGE NAVY MODEL REVOLVER, .36 CALIBER, COMBUSTIBLE CARTRIDGE, PERCUSSION

James D. Julia Auctioneers, Fairfield, Maine

Made by Savage Revolving Fire-Arms Co., Middletown, Connecticut, ca. 1860–62. Total production: approximately 20,000.
Overall length: 14-1/4". Weight: 3 lbs. 6 oz.
Single action, six shot.
"SAVAGE R.F.A. CO. MIDDLETOWN-CT. / H.S. NORTH PATENTED JUNE 17 1856 / JANUARY 18 1859" on top flat of barrel; serial numbered; inspector's marks on some grips. On U.S. Navy contract specimens, there is also an anchor stamped on the top flat of the barrel near the frame, and "P / J.R.G." on the cylinder.

The Savage Navy Model Revolver was similar to the Savage & North Figure 8 Navy Revolver, Fourth Model, except that it had a large, casehardened guard for the trigger and operating lever, extending from the bottom of the frame to the lower part of the front strap. In addition, it had a flat recoil shield instead of the rounded recoil shield of the Figure 8, 4th Model. Some specimens have been reported with 23" barrels instead of the standard 7-1/8" barrel, and some of these have shoulder stocks. The U.S. Army received more than 10,000 Savage Navy Model Revolvers during the Civil War, while the U.S. Navy contracted for about 800 units, with markings as described above.

GOOD—$950 FINE—$4,250

SCHNEIDER AND GLASSICK NAVY MODEL REVOLVER, .36 CALIBER, COMBUSTIBLE CARTRIDGE, PERCUSSION

Made by Schneider & Glassick, Memphis, Tennessee, ca. 1861–62. Total production: Approximately 50.
Overall length: approximately 13". Weight: approximately 2 lbs. 10 oz.
Single action, six shot.
"SCHNEIDER & GLASSICK, MEMPHIS, TENNESSEE" on top of barrel; serial numbered beginning with 1.
This extremely rare revolver was a copy of the Colt Model 1851 Navy Revolver. It featured a blued finish except for an unfinished brass frame, and 7-1/2" octagonal barrel, although at least one example with a part octagonal, part round barrel and iron frame has been reported.

FAIR—$65,000   VERY GOOD—$125,000

SMITH & WESSON NO. 2 ARMY (OR OLD MODEL) REVOLVER, .32 CALIBER, RIMFIRE CARTRIDGE

Made by Smith & Wesson, Springfield, Massachusetts, 1861–74. Total production: 77,155.
Overall length: 10-3/4". Weight: 1 lb. 3 oz. Note: weight and overall length given were for examples with the 6" barrel, and varied according to barrel length.

J.C. Devine, Inc.

Single action, six shot.
"SMITH & WESSON, SPRINGFIELD, MASS." on top of barrel; serial numbered 1–77155 on butt strap; "PATENTED APRL 3, 1855, July 5, 1859 & DEC 18, 1860" on front of cylinder; "2D QUALITY" stamped on 35 specimens with defects.
The Smith & Wesson No. 2 Army Revolver (sometimes called the Old Model Revolver) was not sold to the U.S. government by contract in the Civil War, but large quantities under serial number 35731 were privately acquired and used during the war. The revolver had a sheathed trigger (i.e., no trigger guard bow) and fired a .32-caliber long rimfire cartridge. By pulling down two catches at the bottom front of the frame and flipping the top-hinged barrel upward, the cylinder could be removed for reloading. A fixed ejector rod was mounted below and parallel to the barrel, to aid with ejecting spent cartridges. The frame and barrel were blued. Barrel lengths of 6" and 5" were common; more rare were specimens with 4", 8", and 10" barrels. The two-piece grips were usually of varnished rosewood.

GOOD—$1,000   FINE—$2,500

SMITH & WESSON NO. 2 ARMY (OR OLD MODEL) REVOLVER, B. KITTREDGE & CO. MARKED, .32 CALIBER, RIMFIRE CARTRIDGE

Made by Smith & Wesson, Springfield, Massachusetts, ca. 1861–67. Total production: 2,600.

Overall length: 10-3/4". Weight: 1 lb. 3 oz. Note: Weight and overall length given are for examples with the 6" barrel, and varied with 4" and 5" barrels.

Single action, six shot.

"B. KITTREDGE & Co. / CINCINNATI, O." on side of barrel; "SMITH & WESSON, SPRINGFIELD, MASS." on top of barrel; serial numbered 1–77155 on butt strap; "PATENTED APRL 3, 1855, July 5, 1859 & DEC 18, 1860" on front of cylinder.

Arms dealers B. Kittredge & Company bought 2,600 Smith & Wesson No. 2 Army Revolvers in 1862, marking the barrels with their company name. That September the firm delivered 730 of the revolvers to the State of Kentucky, for the use of the 7th Kentucky Volunteer Cavalry Regiment. Subsequent deliveries were made until a year or two after the end of the Civil War.

Two basic versions exist: those with a 5" or 6" barrel, and those issued after the Civil War, around 1866 or 1867, with a 4" barrel.

GOOD—$1,500   FINE—$3,500

SPILLER & BURR NAVY MODEL REVOLVER REVOLVER, .36 CALIBER, COMBUSTIBLE CARTRIDGE

Made by Spiller & Burr, Atlanta, Georgia, ca. 1862–64; Macon Armory, Macon, Georgia, c. 1864–65. Total production: Approximately 1,450.

Overall length: approximately 12-1/4". Weight: Approximately 2 lbs. 8 oz.

Single action, six shot.

"SPILLER & BURR" on some barrels, omitted on others; serial numbered starting at 1; "C.S." on left or right of most frames.

This Confederate revolver, based on the Whitney Navy Revolver, had a cylinder fabricated by a unique method, in which the iron was twisted. The cylinder had six stop-slots. The blued barrel was octagonal and between 6" and 6-1/2" long. The cylinder was also blued, but the frame was brass. On early-production examples, which had their own serial number range of 1 to about 50, the frame to the front of the cylinder was 5/8"-thick, revealing 1/4" of barrel thread visible. Standard-production specimens had a 7/8"-thick frame section in that location, thus covering the barrel thread, as well as a thicker top strap. About the first 762 units of this revolver were manufactured by Spiller & Burr in Atlanta, while the remainder were produced at the Macon Armory.

FAIR—$17,500   VERY GOOD—$40,000

*James D. Julia
Auctioneers,
Fairfield, Maine*

STARR MODEL 1858 NAVY REVOLVER, .36 CALIBER, COMBUSTIBLE CARTRIDGE, PERCUSSION

Manufactured by Starr Arms Company, New York City, ca. 1858–60. Total production: Approximately 3,000. Overall length: 12". Weight: 3 lbs. 3 oz.

Double action, six shot.

"STARR ARMS CO / NEW YORK" on right side of frame below cylinder; "STARR'S PATENT JAN. 15, 1856" on left side of frame, serial number starting at 1 on cylinder; "JT" inspector's mark on grip of a few U.S. government-purchased examples.

The Starr model 1858 Navy Revolver had a unique, patented double action, featuring a cocking lever that appeared to be a trigger, and behind it and just visible in the curve of the rear of the trigger guard, the actual trigger. Pulling the cocking lever cocked the hammer and rotated the cylinder, and an adjustable lug at the back of the cocking lever actuated the trigger. However, in practice, it was reportedly more common for users to fire the revolver in single-action style, pulling the cocking lever and then pulling the trigger. The revolver had a 6" blued barrel, rifled with six grooves. The cylinder and two-piece frame was also blued, while the hammer, cocking lever, and loading lever were casehardened. The grip was one piece, oiled black walnut. Those examples marked with "JT" inspector's marks on the grip were U.S. government purchases and are rare and bring a premium.

GOOD—$950   **FINE—$3,500**

MARTIALLY MARKED:
GOOD—$1,400   **FINE—$4,500**

STARR MODEL 1858 ARMY REVOLVER, .44 CALIBER, COMBUSTIBLE CARTRIDGE, PERCUSSION

Manufactured by Starr Arms Company, New York City, ca. 1858–60. Total production: Approximately 23,000. Overall length: 11-5/8". Weight: 2 lbs. 14 oz.

Double action, six shot.

"STARR ARMS CO / NEW YORK" on left side of frame below cylinder; "STARR'S PATENT JAN. 15, 1856" on right side of frame, serial numbered starting at 1 on cylinder; inspector's mark on lower part of grip of some U.S. government-purchased examples.

The Starr Model 1858 Army Revolver was similar to the Starr Model 1858 Navy Revolver, except with a .44-caliber bore instead of .36-caliber, and different shaped loading groove and recoil shield. This model of revolver had its own serial number range, starting with number 1.

GOOD—$800   **FINE—$2,500**

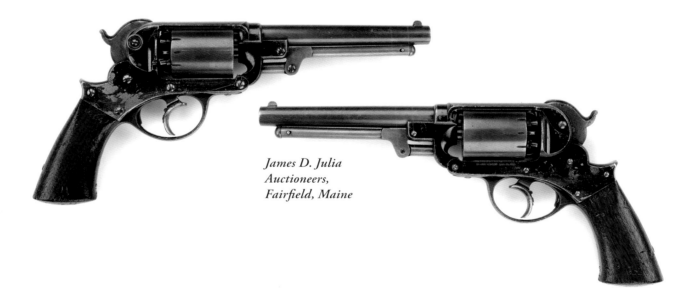

James D. Julia Auctioneers, Fairfield, Maine

STARR MODEL 1863 ARMY REVOLVER, .44 CALIBER, COMBUSTIBLE CARTRIDGE, PERCUSSION

James D. Julia Auctioneers, Fairfield, Maine

Manufactured by Starr Arms Company, New York City, ca. 1863–65. Total production: Approximately 30,900.

Overall length: 13-3/4". Weight: 3 lbs.

Single action, six shot.

"STARR ARMS CO, NEW YORK" on left side of frame below cylinder; "STARR'S PATENT JAN. 15, 1856" on right side of frame, serial numbered starting at 1; government inspector's marks on most examples.

One of the most numerous revolvers bought by the U.S. government in the Civil War, the Starr Model 1863 Army Revolver was similar in appearance to the Starr Model 1858 Army Revolver, except the Model 1863 had an 8", as opposed to 6", and was single action, with an exposed trigger instead of the separate cocking lever and trigger of the Model 1858. Other differences were: the loading groove of the 1863 model had a more pronounced bevel, and the recoil shield had a cutout to aid in capping. Serial numbers commenced where the Starr Model 1858 Army Revolver's serial numbers ended, with a range of about 23,100 to 54,000.

GOOD—$1,100   **FINE—$3,250**

GEORGE TODD NAVY MODEL REVOLVER, .36 CALIBER, COMBUSTIBLE CARTRIDGE, PERCUSSION

Made by George Todd, Austin, Texas, ca. 1857–61. Total production: Unknown; probably very few.
Overall length: Approximately 13". Weight: Approximately 2 lbs. 10 oz.
Single action, six shot.
"GEORGE TODD, AUSTIN" on frame; "GEORGE TODD" on top of barrel; serial numbered beginning with 1.
This exceedingly rare revolver was a copy of the Colt Model 1851 Navy Revolver. Both full-round and half-round, half-octagonal barrels have been reported. The grip straps were brass, and the finish was blued or browned. It is likely that the Todd Navy Model Revolver saw some use in the Confederate service.

FAIR—$35,000   **VERY GOOD—$75,000**

TUCKER, SHERRARD & CO. (OR, L.E. TUCKER & SONS, WEATHERFORD, TEXAS; SHERRARD, TAYLOR & CO.; CLARK, SHERRARD & CO.) NAVY MODEL REVOLVER, .36 CALIBER, COMBUSTIBLE CARTRIDGE, PERCUSSION

Made by L. E. Tucker & Sons, Weatherford, Texas, ca. late 1850s; Tucker, Sherrard & Co., Lancaster, Texas, ca. 1861¬–62; Sherrard, Taylor & Co., Lancaster, Texas, ca. 1862–65; Clark, Sherrard & Co., Lancaster, Texas, ca. 1866–67. Total production: Probably very few during the Civil War; up to 1,500 after the war.
Overall length: Approximately 13". Weight: Approximately 2 lbs. 10 oz.
Single action, six shot.
Pre-Civil War examples by L. E. Tucker & Sons acid-etched "L.E. TUCKER SONS" on barrel; markings of possible Tucker, Sherrard & Co. and Sherrard, Taylor & Co. examples made during the Civil War are unknown; postwar specimens marked "CLARK, SHERRARD & CO., LANCASTER, TEXAS" on barrel, and two acid-etched decorative designs on cylinder: crossed cannon and coat of arms, and five-pointed star with "TEXAS ARMS".
L.E. Tucker & Sons produced a copy of the Colt Model 1851 Navy Revolver before the Civil War, but probably in

Initial	Inspector's Name	Rank/office	Dates	Weapons with this mark
AH	Asabel Hubbard	ASI	1813-47	Barrels and stocks, Whitney and Starr muskets, North and Johnson pistols; barrels of Hall Model 1833 carbines and Model 1819 rifles
AHC	Archibald H. Ceiley	ASI	1862-63	Model 1840 Musician swords
AHC	A.H. Clark	ASI, FI	1859-79	
AHK	Albert H. Kirkham	ASI	1862-65	Model 1840 Musician and NCO swords
AHN	A.H. North	ASI	1862	Spencer Model 1865 carbines
AHT	Albert H. Thompson	ASI	1862-64	Model 1840 Musician swords; Trenton contract Model 1861 rifle muskets
AJN	unknown			Maynard carbines
	A.K. Hengless	Commander, USN		Remington revolvers
ALK	Albert L. Koones	USN	1856-65	Batty Peace flask, 1856
AMB	Armistead M. Ball		1859-60	Harpers Ferry M1855 rifles and rifle muskets
APC	A.P. Casey	ASI	1859-61	Army & Navy percussion double-action revolvers
AR	Alexander Reuben	ASI, FSI	1862-63	
AR	Adam Rhulman	ASI	1830-61	Harpers Ferry muskets and rifles; Hewes & Philips ('H&P') Model 1816 muskets; Traveled in Europe with George Schuyler. In London and approved 10,000 Lefaucheaux revolvers (Schuyler to Simon Cameron, Sept 5, 1861); .54 Austrian rifles
ARW	Abraham R. Woolley	Captain	1813	
ASG	Albert S. Granger	ASI, FSI	1862	
AT	unknown		1814-19	Harpers Ferry muskets
AW	Alexander Wentzel Sr	ASI	1841-51	Proved M1841 rifle barrels
AW	Asaph Wilson		1833-39	Hall rifles and carbines
AW	unknown			Found on double-cartouched Remington revolvers with "CGC"
AWF	unknown	Confederate inspector, Georgia Armory		Georgia Armory Rifle
AWK	A.W. King	Confederate inspector	1863	Ashville Armory Rifle, Type II and III
AWM	unknown	ASI	1864	Colt Special Model 1861 rifle muskets; Sharps New Model 1859 and 1863 rifles
AWN	unknown	Confederate inspector		Georgia Armory Rifle
AWP	unknown	NY inspector		Barrel of a S. Cogswell Troy Model 1817 rifle
B	E.B. Boutwell (or Joseph C. Bragg)		1848	Batty Peace flask
BFQ	B.F. Quimby	ASI	1863	
BH	Benjamin Hannis	ASI	1861-63	Allen & Wheelock, Colt Model 1860, Remington, Savage 'Figure 8', and Starr revolvers; Maynard carbines; Model 1863 Remington rifles
BH	Benjamin Huger	Major	1854-58	
BL	Benjamin Lamphear	ASI	1798	Filed locks
BM	Benjamin Mills		1858-59	Harpers Ferry M1855 rilfes and rifle muskets
BM	Benjamin Moore	ASI	1810-15	North pistols
C	Cloue	ASI	1844-54	
C	R. Chandler		1848	Batty Peace flask
CB	Cyrus Buckland	ASI	1841	

Initial	Inspector's Name	Rank/office	Dates	Weapons with this mark
CB	Charles Boarman	Captain, USN	1847	Batty Peace Flask, 1850
CBC	Calvin B. Cross	ASI	1862-63	
	C.C. Campbell	Confederate Inspector		Cook & Bro. rifles
CDR	unknown			Greene Model Warner carbines
CEB	C.E. Buckland	ASI	1859	
CES	Charles E. Sherman	ASI	1842-47	
CEW	Charles E. Wilson	ASI	1846-65	
CF	Cyrus Foot	ASI	1829-41	Inspector at Springfield Armory; Locks
CFL	C.F. Lewis	ASI, MI	1863	
CG	Calvin Gay	ASI	1818-31	Evans and J.J. Henry, Boulton pistols
CGC	Charles G. Curtis	ASI	1862-63	Remington Beals .36 and .44, Remington Model 1861 .36 and 44; Remington split-breech carbines
CGC	Charles G. Chapman	ASI	1863-64	Henry rifles
CGC	C.G. Chandler	ASI	1861-63	Pettingill and Colt Dragoon revolvers
CHH	C.H. Hunt	ASI	1864	Alfred Jenks contract Model 1861 rifle muskets
CJ	Catesby Jones	Captain, USN	1805-58	Evans pistol barrels
CK	unknown			Starr DA Army revolvers
CNG	Charles N. Goodrich	ASI, FSI	1862-63	
CP	Charles Packard	ASI	1818	1818 Springfield pistols
CR	Cadwalader Ringgold	Captain, USN	1819-66	M1852 Navy officer's swords
CS	Clark Swallow	ASI	1862	
CSC	Charles S. Cotton	Lt., USN	1858-77	
CSL	Charles S. Lowell	Major	1858-64	Starr D.A. .44 revolvers, Colt Model 1860 revolvers and Warner carbines; Model 1840 Naval cutlasses; Spencer Model 1865 rifles
CTJ	C.T. Judd	ASI, MI	1863	
CW	Charles Williams	ASI	1807-14	Harpers Ferry and North pistols, Starr swords and contract muskets; Model 1808 muskets
CWH	C.W. Hartwell	ASI	1831-50	
DA	Daniel Ammen	Lt., USN	1836-78	Batty Peace Flask, 1850
DAP	Dwight A. Perkins	ASI	1862-	Model 1865 Spencer carbines; Colt Special Model 1861 rifle muskets
DC	Daniel Cotton	ASI	1798	Lockmaker
DD	Daniel Dunsmore	USN, gunner	1861-68	Remington revolvers
	D.E. Stanton	USN		Remington revolvers
DFC	David F. Clark	ASI	1861-68	Colt, Starr, Remington and Savage revolvers; Sharps Model 1863 carbines and rifles
DFM	Dexter F. Mossman	ASI	1862-64	Emerson & Silver Model 1860 sabers
DL	D. LeGro	ASI	1826-31	
DLG	D. LeGro		1831-50	
DP	Daniel Pettibone	ASI	1808-09	Evans, Henry and Miles muskets; Henry, Fry and Shuler pistols; Henry rifles; Rose & Sons swords; Model 1807 pistols
	F. Phoenix	Lt. Cdr., USN	1862	Remington-Beals Navy revolvers
DP/B	unknown		1862	Barrel proof on Orison Blunt Pattern 1853 Enfield rifle muskets
DPS	Daniel P. Strong	ASI	1862	
DR	Daniel Reynolds		1861-64	Model 1861 "Plymouth" rifles; Model 1861 cutlasses; Dahlgren bayonets
DR	David Rice	ASI	1835-63	Stocks; Light Cavalry and Artillery sabers
DT	Daniel Tyler	Lt.	1831-50	Starr muskets; Model 1832 Foot Artillery swords; Hall carbines and rifles 1831-33
DW	Decius Wadsworth	Colonel	1802-21	Also found as "W / P" or "P / W" in two lines.

"CGC"—Curtis G. Clarke, inspector of Henry rifles.

Multiple cartouches usually signifies inspector and sub-inspector handling of a weapon. It can also indicate that a weapon went through an arsenal rebuild at some time.

Initial	Inspector's Name	Rank/office	Dates	Weapons with this mark
DWT	D. Waldo Tyler	ASI	1862-64	Watertown contract Model 1861 rifle musket. See also "A"
E	Charles Eberle	ASI	1807	Rose sabers
EA	Ephaphroditus Alis	ASI	1818-41	1815 & 1818 dated Springfield pistol
EAM	E.A. May	ASI	1831 (1819?)-50	
EAW	E.A. Williams		1865	Spencer Model 1860 and 1865 carbines
EB	Edward Barrett	Cdr., USN	1837	
EB	Edmund Byrone	Lt., USN	1814-50	
EB	Elizur Bates	ASI	1838-46	Waters Model 1836 pistol; Hall Model 1840 carbines
EBB	E.B. Boutwell	Cdr., USN	1828-1850	Batty Peace Flask, 1848
EBB	Edgar B. Boyd	ASI	1862	
ECB	Edmund C. Bailey	ASI	1862	Sharps New Model 1859 carbines; Wm. Muir Model 1861 contract rifle-muskets
ECW	E.C. Wheeler	ASI, FSI	1862-82	Springfield rifles, Remington Navy revolvers; Spencer rifles and Model 1865 carbines+E183
EF	E. Farrar	ASI	1860-68	Starr .44 revolvers
EF	Edgar Freeman	Lt., USN	1811-28	
EF	Edward Flather	ASI	1862-63	Starr first model carbines
EH	Edward Hooker	Lt.Cdr., USN	1861-84	
EHP	Edwin H. Perry	ASP	1862	
EJF	E.J. Frost	ASI	1862-64	Barrels
EKC	E.K. Colton	ASI	1860-64	
EM	Edwin Martin	ASI	1862	
EM	Edward McCue	ASI	1862-63	
EMC	E.M. Camp	ASI	1860-65	Colt Model 1860 .44 revolvers; Remington Model 1863 Type 1 rifle muskets
EMD	Edward M. Dustin (see EWD)	ASI	1862-63	Burnside carbines
	Edward M. Yard	Cdr., USN	1863	Remington revolvers
ES	Elisha Shaw	ASI	1796	Forged springs
ESA	Erskin S. Allin (Allen)	SI	1850-65	Model 1861 and 1863 rifle-muskets; Spencer carbines; Norwich arms
ESF	Edward S. Frost	ASI	1862-63	Stocks
	E.S. Hutter	Confederate inspector, Lt.		Danville, VA Ordnance Office. Inspected Keen, Walker & Co. carbines
ET	Elisha Tobey	ASI	1816-32	North Model 1816, 1819 and 1826 Navy pistols; 1817, 1818 Springfield pistols; 1816-21 R. Johnson, Starr and Waters muskets; Starr Model 1826 cutlasses; Model 1832 Foot Artillery swords; Johnson Model 1836 pistols
ET	Edwin Tyler	ASI	1813-19	

Initial	Inspector's Name	Rank/office	Dates	Weapons with this mark
EW	Eber Ward	ASI	1813-15	Charleville and Model 1816 muskets
EWB	E.W. Blake	ASI	1818	
EWD	Edward M. Dustin (see EMD-unconfirmed)	ASI	1862-63	Burnside carbines
	F.A. Parker	Lt. Cdr., USN		Remington revolvers
FAR	Francis A. Roe	USN, gunner	1841-85	Fluted Colt Model 1860 revolvers; Savage Navy revolvers
	Fadoe Butt	ASI	1842	Inspector of filed lockplates at Harpers Ferry; mark unknown
FC	Francis Camp	ASI	1859-62	Colt Special Model 1861 rifle musket barrels
FCH	F.C. Humphreys	Confederate Captain of Ordnance		J.P. Murray Rifles, Types I, II & III. Usually stamped PRO / FCH in two lines
FCW	Frank C. Warner	USN, civilian	1863-68	Plymouth rifles, Whitney revolvers
FDL	unknown			Barrel and stocks of Model 1862 and 1864 Joslyn carbines
FH	Fred Harvey	ASI	1862	
FLR				Barrel of Norris & Clement contract Model 1861 rifle-musket
FMR	Francis M. Ramsay	Cdr., USN	1850-97	Model 1861 Navy signal pistol
FR	Frederick Rodgers	Cdr., USN	1857-99	
FR	Franklin Root	ASI	1862-63	
FRB	F.R. Bull	ASI	1860-61	Sample arms
FSN	F.S. North	ASI	1862-63	
FSS	Frederick S. Strong	ASI	1862-63	C. Robey NCO swords
FW	unknown			R.Johnson Model 1817 contract rifles
FWC	Ferdinand W. Cook	Confederate inspector		Cook & Bro. rifles and carbines
FWS	F.W. Sanderson	ASI	1862-79	Whitney Model 1863 contract Model I rifle-muskets
GAL	George A. Lawrence	ASI	1862-63	Stocks
GAM	George A. Magruder	Captain, USN	1817-61	
GBC	G.B. Cruzen	ASI	1861	Remington New Model 1861 revolvers
GBF	George B. Foote	ASI	1862-63	
GBR	George B. Russell	ASI	1862-63	Cavalry equipment
GC	George Curtis	ASI	1861-	Burnsides Carbine, fifth model; Sharps Model 1863 carbines; Warner carbines; Merrill carbines; Spencer Model 1865 carbines
GDG	Gilbert D. Greason	ASI	1862	
GDL	George D. Little	Ensign, USN	1862-65	Colt Model 1860 revolvers
GDR	G.D. Ramsay Jr.	Captain	1863-65	
GDS	G.D. Shattuck	ASI	1855-60	Colt revolvers
GEC	George E. Chamberlain	ASI	1862-79	Welch and William Mason contract Model 1861 rifle muskets
GES	George E. Saunders	ASI	1862	`
GF	George Flegel	ASI	1812-23	Armorer at Schuylkill Arsenal. Waters muskets and Derringer rifles; Model 1808 Pennsylvania contract muskets; Model 1816 muskets
GF	George Flynn	ASI	1824	Locks
GFM	George F. Morrison	Lt., USN	1849-60	Starr S.A. .44 revolvers
GFT	George F. Tucker	ASI	1862-64	Gwynn & Campbell carbines, Type I
GG	Guert Gansevoort	Cdr., USN	1862-64	Aston M1842 pistols, Ames 1860-61 cutlasses, Colt revolvers, 1865 Dahlgren bayonets, Navy officer's sword, Sharps & Hankins carbines, Remington New Model, Savage and Whitney revolvers; Model 1861 "Plymouth rifles; Model 1849 Colt pocket revolvers
GGB	George G. Bowe	ASI	1862-63	stocks
GGS	George G. Saunders	ASI (civilian inspector?)	1856-70	Colt Dragoon revolvers; Modle 1840 Foot Officers swords; Light Cavalry sabers; Ball carbines

Initial	Inspector's Name	Rank/office	Dates	Weapons with this mark
GH	George Haines	ASI	1860	Ballard carbines
GH	George Hosmer	ASI, FSI	1862-89	Spencer rifles
GHD	George H. Dupee	ASI	1862-63	
GHG	George H. Graham	ASI	1862	
GHH	George H. Hubbard	ASI, FSI	1862-63	
GHS	Gustavus H. Scott	Cdr., USN	1828-73	Colt Model 1860 revolvers
GKC	George K. Charter	ASI	1861-64	Starr revolvers; Cavalry, musician and NCO swords
GKJ	George K. Jacobs		1861-63	Amoskeag government inspector; Lindner carbines
	George Mallory	ASI	1829	Inspector at Harpers Ferry, mark unknown
GMC	George M. Colvocoresses	Cdr., USN	1849-67	Whitney revolvers
GMR	George M. Ransom	Captain, USN	1839-82	Colt Model 1851 revolvers
GP	George Palmer	ASI	1862	
GP	Giles Porter	ASI	1862-75	Remington New Model and Pettingill revolvers; Remington contract Model 1863 rifles
GRC	unknown			Found on double cartouched Remington revolvers with OWA
GSM	G.S. Morse	ASI	1862	Starr revolvers
GT	George Talcott	Lt.	1836-38	
GTB	George T. Balch	Captain	1861-66	Colt and Savage revolvers
GTR	Garland T. Rowland	Captain	1832-34	
GW	George Wells	Lt., USN	1833-62	Aston Model 1842 pistols
GW	George Wright	ASI	1850-62	Aston Model 1842 pistol barrels; U.S. inspector in Europe, 1861-62; .69 Liege rifled muskets; .69 Cologne rifled muskets; Solingen cavalry sabers
GWC	George W. Chapin	ASI	1862-64	Model 1840 Musician swords; Ames Model 1860 cavalry sabers; Starr revolvers
GWH	George W. Hamlin	ASI	1846-64(?)	Colt Model 1851 revolvers; Hall Model 1843 carbines
GWH	George W. Hanger	ASI	1845-46	
GWH	George W. Hartwell		1846-59	
GWP	G.W. Patch	ASI	1846-58	Colt Third Model Dragoon revolvers
GWQ	unknown		1862	Barrel proof on Whitney contract Model 1861 rifle muskets
GWR	George W. Rodgers	Cdr., USN	1839-63	Colt Model 1851 revolvers (stamped in block letters, "I/GWR")
GWS	George W. Schuman	ASI	1858-60	Colt Dragoon revolvers
GWS	G.W. Sherman	ASI	1858-61	Colt Dragoon revolvers
GWS	G.W. Smith	ASI	1857	Colt Dragoon revolvers
GWS	G.W. Sword		1856	Colt Dragoon revolvers
	George Zerger	ASI	1830	Inspector at Harpers Ferry, mark unknown
HBB	Hanson B. Bullock	ASI	1862	
HBC	H.B. Cooley	ASI, FSI	1862-63	A. Jenk & Son contract Model 1861 rifle musket barrels
HBJ	H.B. Johnson	ASI	1862	Remington Beals Navy revolvers
H	Joseph Hall		1863	Amoskeag contract Model 1861 rifle muskets
H	Andrew A. Harwood		1846	Ames Peace flask
	Horace Burpee		1863	Amoskeag assistant inspector
HD	H. Dana	ASI, MI	1862-63	
HDH	Henry D. Hastings	ASI	1862-65	Model 1840 NCO and Musician swords; Model 1863 Sharps and Burnside fifth model carbines; Remington Model 1863 rifles; Smith carbines; Merrill carbines
HDJ	Henry D. Jennings	ASI	1862-63	Model 1863 Remington Rifles
HEH	H.E. Hollister	ASI, FSI	1862-63	
HEV	Henry E. Valentine	ASI	1862-65	Burnside Model 1865 Spencer carbines

"JAS"—John A. Schaeffer

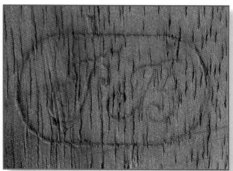

"JB"—Confederate inspector
James Henry Burton

"JH"—At least six inspectors before
1865 could have used this mark.

Initial	Inspector's Name	Rank/office	Dates	Weapons with this mark
HFL	Harry F. Lynch	ASI	1839-40	Colts
HGS	unknown			Stamped on barrel of first model Starr carbines
	H.H. Bell	Commodore, USN	1864	Remington revolvers
HHH	H.H. Hamilton			Sharps rifles
HHH	H.H. Hartzell		1863	Amoskeag contract rifle muskets
	H.H. Herrington	Chief Inspector, CSA	1864-65	Spiller & Burr factory
HHP	Henry H. Perkin	ASI	1810-1817	North Model 1816 Navy pistols and Starr swords
HK	Henry Kirk	ASI	1862-63	
HKC	Henry Knox Craig	Major	1832-38	Waters Model 1836 pistol; Model 1832 Artillery swords and Model 1833 Dragoon sabers; Hall Model 1833 carbines and 1839 rifles, 1832-38
HKH	Henry K. Hoff	Cdr., USN	1862-68	Whitney revolvers, Sharps & Hankins carbines
	H. Lawrence Ingraham	Confederate inspector. Lt.	1862	E&J Johnson & Co. sabers
HLL	H.L. Lathrop	ASI	1862	Colt Model 1860 revolvers
	Henry Miller	ASI	1825	Inspected bayonets. Mark unknown
HMB	unknown		1864	E.Robinson contract Model 1861 rifle musket barrels
HS	Harris Smith	ASI, FSI	1862-79	
HS	H. Stephens	Lt.	1816	Starr swords
HSL	Homer S. Lathe		1862-63	Remington Model 1863 rifle barrels
HT	H. Tracy	ASI	1831-50	
HW	Henry Walke	Cdr., USN	1827-71	Model 1861 "Plymouth" rifles
HWW	Henry W. Wilcos	ASI	1862	
IB	Isack Bartlett	ASI	1808	forged lockplates
	Isaac B. Myers	Chief Inspector, CSA	1862-65	Spiller & Burr factory
IC				Denotes "Inspected and condemned"
IH	Isaac Hull	Captain, USN	1808	
IP	Joseph Perkins	ASI	1785-1805	
JA	John Avis	ASI	1837-38	Waters flintlock pistols
JA	Joel Abbot	Lt., USN	1812-55	
	John A. Gamber	ASI	1844	Proved musket barrels at Lemuel Pomeroy
JAG	James A. Greer	Lt., USN	1848	Batty Peace flask; Colt & Whitney revolvers; Whitney Model 1841 rifles
JAJB	James Andrew Jackson Bradford	Captain	1833-36	Hall Model 1833 carbines and Model 1819 rifles, 1833-36

Initial	Inspector's Name	Rank/office	Dates	Weapons with this mark
JAS	John A. Schaeffer	ASI	1831	Harpers Ferry muskets; Model 1842 muskets; Model 1855 rifles and rifle muskets; Model 1840 Springfield muskets
JB	James Bell	ASI	1827	
JB	James Henry Burton		1845-54; 1861-	Harpers Ferry master armorer; subsequently Confederate inspector, Fayetteville rifles; C.S. Richmond carbines
	James B. Davis	USN		Remington revolvers
JBK	John B. Kirkhan	ASI	1823-41	Locks
JC	James. Cattaway	ASI	1862-63	sample arms
JC	James Carrington	ASI	1803-45	Whitney, Blake and Starr muskets; Model 1832 Foot Artillery swords
JCB	John C. Beaumont	Lt., USN	1843-55	Johnson pistol; M1841 Naval cutlasses; Jenks carbines
JCB	Joseph C. Bragg	ASI	1841-54	R. Johnson, Waters, Ames pistols; Colt Dragoon revolvers; Hall carbines; Robbins & Lawrence Model 1841 rifles; Jenks percussion rifles
JCS	John C. Sharpe	Lt., USN	1825-40	Derringer rifles for Navy
JCS	John C. Stebbins	ASI	1834-41	North-Hall carbines; Waters pistols
JCS	John C. Symmes	Captain	1847-61	
JCW	unknown		1863-1865	Model 1860 cavalry sabers
JD	Joseph Dale	ASI	1815-18	1815 and 1818 Springfield pistol lock maker
JD	J. Dowlar	ASI	1811	Stocks and barrels
JDJ	John D. Johnson	ASI	1819-22	U.S. Model 1819 North pistol barrels
	John D. Kirkham	ASI	1836	Springfield Armory; mark unknown
JEC	J.E. Cummings	ASI, MI	1862-63	
JEC	Joseph Edgar Craig	Lt., USN	1861-99	
JEH	J.E. Hitchcock		1862-63	
JF	unknown		1862-65	Emerson & Silver Light Cavalry, Artillery sabers and Model 1840 NCO swords; Ames Model 1860 sabers
JG	John Garvin (Gravin?)	Lt., USN	1865-74	Colt revolvers
JGB		Confederate inspector		Barrel of Mendenhall, Jones & Gardner Type II rifles
	John G. Corbin	Commander, USN		Remington revolvers
JH	John Hannis	ASI	1862	Wm. Muir contract Model 1861 rifle muskets
JH	Joseph Hannis	ASI	1837-62	Hall Model 1843 carbines; Nipps, Waters, Robert Johnson, Starr, Pomeroy, Edward & Goodrich; Tyron muskets
JH	Joseph Harness (also spelled 'Harniss')	ASI	1841-44	Starr Model 1817 rifles, Waters Model 1836 pistol
JH	James Harris	ASI	1837-51	R. Johnson, I.N. Johnson Model 1842 pistols; Jenks flinlock rifles;Colts Model 1851 revolvers
JH	James Hawkins	ASI	1848-59	Colt Second Model Dragoon revolvers
JH	John Hawkins	ASI	1838-52	Starr Model 1817 rifles; Edward & Goodrich, Nippes, Pomeroy, Starr, Pomeroy, Whitney muskets
JH	John Hill	ASI	1813-35	
	Joseph Hoffman	ASI	1829	Inspector at Harpers Ferry, mark unknown
JHC	James H. Clark		1864	Norwich Arms
	James H. Claspy	Asst. Inspector, CSA	1862-64	Spiller & Burr factory
JHG	John H. Griffith	USN, civilian	1862	Colt and Whitney revolvers; Spencer rifles; Sharps & Hankins carbines; Plymouth rifles
JHH	Joseph H. Hubbard		1862	
JHK	John Henry King		1850	Harpers Ferry Model 1841 rifles prior to 1850
	Jonathon H. Krissell	Lt. Cdr., USN		Remington revolvers
JHL	unknown			Colt Model 1861 Special rifle (Julia 10/07 no. 1473)
JHM	James H. McGuire	ASI	1862	

"JL"—Joseph Lanman

"JLR"—John L. Reseler

"JPC"—James P. Chapman

Initial	Inspector's Name	Rank/office	Dates	Weapons with this mark
	J.H. Russell	Lt. Cdr., USN		Remington revolvers
JJAB	James J.A. Bradford	AI	1834-35	M1832 Foot Artillery swords
JJC	John J. Cornwell	Cdr., USN	1847-67	Model 1936 pistol; Smith carbines
JL	Joseph Lanman (Lenman)	Lt., USN	1825-72	Ames Navy flasks; Model 1841 Naval cutlasses; Jenks (Ames) carbines
JL	Joseph Lombard	ASI	1818-41	Swords, barrels
JLC	Joseph L. Cottle	ASI	1863-75	Spencer Model 1865 rifles
JLH	James L. Henderson	Cdr., USN	1828-61	Colt Model 1851 and 1861 .36 revolvers
JLR	John L. Reseler	ASI	1850	Harpers Ferry Model 1841 rifles after 1850
JM	Julian McAllister	Major	1864-65	M1860 Cavalry Saber, Mansfield and Lamb
JM	John Maggs	ASI	1862	Norwich Arms contract Model 1861 rifle muskets; Providence Tool Co. contract Model 1860 cavalry sabers
JM	Joseph Morgan	ASI	1798-1802	North & Cheney pistols
JM	Justice Murphy	ASI	1841	
JM	Justin Murphy	ASI	1813-40	Jenning, Pomeroy, Starr, Springfield, Waters, North and R. Johnson
	Joseph M. Bradford	Asst. QM, USN		Remington revolvers
JMD	unkown			stamped on barrels of Gallagher carbines
JN	John Newbury	ASI	1817-31	Inspector of contract arms; R. Johnson, Starr, North, Springfield and Pomeroy; Starr Model 1817 Common Rifles; Model 1817 pistols
	J. Nicholson	Cdr., USN		Remington revolvers
JN	John Nicholson Jr.	ASI	1799-1807	
JN	John Nicholson Sr.	ASI	1797-98	Musket barrels
JN	John Norman	ASI	1830-34	
JNS	J.N. Sollace	ASI	1831-1850	
JOB	J.O. Bush	ASI	1864	barrel inspector
JP	James Perkin(s)	ASI	1815	
JP	Jacob Perkin	ASI	1819-21	Waters muskets
JP	Joseph Perkin		1798	
JP	John Pope	Lt.	1843	
JPC	James P. Chapman	ASI	1848-58	Ames Model 1842 pistols; Model 1841 Robbins & Lawrence and E. Whitney rifles
JPO	James P. Oeller(s)	Lt., USN	1813-49	J.J. Henry Boulton Model 1826 pistols, Batty Peace flasks
	J.P. Sanford	Lt., USN	1863	Remington revolvers
JPW	Joseph P. Wells	ASI, MI	1863	
JRE	John R. Esleek	ASI	1863	Parts
JRG	John R. Goldsborough	Captain, USN	1864-65	Whitney, Colt and Savage revolvers; Sharps & Hankins carbines

"JS" is one of the most common marks. Prior to 1865, no fewer than 10 inspectors could have used this stamp.

"JS/[anchor]"—This mark is not attributed, though many believe it was used by an agent purchasing weapons for the Confederacy who worked primarily in the United Kingdom.

Initial	Inspector's Name	Rank/office	Dates	Weapons with this mark
JRMM	J.R.M. Mullaney	USN	1832-79	Colt Model 1851 Navy revolvers
JS	Jacob Shough	ASI	1808-11	Henry, Fry and Guest pistols; Henry rifles and pistols
JS	John Small		1780-1782	
JS	James Smith		1780-1782	
JS	Joseph Smith	Captain, USN	1809-37	
JS	Josiah Snell	ASI	1800-01	North & Cheney pistols
JS	John C. Stebbins	ASI	1819-40	Pomeroy; Edwards & Goodrich, Waters, Whitney, Starr, Nippes, Derringer muskets
JS	Jeremiah Stevens		1837	Hall carbines; Inspector of forgings at Harpers Ferry
JS	James Stillman	ASI	1831-50	
JS	James Stubblefield	ASI	1807-21	Harpers Ferry pistols, rifles and muskets
JS	John Symington	Colonel	1832-63	Model 1855 Springfield rifle-muskets
JSC	James S. Chauncey	Cdr., USN	1812-69	Spencer rifles
JSD	James S. Dudley	Lt.	1861-70	Colt Model 1860 and Starr .44 revolvers
JSD	John S. Dexter	ASI	1798	
JSD	John S. Dunston (Dustin?)	ASI	1862-63	
	J.S. Missroon	Cdr., USN	1862	Remington-Beals Navy revolvers
JSP	James S. Palmer	Lt., USN	1825-67	Adams Navy flasks, 1846-48
	Joseph S. Skerrett	Lt. Cdr., USN		Remington-Beals Navy revolvers
JT	Joseph Tarbell	Captain, USN	1798-1815	
JT	Josiah Tatnal	Captain	1858	Massachusetts Arms Co. Adams revolvers
JT	John Taylor	ASI	1861-62	Colt Model 1860 .44, Starr .36 and Savage .36 revolvers; Colt Model 1861 rifle-muskets; Sharps Model 1859 rifles with double-set triggers
JT	Jerome Towne	ASI	1862-64	Colt Special Model 1861 rifle muskets
JTB	James T. Baden [Reilly calls him "John"]	Lt.	1862-64	Remington, Starr, Whitney & Savage revolvers
JTC	John T. Cleveland	ASI	1856-77	Savage revolvers; Schubarth contract Model 1861 rifle muskets
JTL	J.T. Lerk	Confederate inspector		Inner surface of lockplate and und underside of barrel of Mendenhall, Jones & Gardner Type IV rifles.
JW	Joseph Weatherhead	ASI	1825-47	North Model 1819, 1821 & 1822 pistols; Starr, Waters, R. Johnson and Pomeroy muskets and rifles
JW	John Williamson	Captain	1838-49	
	James Winner		1817	Model 1816 muskets
JWK	John W. Keene	ASI	1862-63	
JWK	John W. Kelly	Lt., USN	1853-64	

"LCA"—Lucius C. Allen.

"LS"—Luther Sage

"MM"—Miles Moulton

Initial	Inspector's Name	Rank/office	Dates	Weapons with this mark
JWR	James W. Reilly	Major	1848-95	Model 1840 Cavalry sabers and Musician swords; Rifleman's knives
JWR	James Wolfe Ripley	Bvt. Lt. Col.	1832-60	
JY	Jonathon Young	Lt. Cdr., USN	1841-82	Whitney revolvers
K	A.D. King (or A.L. Koones)		1849	Batty Peace flask
L	Laley	ASI	1844-54	
LAB	Lester A. Beardslee	Lt. Cdr., USN	1850-98	Starr revolvers and carbines
LAS	unknown			
LB	unknown	Confederate inspector		Stamped on barrels of Mendenhall, Jones & Gardner Type IV rifles. See also LVB
LBC	Luke B. Chase	USN	1861-62	Batty Peace flask, 1849-1850; Remington Model 1841 rifles
LC	Lyman Converse	ASI	1853-1863	Spencer rifles
LCA	Lucius C. Allin	ASI	1859	Colt Dragoon and Model 1851 revolvers; Mass. Arms Co. Adams revolvers and Starr revolvers
LD	L. Dustin (also spelled Duston)	ASI	1861-63	Purchased arms and parts; Model 1840 NCO swords; A. Jenks & Son contract Model 1861 rifle muskets
LF	Lewis Foster Jr.	ASI	1837-39	Waters Model 1836 pistols
LFR	unknown			Smith carbines (marked on barrels); barrels of Norris & Clements contract Model 1863 rifles
LG	Lewis Ghriskey	ASI	1861	Stocks and barrels
LH	Luke Harrington	Mass. Inspector	1825-35	
LH	unknown		1865	Burnside Model 1865 Spencer carbines
LL	Luther Luge	ASI	1841	
LMF	Lewis M. Ferry	ASI	1863	
LS	Luther Sage	ASI	1813-40	Inspector of contract arms. North Model 1813, 1816 and 1819 pistols; R. Johnson, Water, Whitney, Pomeroy and Starr muskets; Springfield pistols and muskets
LVB		Confederate inspector		Stamped on barrels of Mendenhall, Jones & Gardner Type IV rifles. See also LB
LW	Leicester Wheeler	ASI	1818	
M	Joseph Morgan		1798-1801	Usually seen in the form "x / M" in two lines
M	unknown		1863	M1860 Cavalry Saber, Roby
M	Lt. William Murdaugh	Confederate Navy	1861	Transition Model LeMat revolvers
MB	Marin Brittenbaugh		1830	Harpers Ferry Model 1822 muskets
MH	unknown		1795-1815	Found on Harpers Ferry muskets
MH	Michael Hayes	ASI	1860-	Colt revolvers and Model 1861 Special rifle-muskets
MHM	unknown		1864	James D. Mowry contract Model 1861 rifle musket barrels
MLM	Moses L. Morse	ASI	1820-24	Asa Waters Model 1816 muskets

Initial	Inspector's Name	Rank/office	Dates	Weapons with this mark
MM	(Maurice?) Miles Moulton	ASI	1861-64	Savage and Colt Model 1851 revolvers; Burnside 5th Model carbines; Light Cavalry sabers; Greene Model Warner carbines; Ballard carbines; Palmer carbines
MMJ	Martin M. Johnson	ASI	1862-63	Spencer carbines and Model 1860 E422rifles
MNM	unknown		1864	Colt Special Model 1861 rifle muskets barrels; Sharps Model 1863 rifles
MPL	Mann Paige Lomax	Major	1837-42	Waters and R. Johnson pistols; Hall Model 1833 carbines, 1838-40; Jenks flintlock musketoons; Model 1832 Foot Artillery swords; Model 1833 Dragoon sabers
MS	Massachusetts Militia			Edged weapons issued to that state by the federal government
MTK	Marian T. Krepps	ASI	1862-63	
MTW	Marine T. Wickham	ASI	1811-15	Evans muskets and North pistols
MWC	M.W. Carr	ASI	1862-63	
MWM	M.W. Morley	ASI	1862	Arms purchaser; Colt Model 1861 Special rifle-muskets
NB	Nehemiah Baden	Lt.	1813-20	North Model 1816 pistol
NF	Noah Foot	ASI	1824	
NF	Nathan Forbes	ASI	1798-1801	
NJ	State of New Jersey			
NM	unknown			Balllard contract carbines
NO	Noble Orr	ASI	1798-1802	North & Cheney pistols and Whitney muskets
NW	Nathanial Whiting	ASI	1862	
NWP	Nahum W. Patch	ASI (civilian inspector?)	1831-51	Colt Walker and First Model Dragoon revolvers; Ames and R. Johnson pistols; Starr rifles; North-Hall carbines; 1816 US muskets; Model 1841 Naval cutlass; Model 1832 Foot Artillery swords; Model 1840 Light Artillery sabers and Musician swords; Halls Model 1833 and 1840 carbines; Model 1847 Sapper & Miner's musketoons; Jenks flintlock musketoons and rifles
OA	Oliver Allen	ASI	1816-18	North Model 1816 pistol
OBG	O.B. Graham		1861	Norwich Arms contract Model 1861 rifle muskets
	O.C. Badger	Lt. Cdr., USN	1863	Remington revolvers
OD	Otis Dudley	ASI	1830	North, Hall rifles
OHP	Oliver Hazard Perry	Lt., USN	1829-49	Stimpson Navy flask, 1845
ORD	Army Ordnance Dept.		1832-40	Swords purchased by the army
ORR	Robert or Noble Orr		1798-1801	1798 Contract Whitney musket
OS	Oliver Sexton	ASI	1836-1841	Springfield Armory
OWA	O.W. Ainsworth	ASI	1831-74	Colt and Remington revolvers; Savage Model 1861 contract rifle-muskets; Sharps Model 1859 rifles with double-set triggers; Remington Model 1863 rifle muskets
PB	Peter Barrett	USN gunner	1861-71	Colt Model 1860 and 1861 revolvers
PB	Pomeroy Booth	ASI	1862	
PB/P	Philip Burkhart	Armorer/ Inspector, Harpers Ferry and Fayetteville Armory	1835-57	Proved gun barrels; Springfield Model 1840 muskets; Harpers Ferry Model 1842 muskets after 1852; Confederate inspector Fayetteville Armory: Fayetteville Rifle, Type I
PC	unknown	Mass. Inspector		
PC	Pierce Crosby	Cdr., USN	1838-83	
PC	P. Chapman	USN civilian	1844	
	Percival Drayton	Captain, USN	1863	Remington-Beals Navy revolvers
PG	Peter Getz	ASI	1803-08	
PH	Peter V. Hagner	Lieutenant	1838-63	
PH	Philip Hoffman	ASI	1818-1840	Hall rifles; worked at Carruth's Armory, Greenville, SC, in 1818. Returned to Harpers Ferry in 1819; Model 1816 muskets
PS	unknown			Found on early Remington Beals and Elliot revolvers in conjunction with CGC cartouche
PT			1864	Gwynn & Campbell Type I & II (1st-3rd models) carbines
PTC	Patrick Thomas Cunningham	Lt., USN	1863-72	

Initial	Inspector's Name	Rank/office	Dates	Weapons with this mark
PV	P. Valentine	ASI	1862	Purchased arms
P/W	Decius Wadsworth		1798-1801	Also found as "W / P" in two lines.
R	unknown		1846	Model 1841 Naval cutlasses
RAC	Ranaldo A. Carr		1861-66	Model 1851 Colt revolvers
RB	Robert Beals	SI	1862	Colt revolvers
RB	Robert Blanchard	ASI	1831	North Hall carbines
RBH	Robert B. Hitchcock	Lt., USN	1851-53	Model 1852 Naval Officer's sword
RBR	Robert B. Reed	ASI	1820-21	Inspected at Carruth's factory in Greenville, SC
RC	Rufus Chandler	ASI	1831-50	Ames Model 1842 pistol and Ames Cutlass; Model 1840 Cavalry and NCO swords; Jenks carbines
RC	Robert Corbit	ASI	1798	Lock filer
RC	Russel Curtis	ASI	1818	Models 1815, 1817 & 1818 Springfield pistol stocks
RE	Reuben Ellis	ASI	1818	
RHKW	Robert Henry Kirkwood Whiteley	Captain	1838-75	Aston Model 1842 Navy pistols; Schroeder needle-fire carbines; Symmes carbines; Merrill, Latrobe & Thomas carbines; Colt Dragoon and Model 1851 revolvers; Starr and Savage revolvers; Sharps carbines; Burnside 5th Model carbines; Batty Peace flask; Enfield rifles
RJ	Robert Johnson	ASI	1822-26	North Model 1816 pistols; Model 1819 pistols
RKA	Remick K. Arnold	ASI	1862-77	Model 1863 Remington rifle barrels
RKW			1864	Gwynn & Campbell Type II (1st-3rd model) carbines; Burnside fifth model carbines
RL	Roswell Lee	ASI	1818-33	Springfield Model 1816 muskets; Asa Waters muskets, 1821-29
RLB	R.L. Buckland	ASI	1860-61	sample arms
RLB	Rufus L. Baker	Captain	1818-20	
	Richard L. May	Lt. Commander	1863	Plymouth rifles
RO	Robert Orr	ASI	1798-1808	North & Cheney pistols and Whitney muskets
RP	Richard Paine	USN civilian	1839-48	Ames pistols; Jenks carbines by Ames and Remington; Derringer pistol barrels
RP	Richard Parker	Lt.	1838-47	
RPB	Robert P. Barry	Captain	1861-65	
RPB	Robert P. Beales	ASI	1862-79	
RPP	Robert P. Parrott	Captain	1836	
RS	Rufus Sibley	Mass. Inspector	1813-15	Proved contract musket barrels for the U.S. Government at Asa Waters in Millbury, Mass.
RS	Richard Smith	Lt. Col., USMC	1806-30	
RSL	Robert S. LaMotte	Captain	1861-69	Sharps rifles; Model 1863 rifle barrels; Sharps Model 1865 carbines
RSL	Richard S. Lawrence	Superintendent of Robbins & Lawrence	1851	Sharps Model 1851 carbines
RTS	R.T. Safford	ASI	1862-85	
RWM	Richard W. Meade	Cdr., USN	1850-95	Colt Model 1851 and Model 1861 revolvers
S	Shaeffer	ASI	1844-54	
SA	Salmon Adams	ASI	1860-61; 1861-65	C.S. Armory, Richmond
SA	Samuel Alexander		1808	
SAD	S.A. Dinsmore	ASI	1862-63	
SB	Samuel Barron	Lt., USN	1812-61	Whitney Navy revolvers
SB	Samuel Byington		1854-58	Harpers Ferry rifles and rifle muskets
SBB	Samuel B. Bugbee		1862	
SBL	Samuel B. Lathrop	ASI	1818	
SC	Silas Crispin	Captain	1862	Remington Model 1861 revolvers

Initial	Inspector's Name	Rank/office	Dates	Weapons with this mark
SCR	Stephen C. Rowan	Cdr., USN	1826-89	Model 1851 Colt Navy revolvers; Model 1855 Sharps carbines
SD	Samuel Dale	ASI	1817	
SD	Stephen Danks	ASI, SI	1863	
SH	Samuel Hawkins	ASI	1862	
SHW	Sheffield H. Wright		1863	Amoskeag contract Model 1861 rifle musket barrels
SJ	Seth James	ASI	1818-24	Pomeroy muskets
SK	Samuel Keeler	ASI	1848	Colt First Model Dragoon; Batty Peace flasks
SK	Samuel Knowles (Knows/Knous)	ASI	1846-52	Aston Model 1842 pistols; Colt Dragoons/ Sharps Model 1852 Carbines
SL	Samuel Leonard	ASI	1862-75	Colt and Savage revolvers
SLW	Samuel L. Worsley	ASI, FSI	1862-63	
SM	Samuel Marcy	Lt., USN	1838-62	
SM	Stillman Moore	ASI	1846-52	Aston pistols
SPB	Samuel P. Baird	Lt., USN	1861-73	Starr, Whitney revolvers
SRC	unknown			stamped on 1841-dated Springfield musket trigger guard
STB	Samuel T. Bugbee	ASI	1862	Starr revolvers; Burnside fifth model carbines
SWP	S.W. Porter	ASI, FI	1859-63	Whitney contract Model 1863 rifle muskets
TA	Thomas Annely	ASI	1797	Musket and pistol barrels
TAB	Theodore A. Belknap	ASI	1862	
TBH	Thomas B. Hawkins	ASI, FSI	1862-63	
TD	Thomas Dale	ASI	1796	Lock maker
	Thomas Daffin		1862	worked at Frankford Arsenal.E475 P.S. Justice rifles
THS	Thomas H. Stevens	Lt., USN	1816	Starr cutlasses
	T.J. Treadwell	Lt.	1861	Inspected sabers made by Leisenring; sabers and NCO swords by Wilstach & Co.
TKL	unknown		1863-64	Model 1840 NCO swords; Joslyn carbines; Burnside 5th Model carbines
TP	Thomas Palmer	ASI	1808-09	
	Thomas Poynton Ives	Lt., USN	1864	Remington revolvers
TS	Thomas Sangster	Captain	1812	
	Tobias Stanley	Cdr., USN		Remington revolvers
TS	Townsend Stith	Captain	1810	
TS	Thomas Stockton	Captain	1812-25	
TS	Thomas Stuart	Captain	1813	
TTSL	Theodore T.S. Laidley	Major	1862-66	Frankford Arsenal
TV	Thomas Valentine	ASI	1863	need to verify initials. Dixie listed as "TB"
TW	Thomas Warner	ASI	1833-41	R. Johnson pistols; Starr, Wickham, Edwards & Goodrich, Starr, Waters, Pomeroy and Springfield muskets; Model 1833 dragoon sabers
TWB	T.W. Booth	ASI	1861-65	Sharps
TWR	Thomas W. Russell	ASI	1862	Sharps New Model 1863 carbines and Model 1859 Sharps rifles; Spencer Model 1860 carbines
UPS	Urial P. Strong	ASI	1862	
US	Final acceptance stamp		1805-1815	Used at Springfield and Harpers Ferry armories
V	unknown		1795-1805	Most often encountered as "x / V" in two lines
	William A. Moore	ASI	1837	Inspector at Harpers Ferry; lock and mount forgings; mark unknown
WAT	William Anderson Thornton	Captain	1840-66	Model 1836 and 1842 pistols; Model 1842 Navy pistols; Colt Model 1839 carbines; E524Colt's patent flasks; Nippes and Pomeroy Model 1840 musket; Ames, Aston, R. Johnson and Waters pistols; Massachusetts Arms Adams, Remington Beals, Savage and Colt Paterson, Walker and Dragoon revolvers; Hall Model 1840 and 1843 carbines, 1840-52; Model 1841 rifle barrels

"WAT"—William Anderson Thornton

"WB"—Three inspectors could have used this style marking prior to 1865.

Initial	Inspector's Name	Rank/office	Dates	Weapons with this mark
WAT-P	William Anderson Thornton & James S. Palmer		1846	Ames Peace flasks; Ames Navy flasks
WAT-ADK	W.A. Thornton & A.D. King		1858	Batty Peace flasks
WB	William Blanchard	ASI	1831	
WB	William Bradbury	ASI	1860-61	
WB	William Brown	ASI	1862	
WBS	William B. Shubrick	Capt. USN	1806-61	
WC	William Cadwell	ASI	1860-61	
WC	William Chapman	ASI	1860-64	purchased arms and parts
WCK	William C. Kirby	ASI	1841-1858	Whitney and Harpers Ferry Model 1841 rifles with alterations of 1854 and 1855; Model 1855 rifle muskets
WCW	unknown		1865	Sharps & Hankins carbines
WD	William Dickinson	ASI	1848-50	Model 1840 NCO, Musician and Cavalry sabers; Rifleman's Knife
WDE	W.D. Earl	ASI	1863	Parts of arms
WDN	William D. Nicholson	USN	1862-71	
WDW	W.D. Whiting	USN	1841-78	
WEH	unknown		1862	
WF	William Foster	ASI	1863	Parts of arms
WGC	W.G. Chamberlain	ASI	1859-75	
	Wm. Hawksley	Confederate Inspector		Cook & Bro. rifles
WH	Wescom Hudgins	Confederate Inspector		Ridgon & Ansley revolvers
WHB	William H. Barber	ASI	1862	
WHB	William H. Bulkley	ASI	1862	
WHC	Wm H. Carver	ASI	1862-63	
WHC	William H. Chandler	ASI	1862-63	
WHR	William H. Roberts	ASI	1863	Colt Model 1860 revolvers
WHR	William H. Russell	ASI	1862-63	
WKC	unknown		1849	Model 1840 cavalry sabers; Model 1855 Harpers Ferry rifle musket
WLB	William L. Borden	ASI	1844-54	
WM	William Maynadier	Lt. Col.	1838-63	
	William Mitchell	Lt. Commander	1862-63	Spencer rifles; Remington revolvers

"ZB"—Zadock Butt

Initial	Inspector's Name	Rank/office	Dates	Weapons with this mark
	William M. Burdett	Acting Master, USN	1865	Remington revolvers
WMF	William M. Folger	Lt. Cdr., USN	1861-98	
WN	Walter North	ASI	1831-63	Aston pistols, Colt Model 1851 revolvers
WNJ	William N. Jeffers	Commander, USN	1840-78	Navy Model 1861 Coston signal pistols; Whitney revolvers; Remington-Beals Navy revolvers
WP	William Page	ASI	1863	U.S. Providence Tool Co. Model 1861 contract rifle-muskets; Model 1862 Joslyn carbines
W/P	Decius Wadsworth		1798-99	Also found as "P / W" in two lines.
W/P	William F. Wilson	ASI	1852-62	Worked at Frankford Arsenal. Also used mark "WW / P". Proved gun barrels; Harpers Ferry Model 1841 rifles; P.S. Justice rifles
WPMc	William McFarland		1857	Maynard 1st Model carbines
WPT	William P. Taylor	ASI, SI	1862-64	
WR	William Richardson	ASI	1808	
WR	William Russell	ASI	1808	
WS	William Smith	ASI (civilian inspector?)	1828-41	Model 1833 dragoon sabers
	Winfield Scott Schley	Lt., USN	1863	Remington Navy revolvers
WSW	William S. Wood	ASI, FSI	1862-63	
WT	William Taggart	USN, civilian	1838-60	Ames Navy flasks; Ames Navy flasks, 1843
WT	William Turnbull	ASI	1843-51	
WW	William Walters	ASI	1862-64	Remington Model 1861 .44 and Pettingill .44 revolvers; Spencer Model 1860 carbines
	Wallace Whitney		1863	Amoskeag assistant inspector
WW/P	William F. Wilson	ASI	1852-60	Also used mark "W / P". Proved gun barrels; Harpers Ferry Model 1841 rifles
	W.W. Queen	Lt. Cdr., USN	1862	Remington revolvers
Y	Young	ASI	1844-54	
ZB	Zadock Butt	ASI	1862	Merrill breech-loading rifles
	? Marston	civilian inspector	1862	S. Crispin refers to weapons of Hedden & Hoey inspected by "Mr. Marston" in a letter to General Ripley, Feb. 7, 1862 (Report of the Commission on Ordnance...p. 56)
	? Schmidt	ASI	1861	P.V. Hagner refers to weapons inspected by "Schmidt" in a letter to S. Dingee & Co., Dec. 16, 1861 (Report of the Commission on Ordnance...p. 107); Prussian muskets
	? Wainwright	Lt.	1861	Jenks Merrill carbines
Windmill or Maltese Cross stamp	Nathaniel D. Cross	Confederate inspector, Selma Arsenal		Dickinson, Nelson & Co. Rifles; J.P. Murray Type II rifles

BIBLIOGRAPHY

Adams, Doug. *The Confederate LeMat Revolver*. Lincoln, RI: Andrew Mowbray, Inc., 2005.

Albaugh, William A., III. *Tyler, Texas, C.S.A.* Wilmington, NC: Broadfoot Publishing Co., 1993.

Albaugh, William A., III, and Edward N. Simmons. *Confederate Arms*. Philadelphia: Riling and Lentz, 1963.

Albaugh, William A., III, and Richard D. Steuart. *The Original Confederate Colt*. New York: Greenberg Publisher, 1953.

Albaugh, William A., III, Hugh Benet, Jr., and Edward N. Simmons. *Confederate Handguns*. Wilmington, NC: Broadfoot Publishing Company, 1993.

Albaugh, William A., III. *Confederate Brass-Framed Colts & Whitneys*. Wilmington, NC: Broadfoot Publishing Company, 1993.

Bazelon, Bruce S. and William F. McGuinn. *A Directory of American Military Goods Dealers & Makers 1785- 1915*. Manassas, VA: REF Typesetting & Publishing, Inc., 1990.

Bilby, Joseph G. *Civil War Firearms*. Conshockocken, PA: Combined Publishing, 1996.

Coates, Earl J. and Dean Thomas. *An Introduction to Civil War Small Arms*. Gettysburg, PA: Thomas Publications, 1990.

Coates, Earl J. and John D. McAulay. *Civil War Sharps Carbines & Rifles*. Gettysburg, PA: Thomas Publications, 1990.

Coggins, Jack. *Arms and Equipment of the Civil War*. New York: Random House, Inc., 1962.

Curtis, Chris C. *System Lefaucheux*. Santa Ana, CA: Armslore Press, 2002.

Datig, Fred A. *Cartridges for Collectors*. Beverly Hills, CA: Fadco Publishing Company, 1958.

Davies, Paul J. *C.S. Armory Richmond*. Carlisle, PA: Paul J. Davies, 2000.

Davis, Carl. *Arming the Union: Small Arms in the Civil War*. Port Washington, NY: Kennikat Press, 1973.

Delano, Marfé Ferguson and Barbara C. Mallen. *Echoes of Glory: Arms and Equipment of the Union*. Alexandria, VA: Time-Life Books, 1991.

Edwards, William B. *Civil War Guns*. Harrisburg, PA: The Stackpole Company, 1962.

Flayderman, Norm. *Flayderman's Guide to Antique American Firearms...and Their Values 9th ed*. Iola, WI: Krause Publications, 2007.

Fuller, Claud E. and Richard D. Steuart. *Firearms of the Confederacy*. Lawrence, MA: Quarterman Publications, 1944.

Fuller, Claud E. *Springfield Shoulder Arms, 1795-1865*. New York: Francis Bannerman & Son, 1930, reprinted by S & S Firearms, Glendale, NY, 1986.

Fuller, Claud E. *The Breech Loader in Service 1816-1917: A History of All Standard and Experimental U.S. Breechloading and Magazine Shoulder Arms*. New Milfod, CT: N. Flayderman, 1965.

Garavaglia, Louis A. and Charles G. Worman. *Firearms of the American West, 1803-1865*. Albuquerque: University of New Mexico Press, 1984.

Gary, William A. *Confederate Revolvers*. Prescott, AZ: K8 Communications, 1987.

Gluckman, Arcadi. *United States Muskets, Rifles and Cabines*. Buffalo, New York: Otto Ulbrich Co., 1948.

Graf, John F. *Warman's Civil War Collectibles: Identification and Price Guide, 2nd Ed*. Iola, WI: Krause Publications, 2006.

Hartzler, D.D., Yantz, L. and J. Whisker. *The U.S. Model 1861 Springfield Rifle-Musket as Manufactured by the United States Armory at Springfield, Massachusetts, and Various Private Contractors*. Bedford, PA: Bedford Village Press, 2000.

Hassell, J. Alan. *Warner Civil War Cavalry Carbines*. Gettysburg, PA: Thomas Publications, 2000.

Haven, C.T., and F.A. Belden. *A History of the Colt Revolver*. New York: Bonanza Books, 1962.

Hicks, James E. *Notes on United States Ordnance --Small Arms, 1776-1956*. Vol. 1. Mt. Vernon, NY: James E. Hicks, 1957.

Hicks, James E., and Andrew Jandot *U. S. Military Firearms, 1776-1956*. Reprint Ed., La Canada, CA, 1962.

Hill, Richard Taylor and William Edward Anthony. *Confederate Longarms and Pistols*. Charlotte, NC: Taylor Publishing Co., 1978.

Hogg, Ian V., *Weapons of the Civil War*. Greenwich, Connecticut: Brompton Books, 1987. Edison, New Jersey: Book Sales, 1995.

Hopkins, Richard E. *Military Sharps Rifles and Carbines*. Campbell, CA: Published by the author, 1967.

Houze, Herbert G. *Colt Rifles & Muskets from 1847 to 1870*. Iola, WI: Krause Publications, 1996.

Hull, Edward A. *The Burnside Breech Loading Carbines*. Lincoln, RI: Andrew Mowbray Incorporated, 1986.

Hull, Edward A. *Providence Tool Co. Military Arms*. Milton, FL: Santa Rosa Printing, 1978.

Lewis, Berkeley R. *Notes on Ammunition of the American Civil War, 1861-1865*. Washington, DC: American Ordnance Association, 1960.

Layman, George J. *A Guide to the Maynard Breechloader*. Union City, TN: Pioneer Press, 1998

Lewis, Berkeley R. *Small Arms and Ammunition in the United States Service*. Washington, DC: Smithsonian Institution, 1960.

Lord, Francis A. *Civil War Collector's Encyclopedia*. New York: Castle Books, 1963.

Madaus, H. Michael. *The Warner Collector's Guide to American Longarms*. New York, NY: Warner Books, Inc. 1981.

Marcot, Roy. *Spencer Repeating Firearms*. Irvine, CA: Northwood Heritage Press, 1983.

Marcot, Roy M. *U.S. SharpShooters: Berdan's Civil War Elite*. Mechanicsburg, PA: Stackpole Books, 2007.

McAulay, John D. *Carbines of the Civil War*. Union City, TN: Pioneer Press, 1981.

McAulay, John D. *Civil War Carbines, Volume II: The Early Years*. Lincoln, RI: Andrew Mowbray Inc., 1991

McAulay, John D. *Civil War Breech Loading Rifles*. Lincoln, RI: Andrew Mowbray Inc., 1987.

McAulay, John D. *Civil War Pistols*. Lincoln, RI: Andrew Mowbray Inc., 1992.

McAulay, John D. *Civil War Small Arms of the US Navy and Marine Corps*. Lincoln, RI: Andrew Mowbray Publishers, 1999.

McAulay, John D. *Rifles of the U.S. Army 1861-1906*. Lincoln, RI: Andrew Mowbray Publishers, 2003.

McAulay, John D. *U.S. Military Carbines*. Woonsocket, RI: Andrew Mowbray Publishers, 2006.

McKee, W. Reid and Mason, M.E., Jr. *Civil War Projectiles II, Small Arms and Field Artillery, with Supplement*, Mechanicsville: Rapidan Press, 1980.

McQueen, John C. *Spencer: The First Effective and Widely Used Repeating Rifle—And Its Use in the Western Theater of the Civil War*. Marietta, GA: Author, 1989.

Meyer, Jack Allen. *William Glaze and the Palmetto Armory*. Columbia, S.C.: South Carolina State Museum, 1994.

Morrow, John Anderson. *The Confederate Whitworth Sharpshooters*. Atlanta, GA: Author, 1989.

Murphy, John M. *Confederate Carbines & Musketoons*. Santa Ana, CA: Graphic Publishers, 2002.

Murphy, John M. and Howard Michael Madaus. *Confederate Rifles & Muskets*. Newport Beach, CA: Graphic Publishers, 1996.

Noe, David, Larry W. Yantz, and James B. Whisker. *Firearms from Europe—Being a History and Description of Firearms Imported During the American Civil War by the United States of America and the Confederate States of America*. Rochester, NY: Rowe Publications, 1999.

Norman, Matthew W. *Colonel Burton's Spiller & Burr Revolver*. Macon, GA: Mercer University Press, 1996.

Reilly, Robert M. *United States Martial Flintlocks*. Lincoln, RI. Andrew Mowbray Inc., 1986.

Reilly, Robert M. *United States Military Small Arms 1816-1865*. Baton Rouge: The Eagle Press, Inc., 1970.

Rentschler, Thomas B. *Cosmopolitan and Gwyn & Campbell Carbines in the Civil War*. Lincoln, RI: Andrew Mowbray Publishers, 2000.

Rywell, Martin. *Sharps Rifle: The Gun that Shaped American Destiny*. Union City, TN: Pioneer Press, 1984.

Shidler, Dan. *Standard Catalog of Firearms, 17th ed.* Iola, WI: Gun Digest Books, 2007.

Schmidt, Peter A. *Hall's Military Breechloaders*. Lincoln, RI: Andrew Mowbray Publishers, 1996.

Schmidt, Peter A. *U.S. Military Flintlock Muskets and Their Bayonets: The Early years, 1790-1815*. Lincoln, RI: Andrew Mowbray Publishers, 2006.

Schuyler, Hartley and Graham. *Illustrated Catalog of Civil War Military Goods*. New York, NY: Dover Publications, 1985 [Reprint]

Thillmann, John H. *Civil War Cavalry & Artillery Sabers*, Lincoln RI: Andrew Mowbray Publishers, 2001.

Smith, Samuel E., and Edwin W. Bitter. *Historic Pistols: The American Martial Flintlock, 1760-1845*. New York: Scalamandre Publications, 1985.

Smith, Winston O. *The Sharps Rifle*. New York: William Morrow Co., 1943.

Sutherland, Robert Q., and R.L. Wilson. *The Book of Colt Firearms*. Kansas City, MO: Robert Q. Sutherland, 1971.

Sword, Wiley. *Firepower from Abroad: The Confederate Enfield and the Le Mat Revolver, 1861-1863*. Lincoln, RI: Andrew Mowbray, 1986.

Thomas, Dean S. *Ready…Aim…Fire! Small-Arms Ammunition in the Battle of Gettysburg*. Gettysburg, PA: Thomas Publications, 1981.

Thomas, Dean S. *Round Ball To Rimfire. A History of Civil War Small Arms Ammunition, Part Two, Federal Breechloading Carbines & Rifles*. Gettysburg, PA: Thomas Publications, 2002.

Thomas, Dean S. *Round Ball to Rimfire; A History of Civil War Small Arms Ammunition*. Gettysburg, PA: Thomas Publications, 1997.

Thomas, James and Dean. *Handbook of Civil War Bullets and Cartridges*. Gettysburg, PA: Thomas Publications, 1996.

Time Life Books Eds. *Echoes of Glory: Arms and Equipment of the Confederacy*. Alexandria, VA: Time-Life Books, 1991.

Todd, Frederick P. *American Military Equipage, 1851- 1872*. N.P.: Chatham Square Press, Inc., 1983. Ware, Donald L. *Remington Army and Navy Revolvers 1861-1888*. Albuquerque: University of New Mexico Press, 2007.

Whisker, J.B., D. Hartzler, and L.W. Yantz. *Arming the Glorious Cause: Weapons of the Second War for Independenc—A Photographic Study of Confederate Weapons*. State College, PA: RR Books, 1998.

Whisker, James B., Daniel D. Hartzler and Larry W. Yantz. *Firearms from Europe, 2nd ed.* Tom Rowe Books, 2002.

Whisker, J.B., D. Hartzler, and L.W. Yantz. *U.S. Civil War Carbines*. Rochester, NY: Tom Rowe Books, 2001.

Whisker, J.B., D. Hartzler, and L.W. Yantz. *The U.S. Model 1861 Springfield Rifle-Musket, 2nd ed.* Bedford, PA: Bedford Village Press, 2006.

Winders, G.H. *Sam Colt and His Guns*. New York: John Day, 1959.

Wyllie, Arthur. *Regulation U.S. Swords and Their Variations*. N.P., 1980.

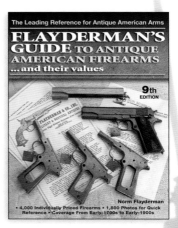
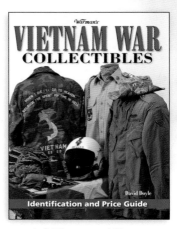

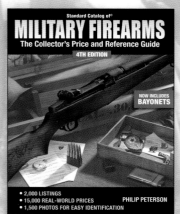